THE ORCHID THIEF

The inspiration for the movie *ADAPTATION*

ballantine reader's circle

A TRUE STORY OF BEAUTY AND OBSESSION

SUSAN ORLEAN

Please turn the page for more reviews. . . .

"OFFBEAT AND ABSORBING . . .

Orleans shows an amazing deftness at weaving such dark history together with portrayals of wacky orchid fanatics, scientific explanations, and personal observation into a compelling, page-turning narrative. Like the best investigative reporters, she has found an eye-opening story in a place where you would have least expected it. Yet her prose is leavened by a down-to-earth sense of humor and poetic insight. Whatever species of book *The Orchid Thief* is, it's a rare one, and one you don't want to pass up while it's in bloom."
　　　　　　　　　　　—*Sunday Tribune Review* (Greensburg, PA)

"Orlean writes in a keenly observant mode reminiscent of John McPhee and Diane Ackerman. . . . In prose as lush and full of surprises as the Fakahatchee itself, Orlean connects orchid-related excesses of the past with exploits of the present so dramatically an orchid will never just be an orchid again."
　　　　　　　　　　　　　　　　　　　—*Booklist*

"The orchid fanatics [Orlean] describes are mesmerizing and her vivid prose brings the intoxicating blooms right up to nose level. For less money than a plane ticket, *The Orchid Thief* will take you on a memorable trip from the dead of winter to Florida's hothouse."
　　　　　　　　　　　　　　　　　—*Free Lance Star*

"Susan Orlean plunges into the world of orchid collectors to create a book that is meticulously researched and written in the pleasing, flowing prose of books like *The Perfect Storm* and *Midnight in the Garden of Good and Evil*. . . . Anyone interested in orchids, Florida, the collecting mentality, fixation, or just good nonfiction will enjoy *The Orchid Thief*. Read it out on the patio, next to your orchid plant, but take care . . . obsession can be contagious."
　　　　　　　　　　　　　　　　　—*Gulfshore Life*

"Between the unearthly landscape, the eccentric orchid growers, and the objects of their desire, Orlean has forged a fascinating adventure inlaid with an oblique commentary on the sterility of mainstream American life. The fact that her story is about plants (plants!) testifies to the book's greatest truth: that passion is blind, often misguided, and impossible to justify—but always worth the ride."
　　　　　　　　　　　　　　　　—*Metro* (San Jose, CA)

ALSO BY SUSAN ORLEAN

Saturday Night

Red Sox and Bluefish

The Bullfighter Checks Her Makeup

The Orchid Thief

THE
ORCHID
THIEF

Susan Orlean

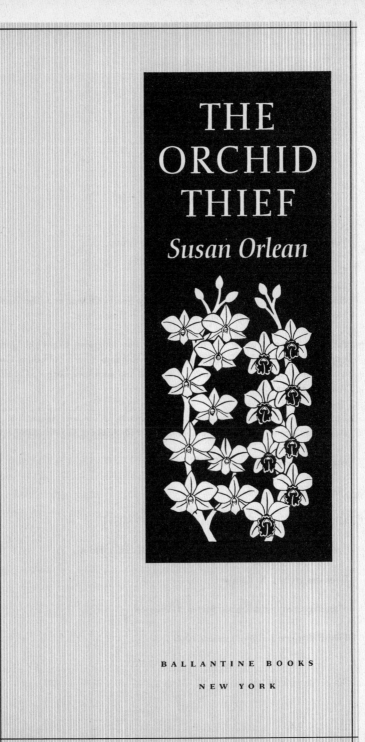

BALLANTINE BOOKS

NEW YORK

A Ballantine Book
Published by The Random House Publishing Group

Copyright © 1998 by Susan Orlean
Book illustrations © 1998 by Regina Scudellari
Reader's Guide copyright © 2000, 2002 by Susan Orlean and The Random
House Publishing Group, a division of Random House, Inc.

All rights reserved under International and Pan-American Copyright Conventions. Published in the United States by The Random House Publishing Group, a division of Random House, Inc., New York, and simultaneously in Canada by Random House of Canada Limited, Toronto.

Ballantine and colophon are registered trademarks of Random House, Inc.
Ballantine Reader's Circle and colophon are trademarks of Random House, Inc.

www.ballantinebooks.com/BRC

ISBN: 0-449-00371-X

Library of Congress Catalog Card Number: 99-90911

This edition published by arrangement with Random House, Inc.

Book design by J. K. Lambert

Manufactured in the United States of America

First Ballantine Edition: January 2000

30 29 28 27 26 25 24 23 22 21

For my parents, Arthur and Edith

Acknowledgments

My thanks to the countless orchid lovers, nursery owners, Florida historians, gardeners, attorneys, thieves, ramblers, wayfarers, adventurers, botanists, naturalists, Seminole Tribe members, staff people at the Loxahatchee and the Big Cypress and the Fakahatchee, and collectors who contributed so much to this book and in many cases do not appear by name in the text.

I am especially grateful to the American Orchid Society for its assistance. Thanks to Ned Nash at AOS, who reviewed my botanical information for accuracy; and very special thanks to James Watson, who was so helpful and generous with his time for all the years this project was germinating.

I am indebted to Tina Brown, who first urged me to pursue the story for *The New Yorker*, then allowed me long leaves of absence to work on the book, and after all that, cheered me on to the finish line.

For Jon Karp, book editor nonpareil and source of great support, good counsel, and encouragement, a million thank-yous would not be enough. And a million more should go to

Ann Godoff and the many people at Random House who helped see this through.

To Richard Pine, I hope you do win that trifecta. In the meantime, thank you for so much, all these many years.

I owe my family, my friends, my boss, and my colleagues for their zeal, tolerance, constancy, credulity, and overall niceness throughout. Oh, and by the way, Debra Orlean takes great frog photographs.

Prologue

Susan Orlean on *ADAPTATION*

Recently, author Susan Orlean agreed to talk about the experience of having her book *The Orchid Thief* used as the inspiration for the movie *Adaptation*. The movie humorously details the chronicles of a screenwriter who suffers writer's block during his attempt to adapt *The Orchid Thief* the book into *The Orchid Thief* the screenplay. The interview was conducted by writer Susan Orlean.

SUSAN ORLEAN: **Welcome. Thanks for agreeing to do this interview.**

SUSAN ORLEAN: You're welcome. I mean, thanks.

SO: **Before we begin, I just have to ask you if we've met before—you look really familiar to me.**

SO: I don't think so, sorry.

SO: **Are you sure?**

SO: I'm sure.

SO: **Okay, if you say so. In any event, my first question is, did you ever think your book would end up as a movie?**

SO: Never. Frankly, I wasn't even sure it would end up as a book. The first time I heard about John Laroche and the orchid poaching, I thought it would be an interesting magazine article, although the story was so strange that I wasn't even sure how it would work for the magazine. I definitely didn't imagine it as a book at that time, and certainly not as a movie. The truth is, when I'm working on a story, I rarely think about whether it could be made into a movie. I'm too busy figuring it out as a piece of writing.

SO: **Really?**

SO: Yes, really.

SO: That surprises me, because everyone I know thinks about writing for the movies.

SO: Then obviously you don't know me.

SO: You don't have to be rude.

SO: I'm not being rude! I'm just saying that I must not be like the people you know, because I don't think constantly about writing for the movies. I love movies. I like to watch them. I don't want to write them.

SO: I stand corrected! When did the idea of turning *The Orchid Thief* into a movie first come up?

SO: The *New Yorker* published my original story "Orchid Fever" in 1995. Immediately after the story came out, I was approached by three or four different producers and studios who were interested in optioning it. At the same time, I suggested to Random House that I'd like to expand the story into a book, because I knew there was so much more I wanted to say. The producers who eventually bought the story, Jonathan Demme and Ed Saxon, agreed to let me write the book before they'd work on the movie.

SO: And when did that happen?

SO: Let's see…I turned my manuscript in sometime around September 1998, if I remember correctly. And I first read the script of *Adaptation* in the spring of 2000.

SO: Did you ask to write the script?

SO: No. I'm not interested in writing screenplays. And I also thought it would be fascinating to see what a screenwriter would do with the book. It's not a typical Hollywood idea: a movie about a guy who steals orchids.

SO: Did you know anything about the script while it was being developed?

SO: All I knew was that the producers had hired a screenwriter who had just written a movie called *Killing John Malkovich*. At least that's what I thought it was called. It sounded pretty odd, but the producers were very excited about this guy and told me that I should be excited, too, so I was.

SO: You mean *Being John Malkovich*.

SO: Yes, that's what the movie is really called, but it wasn't released yet, and I mistakenly thought it was called *Killing John Malkovich*.

SO: How did you feel when you first read the script?

SO: Surprised.

SO: Go on.

SO: I had been warned that the script diverged a lot from the book, and my agent told me that there were a lot of people in the script who were not in the book—and that they were real people, not fictional characters. And she hinted that one of those people was me. But I still wasn't prepared for what I read. The producer gave me the script at lunch. I went back to my office after lunch, shut the door, turned off my phone and started reading. I had to put it down several times to catch my breath. I think it was at the point in the script when I—I mean the character Susan Orlean in the movie—gun down one of the Fish and Wildlife officers in the Fakahatchee that I began to appreciate what an unusual experience this was going to be. The producer asked me to call as soon as I finished reading the script. I waited a day to let it sink in and then called him and said, "It's not what I expected but it's terrific, and please just change my name."

SO: Why?

SO: Because I wasn't sure I really wanted to be a character in a movie, and especially a character who gets kind of . . . unhinged.

SO: I find that hard to believe.

SO: You find what hard to believe?

SO: That you wouldn't want to be a character in a movie. Isn't that everybody's dream? To be a famous movie character?

SO: I don't know if that's everybody's dream or not, but I personally didn't think I wanted to be turned into a movie part. I don't think that is so hard to believe. Would you want to be a character in a movie?

SO: Who's asking the questions here?

SO: You are, obviously. But I'm just asking you to—never mind. What's your next question?

SO: What convinced you to go ahead with being a character?

SO: A couple of things. I realized that if the book—*my* book—was going to be featured prominently in a movie but the author of the book in the movie was going to be named something other than Susan Orlean it would confuse people and eventually annoy me. I wouldn't like seeing the authorship of *The Orchid Thief* attributed to, oh, Mary Smith or Jane Brown or some pseudonymous nonperson. Also, all the other people who were incorporated into the script agreed to allow their real names to be used. I decided, finally, that the best wasy to look at the whole circumstance was as an adventure, a big virtual-reality experiment.

SO: Did you get a lot of money for it?

SO: That's not really anybody's business, is it?

SO: It's an honest question. And anyway, everybody wonders about that.

SO: I don't think it's polite to talk about money.

SO: I don't think it's polite to not answer questions.

[Silence.]

SO: Shall we continue?

SO: Please.

SO: Did you have any particular objections to the script? Did you request any changes?

SO: There were a few things I asked to have taken out—some details that were a little too personal. But I didn't ask for any major changes. I gave them comments on what I liked and didn't like, but only had specific requests about those few details, and they were all taken out.

SO: Who did you want cast as Susan Orlean?

SO: I spent about a year pretend-casting the movie. I considered everyone from Julia Roberts to Nicole Kidman to Holly Hunter to Jodie Foster to Cate Blanchett but I never settled on who my dream choice would be. My friends made suggestions, too—usually they thought of actresses with red hair, since I have red hair. Maybe people don't realize that hair dye is available in Hollywood. Interestingly, no one ever suggested Meryl Streep, probably because she seems larger than life.

SO: Once she accepted the role, did she meet with you and study you and analyze your gestures and accent?

SO: No. I never met with her. I spent a few days on the set during the filming and assumed I would at least meet her there, but she wasn't around. As it happens, I met her once, years ago. I was an extra in the movie *The Deer Hunter*, which was her first film role. I think I said hello to her there.

SO: Did you guys hang out?

SO: No, of course not. I was one of hundreds of extras there. All I did was murmur hello to her in passing. In fact, I wouldn't even say we *met*. I just mean we were in the same place at the same time.

SO: So you just kind of . . . hung out together.

SO: *No.* I just explained to you that we did not hang out together. As a matter of fact, now that I think about it, I believe I murmured to Robert DeNiro, not to Meryl Streep. Anyway, the point I'm trying to make is that I don't know Meryl Streep, I have never talked to Meryl Streep, and I am not Meryl Streep.

SO: What was it like being on the set of *Adaptation*?

SO: It was fun and it was also very weird. The first thing I noticed was that the crew was looking askance at me. Finally one of grips walked over to me and asked if I was *really* me, and if I had *really* done all the things being portrayed in the movie. It was an out-of-body experience. I guess the crew had begun to think Meryl Streep was the real Susan Orlean, and I was...I'm not sure who they thought I was. In the movie, I have a walk-on part as an anonymous shopper. Maybe that's who they thought I was. It was also really exciting to see the whole production, and realize it had all been inspired by my book. That was wonderful.

SO: What exactly does a "grip" do?

SO: I have no idea.

SO: In *Adaptation,* the screenwriter who is trying to adapt *The Orchid Thief* suffers terrible writer's block. Do you ever have writer's block? Did you sympathize with him?

SO: I'm not a fast writer, but so far, fortunately, I haven't ever had real writer's block. I get stuck in places, but I never go through the torture that the character experiences in the movie. I felt sorry for him.

SO: Is Charlie Kaufman a friend of yours?

SO: No, he's not. I met him once, for about two minutes, on the set of *Adaptation*. We were both tongue-tied.

SO: Does he look like Nicholas Cage?

SO: No, he looks like Charlie Kaufman. You don't get it, do you? Movies are movies. Life is life. They aren't the same thing.

SO: Is that remark supposed to make me feel stupid?

SO: No. I'm sorry if I was curt. I am just trying to be clear about what is a movie and what is *reality*.

SO: So when did you finally see the movie? I can ask you that, right?

SO: Of course. I saw the movie—a rough cut of the movie—at a small screening in the spring of 2002. I was so nervous I could hardly watch it. I was really happy to see that the movie portrayed the real heart of the book, which is about the pursuit of passion and how it shapes our lives. But it was very strange to watch it that first time. I think the reality of seeing myself as a character in a movie was a little over-whelming, and so was the reality of seeing my book reinvented as a movie.

SO: So movies are reality sometimes, right?

SO: [Silence]

SO: Right?

SO: Yes, I guess you're right. In this case, anyway.

SO: So are you planning to write any more movies?

SO: You haven't listened to a thing I've said, have you?

SO: One more thing before I let you go. I know it's unprofessional of me to ask this, but the next time you're hanging out with Nicholas Cage, can you get me his autograph?

Contents

The Orchid Thief

The Millionaire's Hothouse

John Laroche is a tall guy, skinny as a stick, pale-eyed, slouch-shouldered, and sharply handsome, in spite of the fact that he is missing all his front teeth. He has the posture of al dente spaghetti and the nervous intensity of someone who plays a lot of video games. Laroche is thirty-six years old. Until recently he was employed by the Seminole Tribe of Florida, setting up a plant nursery and an orchid-propagation laboratory on the tribe's reservation in Hollywood, Florida.

Laroche strikes many people as eccentric. The Seminoles, for instance, have two nicknames for him: Troublemaker and Crazy White Man. Once, when Laroche was telling me about his childhood, he remarked, "Boy, I sure was a *weird* little kid." For as long as he can remember he has been exceptionally passionate and driven. When he was about nine or ten, his parents said he could pick out a pet. He decided to get a little turtle. Then he asked for ten more little turtles. Then he decided he wanted to breed the turtles, and then he started selling turtles to other kids, and then he could think of nothing *but* turtles and then decided that his life wasn't worth living unless he could collect one of every single turtle species known to mankind, including one of those sofa-sized tortoises from the Galapagos. Then, out of the blue, he fell out of love with turtles and fell madly in love with Ice Age fossils. He collected them, sold them, declared that he lived for them, then abandoned them for something else—lapidary I think—then he abandoned lapidary and became obsessed with collecting and resilvering old mirrors. Laroche's passions arrived unannounced and ended explosively, like car bombs. When I first met him he lusted only for orchids, especially the wild orchids growing in Florida's Faka-hatchee Strand. I spent most of the next two years hanging around with him, and at the end of those two years he had gotten rid of every single orchid he owned and swore that he would never own another orchid for as long as he lived. He is usually true to his word. Years ago, between his Ice Age fossils and his old mirrors, he went through a tropical-fish phase. At its peak, he had more than sixty fish tanks in his house and went skin-diving regularly to collect fish. Then the end came. He didn't gradually lose interest: he renounced fish and vowed he would never again collect them and, for that matter, he would never set foot in the ocean again. That was seventeen years ago. He has lived his whole life only a couple of feet west of the Atlantic, but he has not dipped a toe in it since then.

Laroche tends to sound like a Mr. Encyclopedia, but he did not have a rigorous formal education. He went to public school in North Miami; other than that, he is self-taught. Once in a while he gets wistful about the life he thinks he would have led if he had applied himself more conventionally. He believes he would have probably become a brain surgeon and that he would have made major brain-research breakthroughs and become rich and famous. Instead, he lives in a frayed Florida bungalow with his father and has always scratched out a living in unaverage ways. One of his greatest assets is optimism—that is, he sees a profitable outcome in practically every life situation, including disastrous ones. Years ago he spilled toxic pesticide into a cut on his hand and suffered permanent heart and liver damage from it. In his opinion, it was all for the best because he was able to sell an article about the experience ("Would You Die for Your Plants?") to a gardening journal. When I first met him, he was working on a guide to growing plants at home. He told me he was going to advertise it in *High Times*, the marijuana magazine. He said the ad wouldn't mention that marijuana plants grown according to his guide would never mature and therefore never be psychoactive. The guide was one of his all-time favorite projects. The way he saw it, he was going to make lots of money on it (always excellent) *plus* he would be encouraging kids to grow plants (very righteous) *plus* the missing information in the guide would keep these kids from getting stoned because the plants they would grow would be impotent (incalculably noble). This last fact was the aspect of the project he was proudest of, because he believed that once kids who bought the guide realized they'd wasted their money trying to do something illegal—namely, grow and smoke pot—they would also realize, thanks to John Laroche, that crime doesn't pay. Schemes like these, folding virtue and criminality around profit, are Laroche's specialty. Just when you have finally concluded that he is a run-of-the-mill crook, he unveils an ulterior and somewhat principled but always lucrative reason for his crookedness. He likes to describe himself as a shrewd bastard. He loves doing things the hard way, especially if it means that he gets to do what he wants to do but also gets to leave everyone else wondering how he managed to get away with it. He is quite an unusual person. He is also the most moral amoral person I've ever known.

I met John Laroche for the first time a few years ago, at the Collier County Courthouse in Naples, Florida. I was in Florida at the time because I had read a newspaper article reporting that a white man—Laroche—and three Seminole men had been arrested with rare orchids they had stolen out of a Florida swamp called the Fakahatchee Strand State Preserve, and I wanted to know more about the incident. The newspaper story was short but alluring. It described the Fakahatchee as a wild swamp near Naples filled with exceptional plants and trees, including some that don't grow anywhere else in the United States and some that grow nowhere else in the world. All wild orchids are now considered endangered, and it is illegal to take them out of the woods anywhere, and particularly out of a state property like the Fakahatchee. According to the newspaper, Laroche was the ringleader of the poachers. He provided the arresting officers with the proper botanical varietal names for all the stolen plants and explained that the plants were bound for a laboratory where they were going to be cloned by the millions and then sold to orchid collectors around the world.

I read lots of local newspapers and particularly the shortest articles in them, and most particularly any articles that are full of words in combinations that are arresting. In the case of the orchid story I was interested to see the words "swamp" and "orchids" and "Seminoles" and "cloning" and "criminal" together in one short piece. Sometimes this kind of story turns out to be something more, some glimpse of life that expands like those Japanese paper balls you drop in water and then after a moment they bloom into flowers, and the flower is so marvelous that you can't believe there was a time when all you saw in front of you was a paper ball and a glass of water. The judge in the Seminole orchid case had scheduled a hearing a few weeks after I read the article, so I arranged to go down to Naples to see if this ball of paper might bloom.

It was the dead center of winter when I left New York; in Naples it was warm and gummy, and from my plane I could see thick thunderclouds trolling along the edge of the sky. I checked into a big hotel on the beach, and that evening I stood on my balcony and watched the storm explode over the water. The hearing was the next morning at nine. As I pulled out of the hotel garage the parking attendant warned me to drive carefully. "See, in Naples you got to be careful," he said, leaning in my window. He smelled like daiquiris. It was probably suntan lotion. "When it rains here," he added, "cars start to *fly*." There are more golf courses per person in Naples than anywhere else in the world, and in spite of the hot, angry weather everyone around the hotel was dressed to play, their cleated shoes tapping out a *clickety-clickety-clickety* tattoo on the sidewalks.

The courthouse was a few miles south of town in a fresh-looking building made of bleached stone pocked with fossilized seashells. When I arrived, there were a few people inside, nobody talking to anybody, no sounds except for the creaking of the wooden benches and the sound of some guy in the front row gunning his throat. After a moment I recognized Laroche from the newspaper picture I'd seen. He was not especially dressed up for court. He was wearing wraparound Mylar sunglasses, a polyblend shirt printed with some sort of scenic design, a Miami Hurricanes baseball cap, and worn-out grayish trousers that sagged around his rear. He looked as if he wanted a cigarette. He was starting to stand up when the judge came in and settled in her chair; he sat down and looked cross. The prosecutor then rose and read the state's charges—that on December 21, 1994, Laroche and his three Seminole assistants had illegally removed more than two hundred rare orchid and bromeliad plants from the Fakahatchee and were apprehended leaving the swamp in possession of four cotton pillowcases full of flowers. They were accused of criminal possession of endangered species and of illegally removing plant life from state property, both of which are punishable by jail time and fines.

The judge listened with a blank expression, and when the prosecutor finished she called Laroche to testify. He made a racket getting up from his seat and then sauntered to the center of the courtroom with his head cocked toward the judge and his thumbs hooked in his belt loops. The judge squinted at him and told him to state his name and address and to describe his expertise with plants. Laroche jiggled his foot and shrugged. "Well, Your Honor," he said, "I'm a horticultural consultant. I've been a professional horticulturist for approximately twelve years and I've owned a plant nursery with a number of plants of great commercial and ethnobiological value. I have *very* extensive experience with orchids and with the asexual micropropagation of orchids under aseptic cultures." He paused for a moment and grinned. Then he glanced around the room and added, "Frankly, Your Honor, I'm probably the smartest person I know."

———

I had never heard of the Fakahatchee Strand or its wild orchids until I heard about John Laroche, in spite of the fact that I'd been to Florida millions of times. I grew up in Ohio, and for years my family went to Miami Beach every winter vacation, staying at hotels that had fishing nets and crusty glass floats decorating the lobbies and dwarf cabbage palms standing in for Christmas trees. Even then I was of a mixed mind about Florida. I loved walking past the Art Deco hotels on Ocean Drive and Collins Road, loved the huge delis, loved my first flush of sunburn, but dreaded jellyfish and hated how my hair looked in the humidity. Heat unsettles me, and the Florida landscape of warm wideness is as alien to me as Mars. I do not consider myself a Florida person. But there is something about Florida more seductive and inescapable than almost anywhere else I've ever been. It can look brand-new and man-made, but as soon as you see a place like the Everglades or the Big Cypress Swamp or the Loxahatchee you realize that Florida is also the last of the American frontier. The wild part of Florida is really wild. The tame part is really tame. Both, though, are always in flux: The developed places are just little clearings in the jungle, but since jungle is unstoppably fertile, it tries to reclaim a piece of developed Florida every day. At the same time the wilderness disappears before your eyes: fifty acres of Everglades dry up each day, new houses sprout on sand dunes, every year a welt of new highways rises. Nothing seems hard or permanent; everything is always changing or washing away. Transition and mutation merge into each other, a fusion of wetness and dryness, unruliness and orderliness, nature and artifice. Strong singular qualities are engaging, but hybrids like Florida are more compelling because they are exceptional and strange. Once near Miami I saw a man fishing in a pond beside the parking lot of a Burger King right next to the highway. The pond was perfectly round with trim edges, so I knew it had to be phony, not a natural pond at all but just the "borrow pit" that had been left when dirt was "borrowed" to build the roadbed of the highway. After the road was completed and the Burger King opened, water must have rained in or seeped into the borrow pit, and then somehow fish got in—maybe they were dropped in by birds or wiggled in through underground fissures—and pretty soon the borrow pit had turned into a half-real pond. The wilderness had almost taken it back. That's the way Florida strikes me, always fomenting change, its natural landscapes just moments away from being drained and developed, its most manicured places only an instant away from collapsing back into jungle. A few years ago I was linked to Florida again; this time my parents bought a condominium in West Palm Beach so they could spend some time there in the winter. There is a beautiful, spruced-up golf course attached to their building, with grass as green and flat as a bathmat, hedges precision-shaped and burnished, the whole thing as civilized as a tuxedo. Even so, some alligators have recently moved into the water traps on the course, and signs are posted in the locker room saying LADIES! BEWARE OF THE GATORS ON THE GREENS!

The state of Florida does incite people. It gives them big ideas. They don't exactly drift here: They come on purpose—maybe to start a new life, because Florida seems like a fresh start, or to reward themselves for having had a hardworking life, because Florida seems plush and bountiful, or because they have some new notions and plans, and Florida seems like the kind of place where you can try anything, the kind of place that for centuries has made entrepreneurs' mouths water. It is moldable, reinventable. It has been added to, subtracted from, drained, ditched, paved, dredged, irrigated, cultivated, wrested from the wild, restored to the wild, flooded, platted, set on fire. Things are always being taken out of Florida or smuggled in. The flow in and out is so constant that exactly what the state consists of is different from day to day. It is a collision of things you would never expect to find together in one place—condominiums and panthers and raw woods and hypermarkets and Monkey Jungles and strip malls and superhighways and groves of carnivorous plants and theme parks and royal palms and hibiscus trees and those hot swamps with acres and acres that no one has ever even *seen*—all toasting together under the same sunny vault of Florida sky. Even the orchids of Florida are here in extremes. The woods are filled with more native species of orchids than anywhere else in the country, but also there are scores of man-made jungles, the hothouses of Florida, full of astonishing flowers that have been created in labs, grown in test tubes, and artificially multiplied to infinity. Sometimes I think I've figured out some order in the universe, but then I find myself in Florida, swamped by incongruity and paradox, and I have to start all over again.

———

By the time everyone finished testifying at the orchid-poaching hearing, the judge looked perplexed. She said this was one of her most interesting cases, by which I think she meant bizarre, and then she announced that she was rejecting the defendants' request to dismiss the charges. The trial was scheduled for February. She then ordered the defendants—Laroche, Russell Bowers, Vinson Osceola, and Randy Osceola—to refrain from entering the Fakahatchee Strand State Preserve until the case was concluded. Then she excused the orchid people and turned her attention to a mournful-looking man who was up on drug-possession charges. I caught up with Laroche right outside the courthouse door. He was smoking and standing in a huddle with three other men: the Seminole tribe's lawyer, Allan Lerner, and the vice president of the tribe's business operations, Buster Baxley, and one of the codefendants, Vinson Osceola. The other two Seminoles hadn't come to the hearing; according to Allan Lerner, one of them was sick and the other was nowhere to be found.

Buster looked as if he was in a bad mood. "I'm going right now into that swamp with a chain saw, I swear to God," he fumed. "God *damn.*"

Laroche ground out his cigarette. "You know, I feel like I've been screwed," he said. "I've been fucking *crucified.*"

Allan Lerner dribbled his briefcase from hand to hand. "Look, Buster," he said, "I did try to make our point. I reminded the judge that the Indians used to own the Fakahatchee, but she's obviously got something else in mind. Don't *worry.* We'll deal with all of this at trial." Buster scowled and started to walk away. Vinson Osceola shrugged at Allan and walked off after Buster. Allan looked around and then said good-bye to me and followed Buster and Vinson. Laroche lingered for another minute. He drummed his fingers on his chin and then said, "Those swamp rangers are a joke. None of them know anything about the plants in there. Some of them are actually *dumb*—I mean really *dumb.* They were lucky to have arrested me so I could give them the names of the plants. Otherwise I don't think they would have even known what they were. I really don't care what goes on here in court. I've been to the Fakahatchee a thousand times and I'm going to go in there a thousand more."

———

John Laroche grew up in North Miami, an exurb you pass through on the way from Miami to Fort Lauderdale. The Laroches lived in a semi-industrial neighborhood, but it was still pretty close to the swamps and woods. When he was a kid, Laroche and his mother would often drive over and hike through the Big Cypress and the Fakahatchee just to look for unusual things. His father never came along because he really wasn't much for the woods, and then he had broken his back doing construction work and was somewhat disabled. Laroche has no siblings, but he told me that he had a sister who died at an early age. Once, in the middle of re-counting the history of the Laroches, he declared, "You know, now that I think about it, I guess we're a family of ailments and pain." During the months I spent in Florida I met Laroche's father only briefly. I would have loved to have met his mother, who is no longer alive. Laroche described her as overweight and frumpy, and claimed that she was Jewish by birth but at different times in her life she experienced ardent attachments to different religious faiths. She was an enthusiast, a gung ho devotee. She was never the first to call an end to a hike or to chicken out when she and Laroche had to wade into sinkholes. She loved orchids. If the two of them came across an orchid in bloom, she insisted that they tag it and come back in a few months to see if the plant had formed any seeds.

When Laroche was a teenager he was fleetingly obsessed with photography. He decided he had to photograph every single species of Florida orchid in bloom, so every weekend for a while he loaded his mother with cameras and tripods and the two of them would trudge for hours through the woods. He wasn't content for very long with merely photographing the orchids—he soon decided he had to collect the orchids themselves. He stopped bringing cameras on his hikes and started bringing pillowcases and garbage bags to carry plants. In no time he gathered a sizable collection. He considered opening a nursery. He did some construction work after high school to make a living, but just like his father he fell and broke his back and had to take a disability leave. He considers breaking his back a stroke of luck because it cleared the way for him to devote himself to plants. He got married in 1983, and he and his now ex-wife did open a nursery in North Miami. They named it the Bromeliad Tree. They specialized in orchids and in bromeliads, the fam-

ily of dry, spiny air plants that live in trees. Laroche concen-
trated on the oddest, rarest stuff. Eventually he gathered
forty thousand plants in his hothouses, including some that
he claims were the only specimens of their kind in cultivation. Like a lot of nursery owners, Laroche and his wife managed to just get by on their earnings, but he wasn't satisfied
with just scraping by. What he wanted was to find a special
plant that would somehow make him a millionaire.

———

A few days after the hearing, Laroche invited me to go with
him to an orchid show in Miami. He picked me up in a van
dappled with rust. As I opened the door and said hello, he interrupted me and said, "I want you to know that this van is a
piece of shit. As soon as I hit the orchid jackpot I'm buying
myself an awesome car. What are you driving?" I said I had
borrowed my father's Aurora. "Awesome," Laroche said. "I
think I'll get one of those." I leaned in and dug through all
sorts of stuff to try to get to the passenger seat and then sat
down on a few inches of the edge of it, resting my feet on a
bag of potting soil that had split and spilled all over the floor.
Laroche started down the road with great alacrity. I thought
maybe I had suffered whiplash. Each time the van hit a pot-
hole it squeaked and shuddered, and a hundred different
trowels, screwdrivers, terra-cotta planters, Coke cans, and
mystery things rolled around the floor like steel balls in a pin-
ball machine.

I kept my eyes glued to the road because I thought it would
be best if at least one of us did. "See, my whole life—that is,
my whole life in the nursery world—I've been looking for a
goddamn profitable plant," he said. "I had a friend in South
America—he just croaked, as a matter of fact—anyway, this
guy was a major commercial grower and had just *endless*
amounts of money, and he wanted this fantastic bromeliad I

had, so I told him that I'd trade it to him for just a seed or a cutting from the most valuable plant he had. I said, 'Hey, look, I don't care if the plant is gorgeous or butt-ugly.' I just wanted to see the plant that had given him his life of leisure."

"So what was it? What does a profitable plant look like?"

Laroche laughed and lit a cigarette. "He sent me this big box. In the big box was this little box, and then inside of that there was another little box, and then another box, and in the last box was a square inch of lawn grass. I thought, This guy's a real joker! *Fuck* this guy! I called the guy. I said, 'Hey, you son of a bitch! What the hell *is* this?' Well, it turns out that it was a special kind of lawn grass that was green with some tiny white stripes on the edges. That was it! He told me what an asshole I was and said I should have realized what a treasure I was holding. And, you know, he was right. When you think about it, if you could find a really nice-looking lawn grass, some cool new species, and you could produce enough seeds to market it, you would rule the world. You'd be *completely* set for life."

He crushed out his cigarette and steered with his knee while he lit another. I asked him what he had done with the square inch of grass. "Oh, I'm not into lawn grass," he said. "I think I gave it away."

In 1990 Laroche's life as a plant man changed. That year the World Bromeliad Conference was held in Miami. World plant conferences are attended by collectors and growers and plant fanciers from all over. At most shows growers build displays for their plants, and they compete for awards recognizing the quality of the plants and the ingeniousness of their displays. Maybe at one time show displays were uncomplicated, but nowadays the displays have to reflect the theme of the show and usually involve major construction, scores of plants, and props as substantial as mannequins, canoes, Styrofoam mountains, and actual furniture. Laroche suspected he had a knack for display building, and he was certain he had the best bromeliads in the world, so he decided to enter the competition. He designed a twelve- by twenty-five-foot exhibit using hardwood struts and tie beams, Day-Glo paint, a black light to make the Day-Glo paint glow, strings of Christmas lights arranged correctly in the shape of constellations, and dozens of a species of bromeliad that looks like little stars. The display got a lot of attention. This was a turning point for Laroche. As a result of the conference he became well known in the plant community and became even more determined to have a spectacular nursery. He began calling all over the world every day, tracking down unusual plants; his phone bills were thousands of dollars a month. Lots of money flew in and out of his hands, but he put most of it right back into his nursery. He tended to the extravagant. Once he spent five hundred dollars on an air-conditioned box for one little cool-weather fern he had gotten from a guy in the Dominican Republic. The fern died anyway, but even now Laroche says he doesn't regret the expense. He wanted the best of everything. He accumulated what he says was one of the country's largest collections of *Cryptanthus*, a genus of Brazilian bromeliad. He bought a spectacular six-foot-tall *Anthurium veitchii* with weird, corrugated leaves. He still enjoys thinking about that *Anthurium*. He says it was "a gorgeous, gorgeous son of a bitch."

About ten miles outside of Miami Laroche reached the part of his life story that featured orchids. He and his wife had hundreds of them at the Bromeliad Tree, and even though he had been at one time completely fascinated with the bromeliads, he found himself seduced away by the orchids. He became obsessed with breeding them. He especially loved working on hybrids—cross-pollinating different types to create new orchid hybrids. "Every time I'd make a new hybrid, it felt so *cool*," he said. "I felt a little like God." He often took germinating seeds and drenched them with household chemicals or cooked them for a minute in his microwave oven so that they would mutate and perhaps turn into something really interesting, some bizarre new shape or color never seen before in the orchid world. I guess I was a little shocked as he was describing the process, and when he glanced at me and caught my expression he took both hands off the wheel and waved them at me dismissively. "Oh, come *on*," he said. "Mutation's great! Mutation's really fun! It's a great little hobby—you know, mutation for fun and profit. And it's cool as hell. You end up with some cool stuff and some ugly stuff and stuff no one has ever seen before and it's just great."

I asked what the point of it was. "Hey, mutation is the answer to *everything*," he said irritably. "Look, why do you think some people are smarter than other people? Obviously it's because they mutated when they were babies! I'm sure I was one of those people. When I was a baby I probably got exposed to something that mutated me, and now I'm incredibly smart. Mutation is great. It's the way evolution moves ahead. And I think it's good for the world to promote mutation as a hobby. You know, there are an awful lot of wasted lives out there and people with nothing to do. This is the sort of interesting stuff they should be doing."

The more orchids he collected, the more orchid collectors Laroche got to know. He was in the middle of the orchid world, but at the same time he was not really a part of it. Orchids are everywhere in Florida, wild and domesticated ones, natural and hybridized ones, growing in backyards and in shadehouses, being shipped in and out all over the world.

The American Orchid Society, which was founded in 1921, is headquartered on the former estate of an avid collector in West Palm Beach, and many of the biggest and best orchid nurseries in the country—R. F. Orchids, Motes Orchids, Fennell Orchid Company, Krull-Smith Orchids—are in Florida. Some of these nurseries have been around for decades, and some Florida breeders are the third or fourth generation of their family to grow. Orchids have grown in the Florida swamps and hammocks since the swamps and hammocks have existed, and orchids have been cultivated in Florida greenhouses since the end of the 1800s. By the early 1900s, the great estates of Palm Beach and Miami had their own orchid collections and orchid keepers; orchids were considered a rich and romantic accessory, a polished little captive, a bit of wilderness under glass.

Laroche was not at all rich or romantic or polished, so he didn't fit into the Palm Beach plant lovers' world at all, but he did have a wealth of orchids. Day and night, people dropped by his nursery to talk to him about orchids and to admire his collection and to be impressed by him. They came and just hung around so they could be among his plants, or they brought him special flowers in exchange for leading them on hikes through the Fakahatchee, or they invited him over to see their collections and pumped him for advice, or they offered him truckloads of money to help them find the world's most unfindable plants. He thinks some of them called just because they were lonely and wanted to talk to someone, especially someone who shared an interest of theirs. The image of this loneliness seemed to daunt him. He stopped talking about it and then started explaining to me why he loved plants. He said he admired how adaptable and mutable they are, how they have figured out how to survive in the world. He said that plants range in size more than any other living species, and then he asked if I was familiar with the plant that has the largest bloom in the world, which lives parasitically in the roots of a tree. As the giant flower grows it slowly devours and kills the host tree. "When I had my own nursery I sometimes felt like all the people swarming around were going to eat me alive," Laroche said. "I felt like they were that gigantic parasitic plant and I was the dying host tree."

Cloning the Ghost

Near the entrance to the Seminole reservation in
Hollywood, Florida, there is a large wooden sculpture of a Seminole man wrestling a bowlegged,
bucktoothed alligator. Laroche told me once that
his father had been the model for the Seminole
wrestler. I found this improbable, since the
Laroches have no Indian blood at all, but Laroche
explained that the sculptor had been a friend of his
father's and had asked him to pose because he
thought the elder Laroche possessed a quintessen-
tial Seminole build. I still found the story improbable, so I asked Laroche about it several other times,
including once when we were on the phone and I
knew his father was in the room with him. I had
counted on his father to act as a sort of lie detector,
but instead the two of them launched into a discus-
sion of whether the carved Seminole was life-size or
larger than life-size, and whether it had a penis, and
what the scale of the penis implied about Laroche's
father's penis. This was not what I was hoping would

happen, so I dropped the topic and never brought it up again.

———

Before he came to work for the Seminoles Laroche had been on the reservation only now and again, when he was just passing through or when he was buying tax-free cigarettes at the tribal smoke shops. In a sense, it was bad luck that brought him to the reservation full-time. The years right before he went to work for the tribe went miserably. He was in an awful car crash that knocked out his front teeth, put his wife in a coma for weeks, and killed his mother and uncle. Shortly after the crash he and his wife separated. The next year there was a calamitous frost in south Florida that killed a lot of nursery stock, including much of Laroche's. Then in 1991 a contaminated batch of a Du Pont fungicide called Benlate was suspected of killing nursery plants around the country. Orchids seemed especially sensitive to the tainted Benlate, and several commercial orchid nurseries in Florida lost so many that they went out of business. Many of Laroche's plants that hadn't frozen got poisoned. Finally, in August of 1992 Hurricane Andrew hit Florida. The worst of the storm crossed over the part of Dade County south of Miami that was home to a large military base, citrus farms, and nurseries that produced more than a quarter of all the orchids sold in the United States. The towns of Homestead, Naranja, and Florida City were nearly blown away. Most of the nurseries were gone in a minute: greenhouses folded, shade cloth sailed off, pots of flowers tumbled and shattered. Before the hurricane, Laroche had some of his remaining plants at home and the rest in three different rented greenhouses in Miami and Homestead. In the hurricane two of the three greenhouses vanished entirely. The third more or less exploded. A few days after Andrew had passed, Laroche

went to check the third greenhouse. On the way there he
came upon a green hash lying on a road three blocks from
where the greenhouse had been. He stopped to examine it
and realized the hash was one of his plants. He dreaded
going to the greenhouse. Nothing in it was living—saltwater
carried inland by the storm had ruined all the plants that
hadn't blown away. Laroche had been in the plant business
for about twelve years. He had been a famous plant person.
He was now homeless and plantless and alone. He knew
then and there that he would die of a broken heart if he ever
opened his own nursery again.

The Seminole Tribe of Florida has sixteen hundred members; five reservations covering ninety thousand acres; ten
thousand Hereford-cross beef cattle; twenty-six thousand
acres of pastureland; twelve hundred acres of Burriss
lemons; six hundred acres of red and white grapefruit; a catfish farm and a shrimp farm and a turtle farm. The tribe also
owns casinos and cigarette businesses. Most of the businesses do well; their reported annual earnings a few years
ago were $65 million. The casino is especially profitable.
Right now it is limited to poker and video pull-tag machines
and a bingo hall, but the tribe would like to add Las
Vegas–style gambling, including Superpick Lotto and Touch
6 Lotto machines. So far the governor of Florida has opposed
this, even though the tribe has offered to pay the state $100
million a year just to permit the change. Whenever people
figure out that the Seminole tribe has a lot of money, they
feel inspired. Usually they then approach the tribe with investment proposals—say, a shredded-tire-recycling business
or a quarter-horse racetrack or a shopping mall. Usually the
Seminoles politely decline, but on occasion they do form
partnerships with people outside. The day I first visited the
reservation, for instance, Buster Baxley, who was the vice

president of planning and development for the tribe, was meeting with a group of Japanese businessmen about a possible Japanese-Seminole lemon-farm deal. Most of the time the tribe does business on its own, although it often hires white people with expertise in the business to set it up and get it running. Unemployment among the Seminoles is about 40 percent. The white managers of tribe businesses are expected to hire tribe members as assistants and teach them as much about the business as possible. When the system works, the Seminoles end up with training and experience and can eventually put the white managers out of a job.

The idea of starting a Seminole nursery had been kicking around for a while. It was a natural plan. The tribe owned thousands of acres of land covered with plants indigenous to Florida, sabo palms and foxtail grass and finger grass and pop ash trees, the kind of native plants that developers in Florida are required to use on all state-funded projects and many private ones. There were successful nurseries all around, some even on land rented from the tribe. The Florida Seminole reservations are in Hollywood, Brighton, Immokalee, Tampa, and Big Cypress. Hollywood is the most urban of them all, but Buster knew of a spot near tribe headquarters that he thought would be perfect—two and a half acres near the big commercial strip that were empty except for electric towers belonging to Florida Power and Light. The tribal council agreed, and Buster called the local newspaper and placed an ad for a nursery manager. Laroche was still at loose ends when he saw the ad. He had hardly recovered from the hurricane. He was happy to get the job, although now he likes to say he wonders why.

—

Setting up a nursery can be simple if you want it to be, but Laroche managed to make it complicated. He couldn't bear the thought of having an ordinary nursery with cactus planters and potted palms and Christmas trees. He wanted the Seminole nursery to be dazzling, full of extraordinary things. He wanted odd plants from around the world—spiral juniper bushes, cracker roses, confetti shrub, teddy bear palms. He wanted a hundred varieties of what he called "weird-ass vegetables"—spinach that grows on vines, African pumpkins that can be trained onto trellises, carrots that grow in pots, Chinese fuzzy gourds, yard-long green beans, pink Zairean hot peppers shaped like penises.

He had big plans for orchids. He told the tribe that he wanted to build a laboratory where he would propagate fifty or sixty different species. "Sure, the Seminoles could just go into their backyard and dig up grass and twigs and sell it at the nursery," he once said. "Well, big fucking deal. On the other hand, a lab is a fucking *great* idea. It is a *superior* idea. I explained to the tribe that if you have a lab you can take just one or two plants and from that you can grow billions. Once we got the lab running we could just clone huge numbers of orchids and sell them. I could have hundreds of tribe members working in there, learning about cloning and propagation. We could come up with some really cool new hybrids! And we could work with Florida orchids and really blow some minds. I wanted to bring some flair to the place. Screw wax myrtles! Screw saw grass! A lab is the way to make real money, not growing *grass*."

Many wild orchids don't like to live away from the woods. They will usually flourish and produce seeds only if they are in their own little universe with their favorite combination of water and light and temperature and breeze, with the perfect tree bark at the perfect angle, and with the precise kind of bugs and the exact kind of flotsam falling on their roots and into their flowers. Many species of wild orchids aren't propagated commercially, either because they aren't that pretty or because no one has been able to figure out and reproduce exactly what they want and need to survive. The Fakahatchee has several species of orchids that either live wild or die. The prettiest of them is *Polyrrhiza lindenii,* which is also classified botanically as *Polyradicion lindenii* and is commonly known as the ghost orchid. The ghost orchid grows nowhere in this country but the Fakahatchee. If you could figure out how to housebreak any wild orchid, especially a pretty one like the ghost orchid, you would probably become a rich person. You would be able to grow the plants in a greenhouse and then clone hundreds in a lab—hundreds and hundreds of a variety of orchid almost no one on the planet would have. It would be as if you had figured out how to multiply Siberian tigers or gemstones. Orchid fanciers who like to have as many species as possible in their collections would seek you out, and orchid breeders looking for new gene pools would come to you, too. People who bought your plants could eventually grow their own by taking cuttings from their plant, but you would still be acknowledged as the master of growing them from seed, and you would have a seven-year head start, seven years of monopoly, because it takes seven years before a new orchid plant produces its first flowers. The biggest hindrance to all this is that it is now illegal to collect any wild orchids. They are protected under Florida's endangered species law and also the federal endangered species law, and those that are growing in Florida parks and preserves are also protected under administrative rules governing state lands. International buying and selling of wild orchids is severely restricted under the Convention on International Trade in Endangered Species of Wild Fauna and Flora. A few people have had small-scale luck growing wild orchids they'd collected before the laws took effect, but almost anyone who wants a wild orchid now has to steal it from the woods themselves or buy it on the black market from someone else who had.

———

Laroche had a Laroche-style plan in mind. He knew that Florida Indians were exempt from the state laws protecting endangered species. Once he started working for the tribe he believed he would be exempt as well. He would hike into the Fakahatchee with some of the Seminoles working at the nursery, point out the plants he wanted, and have the crew collect them so he wouldn't even touch any plants himself. That was for insurance: even if he wasn't covered by the Indian exemption, he could protect himself by keeping his hands off the plants, and then if they were stopped by rangers he could argue that he'd just gone along for the hike and hadn't done any collecting himself. After he got the plants he would take them to the Seminole plant lab and start cloning them. He'd been fooling around with ghost orchids for years, and he claimed he was one of the only people in the world who'd solved the puzzle of how to clone and grow them. As soon as word got out that he had mastered the cultivation of *Polyrrhiza lindenii*, he would be celebrated in the plant world. The nursery would sell millions of the plants and make millions of dollars, which would please him and impress the tribe. His success with the ghost orchids would also ruin the black-market trade in them because once the species became available commercially there wouldn't be any reason to buy those that had been poached from the wild. This was Laroche's traditional dash of altruism. Finally, the plan would end with a flourish: He would time everything to take place during the Florida legislative session so that as soon as he had gotten what he wanted out of the woods, he would address the legislators and chide them for leaving laws on the books that were too loose to protect endangered plants from cunning people like him. The legislators, shamed, would then change the laws to Laroche's specifications, and thus the woods would be locked up forever and no more ghost orchids would be spirited away. Environmentalists who had despised him for poaching would be forced to admire him. At first he would seem like a demon, but he would end up looking like a saint. Best of all, Laroche thought, was that when everything was settled he would at last end up with his million-dollar plant.

As soon as he started working for the tribe Laroche's new passion became Indian law. He spent a few hours each day ordering materials for the lab and clearing the way for greenhouses and the rest of the day in the University of Miami law library, examining the state of Florida's legal history with Native Americans. Two cases in particular heartened him. The state had prosecuted Miccosukee Indians three times for poaching palm fronds. The Miccosukees and Seminoles use the fronds to thatch the roofs of their chikee huts. Palms are protected trees, but the state lost the cases because the judges ruled that the Miccosukees had a traditional cultural use for the fronds and therefore were entitled to them. The other case that encouraged him was *State of Florida v. James E. Billie*. Chief Billie is the longtime chairman of the Seminole tribe. In 1983 he was arrested for killing a Florida panther on the Big Cypress reservation. The Florida panther is a protected species under both Florida and federal law. The issues of Indian hunting rights and religious freedom snarled the case for years, and eventually neither the state nor the federal government managed to convict the chief.

Laroche was encouraged by both the palm fronds and Chief Billie's panther. He also came across some clumsy contradiction of the state code that made it sound as if laws forbidding removal of plants and animals from Florida state land were overridden by the laws that allow Florida Indians to collect endangered animals and plants for their own use. In Laroche's opinion this was the tool he'd been looking for. He was convinced that this mess of laws allowed him to go with his Seminole crew anywhere he wanted and take anything at all.

———

A few days after Laroche and I went to the orchid show in Miami I drove to Hollywood to visit him at the nursery. I turned on the car radio and tried to find a music station I liked but ended up listening to a talk show about how to keep pet snakes and iguanas happy, and when that was over I listened to an hour-long infomercial for some money-management audiotapes. The announcer had a big, hollow voice and every few minutes he would boom, *"My friends, you are about to enter the promised land of financial independence!"* I drove past Carpet-Marts and Toy-Marts and Car-Marts and the turnoff for Alligator Alley and a highway flyover that leads to the stadium where the Super Bowl is sometimes played, and past signs for all those dreamy-sounding Florida towns like Plantation and Sunrise and Coconut Creek and Coral Springs. The highway median was a low-lying cloud of pink hibiscus bushes. The shoulders were banked with broom grass and sumac and sneezeweed and pennywort, and the road itself looked as if any minute it might just crack and buckle and finally disappear as things grew over it and under it, pushing the roadbed away. As it is, amazing things live on the highway now. Laroche once discovered a rare orchid species growing along an I-95 off-ramp, and so far no one has found it growing anywhere else in the world.

The reservation is midway between Laroche's house and the American Orchid Society headquarters, on a cube of land a few miles west of I-95. People driving by might not realize they are on tribal land. The only hint is a few tax-free tribal smoke shops and tribal gas stations and the low gray Seminole casino that takes up an entire block. From the road you can't see the tribe headquarters or the rodeo arena or the blocks of neat white reservation houses where most tribe members live. I ended up at the reservation many times during my trips to Florida, and every time I almost accidentally passed it by.

I was developing mixed feeling about spending time with Laroche. I didn't enjoy driving with him but I did enjoy hearing his version of his life. We weren't natural friends. He struck me as the late-sleeping, heavy-smoking, junk-food-eating, law-bending type, whereas I am not, but I am the sort of person who finds his sort of person engaging. Many things he said were incredible or staggering or cracked or improbable, but they were never boring. The current of his mind and behavior was more riptide than rivulet. I didn't care all that much whether what he said was true or not; I just found the flow irresistible. That day I wanted to get a tour of the nursery and he had promised that was what he would give me, but when I arrived he was waiting near the nursery's front gate and said that it was very important that we leave immediately because there was something he absolutely had to do. I parked and got into his van and asked him where the fire was. He snorted at me and said that he needed to go visit a friend he'd given some plants to a few years earlier because he had just decided, based on nothing in particular, that he wanted to repossess the plants.

We drove off, and he started talking about his orchid plans to me, and then suddenly he pulled over onto the shoulder of the road under a palm, put the van in neutral, and hauled on the hand brake. He patted himself down for cigarettes and then dug around under his seat and at last unfolded with a triumphant grin on his face and a crushed pack of Marlboros in his hand. His match hissed. The palm fronds made scratchy sounds on the roof of the van. "Look," he said at last, "I don't think you ought to have a bunch of Indians just running through the Fakahatchee pulling up plants. I mean, someone like Buster—well, Buster's pretty belligerent. In the meantime, though, *someone* is going to figure out how to benefit from the law the way it is now and I just figured it might as well be me." He shifted in his seat and leaned back against the window. His knees bracketed the steering wheel. He had the longest, skinniest lap I think I have ever seen. "I figured we'd get what we needed out of the swamp and then the legislature would change the laws. That's what I wanted to say in court: The state needs to *protect* itself. I'm working for the Seminoles but I'm really on the side of the plants. Is what I did ethical? I don't know. I'm a shrewd bastard. I could be a great criminal. I could be a great con man, but it's more interesting to live your life within the confines of the law. It's more challenging to do what you want but try to do it so you can justify it. People look at what I do and think, Is that moral? Is that right? Well, isn't every great thing the result of that kind of struggle? Look at something like atomic energy. It can be diabolic or it can be a blessing. Evil or good. Well, that's where the give is—at the edge of ethics. And that's *exactly* where I like to live."

He started the van and drove down the block into the parking lot of a nursery. Laroche said the owner of the nursery was a man he met when he and his wife still owned the Bromeliad Tree. He mentioned that the man was gay. "You don't have any problems with homosexuals, do you?" he asked me.

"Of course not," I said. "What are you talking about?"

"I just needed to check," he said. "Because whatever your personal issues are, when you're in the plant business you realize that gay people *are* your friends."

After the hurricane Laroche hadn't had anywhere to keep his few remaining plants and he had no stomach for trying to care for them, so he had given them to the nursery owner. None of the plants were orchids—those had all died; they were mostly hoyas, a species of plant with tough, rubbery leaves and long, loopy vines. Laroche hadn't been especially fond of the hoyas back then and he wasn't especially fond of them now, but for some reason he had decided that he wanted the plants back. He seemed to think there was nothing wrong with taking them. We got out of the van and walked down a crunchy gravel path to a shadehouse. Along the path there were enormous tropical trees with pimply bark and flowers the color of bubble gum, the kind of trees you would draw in a tropical cartoon. The hoyas were hanging by themselves in a small shadehouse with a padlock on the door, and for a moment I wondered if the nursery owner had ever worried that Laroche might someday come back for them. We waited next to the shadehouse looking in at the hoyas and smacking mosquitoes. The plants were in pots suspended from the ceiling. The tips of the vines dusted the floor. "They were pretty good plants to begin with," Laroche said. "It looks like he's kept them happy." It had gotten dopey and warm, an afternoon with a lazy pace, and the light in and around the greenhouses was peculiar and still, as if it were captured inside a bubble, and all the sounds—the crackling of the gravel paths, the mumbling of leaves in the wind, the squeak of doors, the abstract tropical animal sounds of ticking and cheeping and crying—all the sounds were clear but blunted, like sounds inside a covered bowl. I don't know how long we just stood there before the nursery owner drove up in one of those little golf carts that nurserymen use to survey their property. When he saw Laroche he looked mildly pleased. "Well, John," he said. "My goodness, if it isn't John." He turned off the cart, cracked a few of his knuckles, and stepped out. He was a bald, muscular guy with a pruned beard and a cashew-colored tan. Laroche said hello and that the nursery looked terrific and that I was hanging around because I was writing a book about him. The nursery owner looked alarmed and said he didn't want his name in any book about Laroche. Laroche chuckled and then motioned toward the plants and said that for sentimental reasons he wanted to visit them. The man fished around on a key ring and then unlocked the shadehouse. A toucan sitting on a perch near the door glared at us with a yellow eye and then without opening its beak it yelled like a jackhammer. Laroche stepped into the shadehouse and twirled one of the long hoya vines. "By the way," he said, "I'm here to get my plants back. I'll even buy them back or whatever."

"Not interested," the owner said, stroking a leaf.

"I've come back for them," Laroche repeated. "Hey, come on, buddy."

The man stroked another leaf and then said, "No, John. I love them now. At this point they're really mine, not yours."

They quarreled for a few minutes. Finally Laroche persuaded him to give him some cuttings in a couple of months, and that seemed to satisfy both of them. We left the shadehouse and walked through another one that smelled like ripe bananas. The nursery owner petted each plant as we passed. "Hey, John," he said. "You know, I have hardly any orchids anymore. You know, I decided that orchid people are too crazy. They come here and buy an orchid and they kill it. Come, buy, kill. I can't stand it. Fern people are almost worse, but the orchid people are too—oh, you know. They think they're superior." He looked at Laroche. "You collecting anything now, John?"

"Nah," Laroche said. "I don't want to collect anything for myself right now. I really have to watch myself, especially around plants. Even now, just being here, I still get that collector feeling. You know what I mean. I'll see something and then suddenly I get that *feeling*. It's like I can't just have something—I have to have it and learn about it and grow it and sell it and master it and have a million of it." He shook his head and scuffed up some gravel. "You know, I'll see something, just *anything*, and I can't help but thinking to myself, Well, Jesus Christ, now *that's* interesting! Jesus, I'll bet you could find a *lot* of those."

A Green Hell

You would have to want something very badly to go looking for it in the Fakahatchee Strand. The Fakahatchee is a preserve of sixty-three thousand coastal lowland acres in the southwestern corner of Florida, about twenty-five miles south of Naples, in that part of Collier County where satiny lawns and golf courses give way to an ocean of saw grass with edges as sharp as scythes. Part of the Fakahatchee is deep swamp, part is cypress stands, part is wet woods, part is estuarine tidal marsh, and part is parched prairie. The limestone underneath it is six million years old and is capped with hard rock and sand, silt and shell marls, and a grayish-greenish clay. Overall, the Fakahatchee is as flat as a cracker. Ditches and dents fill up fast with oozing groundwater. The woods are dense and lightless. In the open stretches the land unrolls like a smooth grass mat and even small bumps and wrinkles are easy to see. Most of the land is at an elevation of only five or ten feet, and it slopes millimeter by millimeter until it is dead even with the

sea. The Fakahatchee has a particular strange and exceptional beauty. The grass prairies in sunlight look like yards of
raw silk. The tall, straight palm trunks and the tall, straight
cypress trunks shoot up out of the flat land like geysers. It is
beautiful the way a Persian carpet is beautiful—thick, intricate, lush, almost monotonous in its richness.

People live in the Fakahatchee and around it, but it is an
unmistakably inhospitable place. In 1872 a surveyor made
this entry in his field notes: "A pond, surrounded by bay and
cypress swamp, impracticable. Pond full of monstrous alligators. Counted fifty and stopped." In fact, the hours I spent in
the Fakahatchee retracing Laroche's footsteps were probably
the most miserable I have spent in my entire life. The
swampy part of the Fakahatchee is hot and wet and buggy
and full of cottonmouth snakes and diamondback rattlers
and alligators and snapping turtles and poisonous plants and
wild hogs and things that stick into you and on you and fly
into your nose and eyes. Crossing the swamp is a battle. You
can walk through about as easily as you could walk through
a car wash. The sinkholes are filled with as much as seven
feet of standing water, and around them the air has the slack,
drapey weight of wet velvet. Sides of trees look sweaty.
Leaves are slick from the humidity. The mud sucks your feet
and tries to keep ahold of them; if it fails it will settle for your
shoes. The water in the swamp is stained black with tannin
from the bark of cypress trees that is so corrosive it can cure
leather. Whatever isn't wet in the Fakahatchee is blasted.
The sun pounds the treeless prairies. The grass gets so dry
that the friction from a car can set it on fire, and the burning
grass can engulf the car in flames. The Fakahatchee used to
be littered with burned-up cars that had been abandoned by
panfried adventurers—a botanist who traveled through in
the 1940s recalled in an interview that he was most im-

pressed by the area's variety of squirrels and the number of charred Model T's. The swamp's stillness and darkness and thickness can rattle your nerves. In 1885 a sailor on a plume-collecting expedition wrote in his diary: "The place looked wild and lonely. About three o'clock it seemed to get on Henry's nerves and we saw him crying, he could not tell us why, he was just plain scared."

Spooky places are usually full of death, but the Faka-hatchee is crazy with living things. Birders used to come from as far away as Cuba and leave with enough plumes to decorate thousands of ladies' hats; in the 1800s one group of birders also took home eight tons of birds' eggs. One turn-of-the-century traveler wrote that on his journey he found the swamp's abundance marvelous—he caught two hundred pounds of lobsters, which he ate for breakfasts, and stumbled across a rookery where he gathered "quite a supply of cormorant and blue heron eggs, with which I intend to make omelets." That night he had a dinner of a fried blue heron and a cabbage-palm heart. In the Fakahatchee there used to be a carpet of lubber grasshoppers so deep that it made driving hazardous, and so many orchids that visitors described their heavy sweet smell as nauseating. On my first walk in the swamp I saw strap lilies and water willows and sumac and bladderwort, and resurrection ferns springing out of a fallen dead tree; I saw oaks and pines and cypress and pop ash and beauty-berry and elderberry and yellow-eyed grass and camphor weed. When I walked in, an owl gave me a lordly look, and when I walked out three tiny alligators skittered across my path. I wandered into a nook in the swamp that was girdled with tall cypress. The rangers call this nook the Cathedral. I closed my eyes and stood in the stillness for a moment hardly breathing, and when I opened my eyes and looked up I saw dozens of bromeliad plants roosting in the branches of almost every tree I could see. The bromeliads were bright red and green and shaped like fright wigs. Some were spider-sized and some were as big as me. The sun shooting through the swamp canopy glanced off their sheeny leaves. Hanging up there on the branches the bromeliads looked not quite like plants. They looked more like a crowd of animals, watching everything that passed their way.

I had decided to go to the Fakahatchee after the hearing because I wanted to see what Laroche had wanted. I asked him to go with me, but because the judge had banned him from the swamp until the case was over I had to look around for someone else. I suppose I could have gone alone, but I had heard the Fakahatchee was a hard place and even a few brave-seeming botanists I'd talked to told me they didn't like to go in by themselves. At last I was introduced to a park ranger named Tony who said he would go with me. I then spent the next several days talking myself into being un-afraid. A few days before we were supposed to go, Tony called and asked if I was really sure I wanted to make the trip. I said I was. I'm actually pretty tough. I've run a marathon and trav-eled by myself to weird places and engaged in conversations with a lot of strangers, and when my toughness runs out I can rely on a certain willful obliviousness to keep me going. On the other hand, my single most unfavorite thing in life so far has been to touch the mushy bottom of the lake during swimming lessons at summer camp and feel the weedy slime squeeze between my clenched toes, so the idea of walking through the swamp was a little bit extra-horrible to me. The next day Tony called and asked again if I was really ready for the Fakahatchee. At that point I gave up trying to be tough and let every moment in the lake at Camp Cardinal ooze back into my memory, and when I finally met Tony at the ranger station I almost started to cry.

But I was determined to see orchids, so Tony and I went deep into the Fakahatchee to try to find them. We walked from morning until late in the afternoon with little luck. The light was hot and the air was airless. My legs ached and my head ached and I couldn't stand the sticky feel of my own skin. I began having the frantic, furtive thoughts of a deserter and started wondering what Tony would do if I suddenly sat down and refused to keep walking. He was a car-length ahead of me; from what I could tell he felt terrific. I mustered myself and caught up. As we marched along Tony told me about his life and mentioned that he was an orchid collector himself and that he had a little home orchid lab, where he was trying to produce a hybrid that would have the wraparound lip of an *Encyclia* but would be the color of a certain *Cattleya* that is maroon with small lime-green details. He said that he would find out if he had succeeded in seven or eight years, when the hybrid seedlings would bloom. I said nothing for the next mile or so. When we stopped to rest and Tony tried to figure out what was wrong with his compass, I asked him what he thought it was about orchids that seduced humans so completely that they were compelled to steal them and worship them and try to breed new and specific kinds of them and then be willing to wait for nearly a decade for one of them to flower.

"Oh, mystery, beauty, unknowability, I suppose," he said, shrugging. "Besides, I think the real reason is that life has no meaning. I mean, no *obvious* meaning. You wake up, you go to work, you do stuff. I think everybody's always looking for something a little unusual that can preoccupy them and help pass the time."

The orchid I really wanted to see was *Polyrrhiza lindenii*, the ghost orchid. Laroche had taken more of other orchid and bromeliad species when he went poaching, but he told me that the ghost orchids were the ones he had wanted the most. *Polyrrhiza lindenii* is the only really pretty orchid in the Fakahatchee. Technically it is an orchid of the Vandaneae tribe, Sarcanthinae subtribe; *Polyrrhiza* is its genus (the genus is sometimes also called *Polyradicion*). The ghost is a leafless species named in honor of the Belgian plantsman Jean-Jules Linden, who first discovered it in Cuba in 1844. It was seen for the first time in the United States in 1880 in Collier County. The ghost orchid usually grows around the trunks of pop ash and pond apple and custard apple trees. It blooms once a year. It has no foliage—it is nothing but roots, a tangle of flat green roots about the width of linguine, wrapped around a tree. The roots are chlorophyllus; that is, they serve as both roots and leaves. The flower is a lovely papery white. It has the intricate lip that is characteristic of all orchids, but its lip is especially pronounced and pouty, and each corner tapers into a long, fluttery tail. In pictures the flower looks like the face of a man with a Fu Manchu mustache. These tails are so delicate that they tremble in a light breeze. The whiteness of the flower is as startling as a spotlight in the grayness and greenness of a swamp. Because the plant has no foliage and its roots are almost invisible against tree bark, the flower looks magically suspended in midair. People say a ghost orchid in bloom looks like a flying white frog—an ethereal and beautiful flying white frog. Carlyle Luer, the author of *The Native Orchids of Florida,* once wrote of the ghost orchid: "Should one be lucky enough to see a flower, all else will seem eclipsed."

Near a large sinkhole Tony pointed out some little green straps on a young tree and said they were ghost orchids that were done blooming for the year. We walked for another hour, and he pointed out more green ghost-orchid roots on more trees. The light was flattening out and I was muddy and scratched and scorched. Finally we turned around and walked five thousand miles or so back to Tony's Jeep. It had been a hard day and I hadn't seen what I'd come to see. I kept my mind busy as we walked out by wondering if the hard-to-find, briefly seen, irresistibly beautiful, impossible-to-cultivate ghost orchid was just a fable and not a real flower at all. Maybe it really was a ghost. There are certainly ghosts in the Fakahatchee—ghosts of rangers who were murdered years ago by illegal plume hunters, and of loggers who were cut to pieces in fights and then left to cool and crumble into dirt, and for years there has been an apparition wandering the swamp, the Swamp Ape, which is said to be seven feet tall and weigh seven hundred pounds and have the physique of a human, the posture of an ape, the body odor of a skunk, and an appetite for lima beans. There is also an anonymous, ghostly human being whom the Fakahatchee rangers call the Ghost Grader, who brings real—not imaginary—construction equipment into the swamp every once in a while and clears off the vine-covered roads.

If the ghost orchid was really only a phantom it was still such a bewitching one that it could seduce people to pursue it year after year and mile after miserable mile. If it was a real flower I wanted to keep coming back to Florida until I could see one. The reason was not that I love orchids. I don't even especially *like* orchids. What I wanted was to see this thing that people were drawn to in such a singular and powerful way. Everyone I was meeting connected to the orchid poaching had circled their lives around some great desire—Laroche had his crazy inspirations and orchid lovers had their intense devotion to their flowers and the Seminoles had their burning dedication to their history and culture—a desire that then answered questions for them about how to spend their time and their money and who their friends would be and where they would travel and what they did when they got there. It was religion. I *wanted* to want something as much as people wanted these plants, but it isn't part of my constitution. I think people my age are embarrassed by too much enthusiasm and believe that too much passion about anything is naive. I suppose I do have one unembarrassing passion—I want to know what it feels like to care about something passionately. That night I called Laroche and told him that I had just come back from looking for ghost orchids in the Fakahatchee but that I had seen nothing but bare roots. I said that I was wondering whether I had missed this year's flowers or whether perhaps the only place the ghost orchid bloomed was in the imagination of people who'd walked too long in the swamp. What I didn't say was that strong feelings always make me skeptical at first. What else I didn't say was that his life seemed to be filled with things that were just like the ghost orchid—wonderful to imagine and easy to fall in love with but a little fantastic and fleeting and out of reach.

I could hear a soft puckery gulp as he inhaled cigarette smoke. Then he said, "Jesus Christ, of course there are ghost orchids out there! I've *stolen* them, for Chrissake! I know exactly where they are." The phone was silent for a moment, and then he cleared his throat and said, "You *should* have gone with me."

Orchid Fever

The Orchidaceae is a large, ancient family of perennial plants with one fertile stamen and a three-petaled flower. One petal is unlike the other two. In most orchid species this petal is enlarged into a pouch or lip and is the most conspicuous part of the flower. There are more than thirty thousand known orchid species, and there may be thousands more that haven't yet been discovered and maybe thousands that once lived on earth and are now extinct. Humans have created another hundred thousand hybrids by cross-fertilizing one species with another or by crossing different hybrids to one another in plant-breeding labs.

Orchids are considered the most highly evolved flowering plants on earth. They are unusual in form, uncommonly beautiful in color, often powerfully fragrant, intricate in structure, and different from any other family of plants. The reason for their unusualness has always been puzzled over. One guess is that orchids might have evolved in soil that was naturally irradiated by a meteor or mineral deposit, and that the radiation is what mutated them into thousands of amazing forms. Orchids have diverse and unflowerlike looks. One species looks just like a German shepherd dog with its tongue sticking out. One species looks like an onion. One looks like an octopus. One looks like a human nose. One looks like the kind of fancy shoes that a king might wear. One looks like Mickey Mouse. One looks like a monkey. One looks dead. One was described in the 1845 Botanical Registry as looking like "an old-fashioned head-dress peeping over one of those starched high collars such as ladies wore in the days of Queen Elizabeth; or through a horse-collar decorated with gaudy ribbons." There are species that look like butterflies, bats, ladies' handbags, bees, swarms of bees, female wasps, clamshells, roots, camel hooves, squirrels, nuns dressed in their wimples, and drunken old men. The genus *Dracula* is blackish-red and looks like a vampire bat. *Polyrrhiza lindenii,* the Fakahatchee's ghost orchid, looks like a ghost but has also been described as looking like a bandy-legged dancer, a white frog, and a fairy. Many wild orchids in Florida have common names based on their looks: crooked-spur, brown, rigid, twisted, shiny-leafed, cow horn, lipped, snake, leafless beaked, rat tail, mule-ear, shadow witch, water spider, false water spider, ladies' tresses, and false ladies' tresses. In 1678 the botanist Jakob Breyne wrote: "The manifold shape of these flowers arouses our highest admiration. They take on the form of little birds, of lizards, of insects. They look like a man, like a woman, sometimes like an austere, sinister fighter, sometimes like a clown who excites our laughter. They represent the image of a lazy tortoise, a melancholy toad, an agile, ever-chattering monkey." Orchids have always been thought of as beautiful but strange. A wildflower guide published in 1917 called them "our queer freaks."

The smallest orchids are microscopic, and the biggest ones have masses of flowers as large as footballs. Botanists reported seeing a cow horn orchid in the Fakahatchee with normal-sized flowers and thirty-four pseudobulbs, which are the bulging tuber-shaped growths at the base of the plant where its energy is stored, each one over ten inches long. Some orchid flowers have petals as soft as powder, and other species have flowers as rigid and rubbery as inner tubes. Raymond Chandler wrote that orchids have the texture of human flesh. Orchids' colors are extravagant. They can be freckled or mottled or veiny or solid, from the nearly neon to spotless white. Most species are more than one color—they'll have ivory petals and a hot pink lip, maybe, or green petals with burgundy stripes, or yellow petals with olive speckles and a purple lip with a smear of red underneath. Some orchids have color combinations you wouldn't be caught dead wearing. Some look like the results of an accident involving paint. There are white orchids, but there is no such thing as a black orchid, even though people have been wanting a black orchid forever. It was black-orchid extract that Basil St. John, the comic-book character who was the boyfriend of comic-book character Brenda Starr, needed in order to control his rare and mysterious blood disease. I once asked Bob Fuchs, the owner of R. F. Orchids in Homestead, Florida, if he thought a black orchid would ever be discovered or be produced by hybridizing. "No. Never in real life," he said. "*Only* in *Brenda Starr.*"

Many plants pollinate themselves, which guarantees that they will reproduce and keep their species alive. The disadvantage of self-pollination is that it recycles the same genetic material over and over, so self-pollinating species endure but don't evolve or improve themselves. Self-pollinated plants remain simple and common—weeds. Complex plants rely on cross-fertilization. Their pollen has to be spread from one plant to another, either by the wind or by birds or moths or bees. Cross-pollinating plants are usually complex in form. They have to be shaped so that their pollen is stored somewhere where it can be lifted by a passing breeze, or they have to be found attractive by lots of pollinating insects, or they must be so well suited and so appealing to one particular insect that they will be the only plant on which that insect ever feeds. Charles Darwin believed that living things produced by cross-fertilization always prevail over self-pollinated ones in the contest for existence because their offspring have new genetic mixtures and they then will have the evolutionary chance to adapt as the world around them changes. Most orchids never pollinate themselves, even when a plant's pollen is applied artificially to its fertile stigma. Some orchid species are actually poisoned to death if their pollen touches their stigma. There are other plants that don't pollinate themselves either, but no flower is more guarded against self-pollination than orchids.

The orchid family could have died out like dinosaurs if insects had chosen to feed on simpler plants and not on orchids. The orchids wouldn't have been pollinated, and without pollination they would never have grown seeds, while self-pollinating simple plants growing nearby would have seeded themselves constantly and spread like mad and taken up more and more space and light and water, and eventually orchids would have been pushed to the margins of evolution and disappeared. Instead, orchids have multiplied and diversified and become the biggest flowering plant family on earth because each orchid species has made itself irresistible. Many species look so much like their favorite insects that the insect mistakes them for kin, and when it lands on the flower to visit, pollen sticks to its body. When the insect repeats the mistake on another orchid, the pollen from the first flower gets deposited on the stigma of the second—in other words, the orchid gets fertilized because it is smarter than the bug. Another orchid species imitates the shape of something that a pollinating insect likes to kill. Botanists call this pseudoantagonism. The insect sees its enemy and attacks it—that is, it attacks the orchid—and in the process of this pointless fight the insect gets dusted with orchid pollen and spreads the pollen when it repeats the mistake. Other species look like the mate of their pollinator, so the bug tries to mate with one orchid and then another—pseudocopulation—and spreads pollen from flower to flower each hopeless time. Lady's slipper orchids have a special hinged lip that traps bees and forces them to pass through sticky threads of pollen as they struggle to escape through the back of the plant. Another orchid secretes nectar that attracts small insects. As the insects lick the nectar they are slowly lured into a narrowed tube inside the orchid until their heads are directly beneath the crest of the flower's rostellum. When the insects raise their heads the crest shoots out little darts of pollen that are instantly and firmly cemented to the insects' eyeballs but then fall off the moment the insects put their heads inside another orchid plant. Some orchids have straight-ahead good looks but have deceptive and seductive odors. There are orchids that smell like rotting meat, which insects happen to like. Another orchid smells like chocolate. Another smells like an angel food cake. Several mimic the scent of other flowers that are more popular with insects than they are. Some release perfume only at night to attract nocturnal moths.

No one knows whether orchids evolved to complement insects or whether the orchids evolved first, or whether somehow these two life forms evolved simultaneously, which might explain how two totally different living things came to depend on each other. The harmony between an orchid and its pollinator is so perfect that it is kind of eerie. Darwin loved studying orchids. In his writings he often described them as "my beloved Orchids" and was so certain that they were the pinnacle of evolutionary transformation that he once wrote that it would be "incredibly monstrous to look at an Orchid as having been created as we now see it." In 1877 he published a book called *The Various Contrivances By Which Orchids are Fertilised by Insects*. In one chapter he described a strange orchid he had found in Madagascar—an *Angraecum sesquipedale* with waxy white star-shaped flowers and "a green whip-like nectary of astonishing length." The nectary was almost twelve inches long and all of the nectar was in the bottom inch. Darwin hypothesized that there had to be an insect that could eat the unreachable nectar and at the same time fertilize the plant—otherwise the species couldn't exist. Such an insect would have to have a complementarily strange shape. He wrote: "In Madagascar there *must* be moths with proboscis capable of extension to a length of ten to twelve inches! This belief of mine has been ridiculed by some entomologists, but we now know from Fritz Muller that there is a sphinx-moth in South Brazil which has a proboscis of nearly sufficient length, for when dried it was between ten and eleven inches long. When not protruded the proboscis is coiled up into a spiral of at least twenty windings . . . some huge moth with a wonderfully long proboscis could drain the last drop of nectar. If such great moths were to become extinct in Madagascar, assuredly the *Angraecum* would become extinct." Darwin was very interested in how orchids released pollen. He experimented by poking them with needles, camel-hair brushes, bristles, pencils, and his fingers. He discovered that parts were so sensitive that they released pollen upon the slightest touch, but that "moderate degrees of violence" on the less sensitive parts had no effect, which he concluded meant that the orchid wouldn't release pollen haphazardly—it was smart enough to save it for only the most favorable encounters with bugs. He wrote: "Orchids appeared to have been modelled in the wildest caprice, but this is no doubt due to our ignorance of their requirements and conditions of life. Why do Orchids have so many perfect contrivances for their fertilisation? I am sure that many other plants offer analogous adaptations of high perfection; but it seems that they are really more numerous and perfect with the Orchideae than with most other plants."

The schemes orchids use to attract a pollinator are elegant but low-percentage. Botanists recently studied one thousand wild orchids for fifteen years, and during that time only twenty-three plants were pollinated. The odds are bad, but orchids compensate. If they are ever fertilized, they will grow a seedpod that is supercharged. Most other species of flowers produce only twenty or so seeds at a time, while orchid pods may be filled with millions and millions of tiny dust-sized seeds. One pod has enough seeds to supply the world's prom corsages for the rest of eternity.

Some species of orchids grow in the ground and others don't live in soil at all. The ones that don't grow in soil are called epiphytes, and they live their lives attached to a tree branch or a rock. Epiphytic orchid seeds settle in a comfortable spot, sprout, grow, dangle their roots in the air, and live a lazy life absorbing rainwater and decayed leaves and light. They aren't parasites—they give nothing to the tree and get nothing from it except a good place to sit. Most epiphytes evolved in tropical jungles, where there are so many living things competing for room on the jungle floor that most species lose the fight and die out. Orchids thrived in the jungle because they developed the ability to live on air rather than soil and positioned themselves where they were sure to get light and water—high above the rest of the plants on the branches of trees. They thrived because they took themselves out of competition. If all of this makes orchids seem smart— well, they *do* seem smart. There is something clever and unplantlike about their determination to survive and their knack for useful deception and their genius for seducing human beings for hundreds and hundreds of years.

Orchids grow slowly. They languish. They will produce a flower and a seedpod, maybe, and then rest for months at a time. A pollinated orchid seed will mature into a flowering plant in about seven years. Over time, an orchid will wither away in back but it will keep growing from the front. It has no natural enemies except bad weather and the odd virus. Orchids are one of the few things in the world that can live forever. Cultivated orchids that aren't killed by their owners can outlive their owners and even generations of owners. Many people who collect orchids designate an orchid heir in their wills, because they know the plants will outlast them. Bob Fuchs of R. F. Orchids has some plants in his nursery that were discovered by his late grandfather in South America at the turn of the century. Thomas Fennell III, of Fennell Orchids, has plants that his grandfather collected when he was a young man orchid-hunting in Venezuela. Some orchids at the New York Botanical Garden have been living in greenhouses there since 1898.

Orchids first evolved in the tropics, but they now grow all over the world. Most of them spread from the tropics as seeds that were lifted and carried on air currents. A hurricane can carry billions of seeds thousands of miles. Orchid seeds blown from South America to Florida will drop in swimming pools and barbecue pits and on shuffleboard courts and gas stations, on roofs of office buildings and on the driveways of fast-food restaurants, and in hot sand on a beach and in your hair on a windy day, and those will be swept away or stepped on or drowned without being felt or seen. But a few might drop somewhere tranquil and wet and warm, and some of those seeds might happen to lodge in a comfortable tree crotch or in a crack on a stone. If one of those seeds encounters a fungus that it can use for food, it will germinate and grow. Each time a hurricane hits Florida, botanists wonder what new orchids might have come in with it. At the moment, they are waiting to see what was blown in by Hurricane Andrew. They will know the answer around the seventh anniversary of the storm, when the seeds that landed will have sprouted and grown.

—

Nothing in science can account for the way people feel about orchids. Orchids seem to drive people crazy. Those who love them love them madly. Orchids arouse passion more than romance. They are the sexiest flowers on earth. The name "orchid" derives from the Latin *orchis*, which means testicle. This refers not only to the testicle-shaped tubers of the plant but to the fact that it was long believed that orchids sprang from the spilled semen of mating animals. The British Herbal Guide of 1653 advised that orchids be used with discretion. "They are hot and moist in operation, under the dominion of Venus, and provoke lust exceedingly." In Victorian England the orchid hobby grew so consuming that it was sometimes called "orchidelirium"; under its influence many seemingly normal people, once smitten with orchids, became less like normal people and more like John Laroche. Even now, there is something delirious in orchid collecting. Every orchid lover I met told me the same story—how one plant in the kitchen had led to a dozen, and then to a backyard green-house, and then, in some cases, to multiple greenhouses and collecting trips to Asia and Africa and an ever-expanding or-chid budget and a desire for oddities so stingy in their re-wards that only a serious collector could appreciate them—orchids like the *Stanhopea,* which blooms only once a year for at most one day. "The bug hits you," a collector from Guatemala explained to me. "You can join A.A. to quit drinking, but once you get into orchids you can't do anything to kick the habit." I didn't own any orchids before I went down to Florida, but Laroche always teased me and said that I'd never get through a year around orchid people without getting hooked. I didn't want to get hooked—I didn't have the room or the patience to have plants in my apartment, and I suppose I also didn't want Laroche to feel too smug about his predictive powers. In fact, nearly every orchid grower I talked to insisted on giving me a plant and I was so leery of getting attached that I immediately gave them all away.

Currently, the international trade in orchids is more than $10 billion a year, and some individual rare plants have sold for more than twenty-five thousand dollars. Thailand is the world's largest exporter of cut orchids, sending $30 million worth of corsages and bouquets around the world. Orchids can be expensive to buy and expensive to maintain. There are orchid baby-sitters and orchid doctors and orchid boarding-houses—nurseries that will kennel your plants when they're not in bloom and then notify you when they've developed a bud and are ready to take home to show off. One magazine recently reported that a customer of one orchid kennel in San Francisco had so many plants that he was paying two thousand dollars in monthly rent. There are dozens of orchid sites on the Internet. For a while I checked in on "Dr.

Tanaka's Homepage"; Dr. Tanaka described himself as "A comrade who love Paph!" and also as "so bad-looking, I can not show you my photo." Instead, his homepage had stories about new "splendid and/or marvelous Paphiopedilums in the Recent Orchid Show in JAPAN" and photographs of his greenhouse and his family, including one of his daughter, Paphiopedilum. "Junior high school, 1st year," he wrote under the picture of a smiling Miss Paphiopedilum Tanaka. "She is at a cheeky age. But I put her name to almost all selected clones of Paphs. First of all, I put 'Maki' and the next, 'Dreamy Maki', 'Maki's Happiness', etc." As for his wife, Kayoko, Dr. Tanaka wrote, "Her age is secret. She is worried about developing a middle aged spread as me. She never complain of my growing orchids, Paphiopedilums, and let me do as I like. . . . Before we have a daughter, I have put my wife's name to the all of selected clones of my Paphs. But after that, I have forgotten her name entirely."

I heard countless stories of powerful orchid devotion during the time I hung around with Laroche. I heard about a collector who had two greenhouses on top of his town house in Manhattan where he kept three thousand rare orchids; the greenhouses had automatic roof vents, gas heaters, an artificial cloud system, and breeze-simulating fans, and he, like many collectors, took vacations separately from his wife so one of them could always be home with the orchids. I heard about Michihiro Fukashima, the man who founded Japan Airlines, who said he found the business world too cruel, so he retired early, turned his assets over to his wife, severed all other ties to his family, and moved to Malaysia with his two thousand orchid plants. He had been married twice before and told a reporter that he felt "he had made his wives unhappy because of his orchid obsession." Charles Darrow, who invented the game Monopoly, retired with all his Monopoly money at the age of forty-six to devote himself to gathering and breeding wild orchids. A young Chinese collector, Hsu She-hua, recently described himself as a fanatic and said that even though he had been hauled into court four times for possessing wild orchids he considered it worthwhile.

Collecting can be a sort of love sickness. If you collect living things, you are pursuing something imperfectible, because even if you manage to find and possess the living things you want, there is no guarantee they won't die or change. A few years ago, thirty thousand orchids belonging to a man in Palm Beach all died. He blamed methane fumes from a nearby sewage station. He sued the county and received a settlement, but began what his family called "a downhill slide." He was arrested for attacking his father, then for firing a sixteen-gauge shotgun into a neighbor's house, then for carrying a concealed knife, pistol, and shotgun. "It was the death of his orchids," his son told a reporter. "That's where it all began." Beauty can be painfully tantalizing, but orchids are not simply beautiful. Many are strange-looking or bizarre, and all of them are ugly when they aren't flowering. They are ancient, intricate living things that have adapted to every environment on earth. They have outlived dinosaurs; they might outlive human beings. They can be hybridized, mutated, crossbred, and cloned. They are at once architectural and fanciful and tough and dainty, a jewel of a flower on a haystack of a plant. The botanical complexity of orchids and their mutability makes them perhaps the most compelling and maddening of all collectible living things. There are thousands and thousands of orchid species. New orchids are being created in laboratories or being discovered every day, and others are nearly unfindable because they exist in tiny numbers in remote places. In a sense, then, the number of orchid species on the planet is uncountable because it is constantly changing. To desire orchids is to have a desire that will never be, can never be, fully requited. A collector who wants one of every orchid species on earth will certainly die before even coming close.

A Mortal Occupation

The great Victorian-era orchid hunter William Arnold drowned on a collecting expedition on the Orinoco River. The orchid hunter Schroeder, a contemporary of Arnold's, fell to his death while hunting in Sierra Leone. The hunter Falkenberg was also lost, while orchid hunting in Panama. David Bowman died of dysentery in Bogotá. The hunter Klabock was murdered in Mexico. Brown was killed in Madagascar. Endres was shot dead in Rio Hacha. Gustave Wallis died of fever in Ecuador. Digance was gunned down by locals in Brazil. Osmers vanished without a trace in Asia. The linguist and plant collector Augustus Margary survived toothache, rheumatism, pleurisy, and dysentery while sailing the Yangtze only to be murdered when he completed his mission and traveled beyond Bhamo. Orchid hunting is a mortal occupation. That has always been part of its charm. Laroche loved orchids, but I came to believe he loved the difficulty and fatality of getting them almost as much as the flowers themselves. The worse a time he had in the swamp the more enthusiastic he would be about the plants he'd come out with.

Laroche's perverse pleasure in misery was traditional among orchid hunters. An article published in a 1906 magazine explained: "Most of the romance in connection with the cult of the orchid is in the collecting of specimens from the localities in which they grow, perhaps in a fever swamp or possibly in a country full of hostile natives ready and eager to kill and very likely eat the enterprising collector." In 1901 eight orchid hunters went on an expedition to the Philippines. Within a month one of them had been eaten by a tiger; another had been drenched with oil and burned alive; five had vanished into thin air; and one had managed to stay alive and walk out of the woods carrying forty-seven thousand *Phalaenopsis* plants. A young man commissioned in 1889 to find cattleyas for the English collector Sir Trevor Lawrence walked for fourteen days through jungle mud and never was seen again. Dozens of hunters were killed by fever or accidents or malaria or foul play. Others became trophies for headhunters or prey for horrible creatures such as flying yellow lizards and diamondback snakes and jaguars and ticks and stinging marabuntas. Some orchid hunters were killed by other orchid hunters. All of them traveled ready for violence. Albert Millican, who went on an expedition in the northern Andes in 1891, wrote in his diary that the most important supplies he was carrying were his knives, cutlasses, revolvers, daggers, rifles, pistols, and a year's worth of tobacco. Being an orchid hunter has always meant pursuing beautiful things in terrible places. From the mid-1800s to the early 1900s, when orchid hunting was at its prime, terrible places were really terrible places, and any man advertising himself as a hunter needed to be hardy, sharp, and willing to die far from home.

Some Victorian orchid collectors went to the tropics themselves, but most stayed home and paid professional hunters
to travel around the world and collect for them. Having tropical orchids therefore indicated you were rich enough to hire
a man to do a task that might kill him. As soon as the English
got interested in tropical orchids there were Englishmen who
set up tropical-orchid businesses. These commercial growers
depended entirely on orchid hunters. No one in England was
very good at cultivating or breeding tropical orchids at the
time, so hunters were the only way to get nursery stock, let
alone new species. The large nurseries employed whole
crews of hunters. In 1894, for instance, the preeminent Victorian orchid grower Frederick Sander, who had sixty greenhouses at his estate in St. Albans, employed twenty-three
hunters collecting around the world for him, including a
man in Mexico, two in Brazil, two in Colombia, two in Peru,
one in Madagascar, one in New Guinea, three in India, and
one in the Straits Settlement. One of Sander's best hunters
was Benedict Roezl, a tough-looking Czech. Roezl had cut
off his left hand accidentally while in Havana demonstrating
a machine he had invented for extracting fiber from hemp;
the iron hook he used in its place added to his grim appearance. Roezl combed across South America and discovered
eight hundred new orchid species in his travels. At the peak
of Victorian orchid fever there were scores of orchid hunters
crisscrossing the world for different growers. In 1863 a boat
sailing to the Andes had among its passengers John Weir of
the Royal Horticultural Society; John Blunt, working for
Frederick Sander's archrival John Lowe; and a hunter named
Schlim, working for Jean-Jules Linden, a distinguished Belgian nurseryman. All three of these men were heading for exactly the same part of the Andes, looking for exactly the same

Peruvian odontoglossums, and each had promised his employer that he would be the first to bring the plants home. The wide world was crowded as far as orchid hunters were concerned. When men working for rival growers crossed paths they sometimes killed each other, or at least came close. William Arnold—the hunter who later drowned in the Orinoco—was a young German who often worked for Frederick Sander. Arnold was a defiant and irritable man known to be picky about the weapons he traveled with. He supposedly bragged to other hunters that he turned down an assignment because the sponsor offered him a lot of money but only a secondhand gun. Sander once sent Arnold to Brazil to look for cattleyas. On the boat ride over, Arnold got into a fight with another hunter on board who was also going to Brazil, also looking for cattleyas, but for Sander's rival John Lowe. Both hunters were heavily armed and belligerent. After boasts and threats and a display of side arms they nearly ended up in a duel. Once Arnold arrived in Brazil he wrote to Sander about the incident. According to his biographer Arthur Swinson, Sander wrote back to Arnold: "This makes me *very* excited and gives me much pleasure for I love these battles *very* much." He advised Arnold to stop hunting for orchids immediately and instead start tracking Lowe's orchid hunter to see what kinds of plants he was collecting and to get any he might overlook. Then Sander told Arnold to try to urinate on his competitor's plants when they were packed for shipping because the urine would cause the plants to bolt and die on the boat ride home.

Hunters worked solo and evidently enjoyed very little fraternity. They never traveled with their peers, but they were sometimes accompanied by huge crews—Joseph Hooker's sixty-man entourage included a valet, coolies, seed gatherers, cooks, tree climbers, a taxidermist, and a plant dryer. They

undoubtedly got lonely. When Augustus Margary was homesick he would stand outside his tent and sing "Polly Wolly
Doodle" and "My Darling Clementine." Nevertheless, if one
hunter encountered another in the jungle they would not so-
cialize, and they would certainly say nothing at all about
their orchids. Or they might offer false information and
phony directions to some imaginary hillside carpeted with
flowers, and sometimes they planted fake maps with orchid
habitats marked on them so that they could steer their rivals
the wrong way. They were either prideful or greedy or both.
Most took every orchid specimen they found. The Czech orchid hunter Roezl once sent Sander a shipment from South
America that weighed eight tons. Because orchid hunters
hated the thought of another hunter's finding any plants they
might have missed, they would "collect out" an area, and
then they would burn the place down. Even hunters working
for the same grower were dog-eat-dog. Competition between
them was so intense that it could even take their minds off
orchids. Whenever some of Sander's hunters came upon
each other they would stop looking for orchids and spend
days or weeks pursuing each other through the jungle for no
reason at all.

Hunters had to travel to scary and dangerous faraway
places, but that hardly ever deterred them. Benedict Roezl
was said to have been robbed seventeen times in his travels.
The English plant hunter Joseph Hooker spent two years
trekking through the Himalayas outfitted in nothing more
protective than his spectacles and a tartan shooting jacket.
He had no mountaineering equipment at all, although the
wife of a friend gave him some woolly stockings and a little
antiglare eyeshade she made for him out of one of her veils.
On his climbs Hooker had biscuits and tea and fine brandy,
carried a solid-oak traveling desk and brass-bound ditty

boxes, and slept with a copy of Darwin's *Journal of the Voyage of the Beagle* under his pillow. He rarely had a good night's sleep because the yaks he used as pack animals were insomniacs and so inquisitive that they would stick their heads into Hooker's tent and snort on him until he woke up. In his seven months in Assam he was drenched by nearly three hundred inches of rain. Nevertheless Hooker persevered, and by the end of his odyssey he had collected thousands of new species and had traveled higher and farther on Kanchenjunga, the world's third highest mountain, than any European before him. In 1865, done with his adventuring, Hooker became director of the Royal Botanical Gardens at Kew.

Commercial growers never hesitated to send their hunters somewhere unwholesome. A grower probably did mind losing a man by misadventure but maybe not as much as losing an opportunity for collecting. Carl Roebelin was another one of the great Victorian orchid hunters. He was German, mentally hard and physically fearless. At Sander's request he once went hunting on a small island in the Philippines. Just after he arrived an earthquake turned the island inside out and Roebelin was almost killed. As soon as he made it to safety he wired Sander to tell him that he was returning to England because the island had been devastated. At the end of the wire he mentioned that he'd seen some astounding cinnamon-scented lilac vandas in the jungle right before the earthquake. If Roebelin had really wanted to leave the Philippines and come home, this was exactly the wrong thing to say. Sander wired back immediately and demanded that Roebelin return to the island and find those lilac vandas or find another employer to pay his passage home. Roebelin refused and Sander's threats became more strenuous. Roebelin finally gave in. The plant he retrieved from the wreckage was a new species that was later given the name *Vanda sanderiana*. It was put on display in the Royal Botanic Gardens at Kew when it bloomed and was such a spectacle that it drew a crowd of thousands. Many vandas grown commercially now can be traced back to Roebelin's salvaged plant.

Sander's greatest hunter was another German named William Micholitz. He was tireless, productive, and canny, and Sander's preeminence as a commercial grower was largely due to Micholitz's many discoveries. Even so, Sander never seemed particularly tender toward him. Once when Micholitz was sailing from Ecuador back to England the ship he was sailing on caught fire. The ship was lost and the orchids he had collected for Sander burned and Micholitz almost died. He sent Sander a telegram saying, "Ship Burnt! What do?" Sander wired back: "Go Back!" Micholitz wired again: "Too late. Rainy season." Sander: "GO BACK." In 1899 Micholitz disappeared for several months, which apparently annoyed Sander more than it worried him. He complained in a letter to a friend: "Micholitz is perhaps eaten—we hear *nothing*." Micholitz had not been eaten and he did finally reappear; Sander greeted him and then commanded him to go collecting in Colombia at once even though the country was in the middle of a revolution. Sander once sent Micholitz to the Tanimbar Islands, remote bits of land southwest of New Guinea. After a few months Sander wrote to Micholitz demanding to know what orchids he had found in Tanimbar. Micholitz explained in his reply that he had successfully located orchids and had successfully found locals to help him collect but that he had run into interference: "A big battle has taken place. In the evening the people brought back their dead and wounded. Three had been decapitated by the enemy, and one of them was also minus hands and feet and last but not least his penis, which with one hand they hung up over the gate of the village. After the fight the people did not want to collect any plants."

Sander and Micholitz seem like a miserable couple, but what drew them together was that they were both in love with the same thing. Everything was less important and less interesting to them than orchids—even death and war. On the brink of World War I, Micholitz wrote to Sander that he worried about the approaching conflict but just for one reason, one that Sander certainly understood: "I suppose if it comes to a universal war, there will be very little demand for orchids." A few years later Sander was on his deathbed. Just before he fell into his final coma, he sent a note to a garden director in Frankfurt and signed off with a few lines Micholitz would have appreciated: "This illness will be the end of me. Tell me, how are the plants I sent you? Are they still alive?"

———

Some hunters traveled for so long that they became attached to the jungle and became strangers at home. Carl Roebelin dated local women and adopted the language of wherever he was hunting, and after a few years he settled in Burma with a Burmese woman and just shipped the plants he collected back to England by themselves. Charles Waterton, who wrote a book called *Wanderings in South America*, declared that while on his travels he had been "seized with an unconquerable aversion to Piccadilly" and went to live permanently with the Orinoco Indians. There is no record of what residents of places like Tanimbar and Assam and Belize felt about European hunters arriving out of the blue and harvesting their native flowers. Often local people worked for the hunters as guides. To say that most hunters respected them for anything other than their ability to find flowers would be untrue. Joseph Hooker, for one, scorned the locals he met; he called the Bhotias "queer and insolent," the Lepchas "veritable coward[s]," and the Khasi "sulky, intractable fellows." Orchid fever usually prevailed over common decency. At its worst it was the same arrogance and sense of entitlement of European colonization, only in miniature. In the late 1880s an Englishman in New Guinea discovered a new variety of orchid growing in a cemetery. Without bothering to get permission he dug up the graves and collected the flowers. As an afterthought he gave the people whose ancestors he had disinterred a few glass beads for the disturbed graves and to persuade them to help him carry the plants to port. After this graveyard shipment arrived in London it was sold in a deluxe auction house for a record amount of money. Another hunter in New Guinea found some good orchids growing on human remains. He collected the plants and sent them to England still attached to ribs and shinbones. That same year a *Dendrobium* from Burma was auctioned off at Protheroe's of London still attached to the human skull on which it had been found.

Sometimes orchid species were discovered and brought back to Europe but then couldn't be found again in the wild. These were known as lost orchids, and every orchid fancier and every ambitious commercial grower and every prideful hunter was determined to find one of them. *Paphiopedilum fairrieanum* was one of the lost orchids. It had been discovered in north India in the early 1800s and then seemed to vanish. Hunters scoured India and Burma for it without success, but their sponsors kept sending them back to look again. Frederick Sander's hunters once collected a few species that looked so much like *Paphiopedilum* that Sander was sure he had hit the jackpot. He sent the specimens to the dean of botanists, William Reichenbach, who examined the plants, identified them as cattleyas rather than the lost *Paphiopedilum,* and sent a nasty and dismissive note to Sander saying, "Don't talk to me about your stupid *Cattleya*—it's too piddling!" *Paphiopedilum fairrieanum* was eventually rediscovered by a hunter in the Himalayas forty years later. *Cattleya labiata vera* was, at one time, common in European greenhouses, but then one by one each mysteriously died until there was only a single plant left in all of western Europe. No nurseryman or plant hunter could remember where the flower had originally been found. Then the greenhouse with the sole surviving specimen burned down, incinerating the final domesticated *Cattleya labiata vera*. Hunters pined for it without luck for seventy years and finally more or less abandoned the search. One evening, seven decades after the last one had burned, a British diplomat spotted a woman at an embassy dinner in Paris with a corsage that reminded him of *Cattleya labiata vera*. He traced the flower to Brazil and confirmed that it was the lamented *Cattleya,* and soon hunters were able to restock Europe's greenhouses. Most other lost orchids, though, have never been seen again.

Orchid hunters' hauls got bigger and bigger toward the middle of the 1800s. This was partly motivated by rapacity and shortsightedness, but also by the fact that plant transportation was so unreliable that most of the plants shipped to Europe arrived dead—you needed to collect a huge haul to end up with even a small surviving heap of plants in London. In a letter to the Royal Horticultural Society in 1819 a nurseryman noted that only a few of a thousand plants shipped to him survived the trip. In 1827 a Whitechapel surgeon named Nathaniel Bagshaw Ward put a caterpillar to pupate in a glass jar and promptly forgot about it. Probably there was a little soil in the jar, because months later when Ward remembered the caterpillar, he noticed that a tiny fern and a few sprigs of grass had sprung up in the jar. Ward surmised that plants might flourish if they were kept in a sealed glass container with a little moisture and protected from London's dirty air, and that it might be possible for someone to cultivate exotic plants this way even inside a dark apartment. He then took a bigger jar and put in more plants and eventually created a miniature garden that was so extraordinary that landscape designers and horticulturists came to his house just to admire it. Word of Dr. Ward's indoor jungle got around, and soon a fern-filled "Wardian case" became a fixture in Victorian living rooms. Ward himself created the most elaborate of Wardian cases, which contained a fish tank, a fern garden, a chameleon, and a Jersey toad.

Dr. Ward further surmised that his glass cases might overcome the difficulties of plant transportation, and in 1834 he built a prototype, filled it with English ferns, and sent it on a six-month ship ride to New South Wales. The ferns thrived. He then shipped tender Australian ferns back to England in a sealed case, and they also survived. Ward published a magazine article in 1839 describing his Wardian cases; and in 1842 expanded it into a book called *On the Growth of Plants in Closely Glazed Cases*. Wardian cases were adopted directly by European gardeners. Now instead of only one in a thousand plants surviving a journey, more than nine hundred of a thousand plants would make it alive. The Wardian case made possible a new economy of botany. Profit-making plants like tea trees, tobacco, cork oak, and coffee bushes could be moved from their native continents to another, and from one region of a country to another. Natural boundaries melted; the world shrank to the size of a glass caterpillar jar. Inside a Wardian case, Joseph Paxton could ship an *Amherstia nobilis* from India to Chatsworth Hall; Joseph Hooker could send a consignment from Tierra del Fuego to the Royal Botanic Gardens at Kew of full-grown Argentinean trees.

Even after the Wardian case improved plant transportation, the huge hauls continued anyhow, and garden journals in England began publishing warnings about emptying the jungles. Some well-traveled places were already so deflowered that to find any orchids or to hope to find new species, hunters traveled to more and more remote jungles in places such as Surabaja, the Naga Hills, the Irrawaddy River area, Yap, and Fakfak. They combed through the East Indies island by island. In one journal a Malaysian botanist wrote that there were barely any orchids left in his country. In 1878 a Swiss botanist wrote: "Not satisfied with taking 300 or 500 specimens of a fine orchid, [collectors] must scour the whole country and leave nothing for many miles around. . . . These modern collectors spare nothing. This is no longer collecting; it is wanton robbery." A collector returning from Colombia reported that the places where *Miltonia* used to flourish were now "cleared as if by forest fire." Even the most inaccessible places were crowded with orchid hunters. Joseph Hooker climbed through the Khasia Mountains in Assam; the place was mobbed when he got there. He wrote to his father: "What with Jenkins' and Simon's collectors here, twenty or thirty of Falconer's, Lobb's, my friends Raban and Cave and Inglis's friends, the roads here are becoming stripped like the Penang jungles, and for miles it sometimes looks as if a gale had strewed the road with rotten branches and Orchidae. Falconer's men sent down 1000 baskets the other day." Early shipments from the tropics to England consisted of maybe fifty plants. Glass was so expensive that most greenhouses were small; fifty plants amounted to something in a small greenhouse. Then in 1845 Britain repealed the high tax on glass and thus launched the era of enormous plant houses, such as the Palm House at Kew Gardens, with its forty-five thousand square feet of pale green glass panels. Collectors and nurserymen wanted more of everything. In 1869 the Suez Canal opened, making the voyage from Africa, Madagascar, and Asia to Europe much shorter and more survivable. Hunters got better at their work, and by the 1870s shipments contained thousands and even tens of thousands of flowers. On one expedition for odontoglossums in Colombia, four thousand trees were chopped down and ten thousand orchids peeled off them. Even that number was soon surpassed. On May 4, 1878, an English grower named William Bull announced he was about to receive a record-sized consignment of two million plants.

—

Almost nothing is recorded about the lives of most orchid hunters except for whom they worked for, what species they discovered, and how they met their fate if they happened to die on the job. One hunter wrote to his sponsor that in spite of all his discoveries he expected to die anonymously "except for the doubtful immortality of a seed catalogue." Most hunters were German or Dutch or English, most were young, probably very few had families. No journal of the time mentions exactly where they grew up, how they fell into their profession, how well they were schooled if they were schooled at all. No mention is made of how they found their way around the world when finding your way around the world was not an easy thing to do, or how they taught themselves to identify plants that were nearly unknown. Obviously they were all adventuresome and able-bodied. Apparently they had a good sense of direction, mastery of a few foreign languages, and a tolerance for being alone. Certainly they were men who chose to live a life that offered little ordinary comfort, maybe no domestic life at all, most likely only a sprinkling of money. Chances are they were refugees from the conventions of the middle class. Instead they chose lives that would take them to the corner pockets of the world where they would see things maybe no one else ever would, things they thought were more mysterious and different and beautiful than ever imagined. The great travelers of the eighteenth century had sought out the marvels of the civilized world, those achievements that were man-made and had in fact won out over nature. By the nineteenth century curiosity had changed. It might have been the moment when cynicism was born. The Industrial Revolution was proving that not all man-made advances were perfect and many could be awful. Alfred Wallace, a colleague of Darwin's, once noted that the English working class lived in squalor unknown to the "primitives" he studied in the Amazon. Nature by contrast seemed pure and bewitching. The great travelers turned away from civilization and went to explore the wild world. Fascination with what man could create gave way to the question of how man was created and what if anything distinguished humankind from the rest of the natural world.

The British Isles have a limited number of native species of plants and animals, whereas the places British orchid hunters explored had an unimaginable profusion of natural forms. The Victorians were tireless name-givers and classifiers, and they set out to categorize the living diversity they were finding on other continents. At the center of this enterprise was the locating, identifying, and classifying of orchids, the greatest of all plant families. As modern living became chaotic and bewildering, the Victorians looked for order in the universe, an outline that could organize their knowledge of every living thing and maybe at the same time rationalize the meaning of existence.

Orchid hunters had important and consequential but ultimately invisible lives. They discovered hundreds of plant species, but they are mostly unremembered for it. They were the first to trail-blaze many parts of the world, but no place is named for them, no plaque marks their landings, no one recalls that they traveled across many of those places long before the royally commissioned explorers who are credited with discovering them. What they brought out of the roughest jungles was not just gorgeous and astonishing but also essential to science. They saw more of the world than most men of their time, but finally the world forgot them. I used to think that John Laroche was irascible and self-reliant and enterprising enough to have been the perfect Victorian orchid hunter, but I think it would have galled him too much to have no one remember his name.

—

The very first tropical orchid to bloom in England had not been collected by an professional orchid hunter. It was a *Bletia verecunda* that a Quaker cloth merchant named Peter Collinson had found in the Bahamas in 1731, a hundred years before orchid hunting was in its prime. When Collinson returned to England he gave the *Bletia* to a friend named Sir Charles Wager, who put the plant in his garden and mulched it with bark for the winter. The plant looked weedy and dry, but the next summer it produced a lovely flower. Other orchids were brought to England during the next few decades by colonial administrators and returning missionaries who had collected the flowers as souvenirs. Captain Bligh of the HMS *Bounty* brought some back on one of his expeditions to Jamaica. *Cattleya labiata* came to England in 1818, when a horticulturist named William Cattley found and cultivated some strange-looking plants that had been used as packing material in a shipment of moss and lichens. Orchids had been a high-class hobby in China for three thousand years. The world's first orchid books were published in 1228, when Chao Shih-ken wrote *Orchid Guide for Kuei-men and Chang-chou*, and in 1247, when Wang Kuei-hsueh wrote *Wang's Orchid Guide*. During the Ming Dynasty, orchids were used to treat venereal diseases, diarrhea, boils, neuralgia, and sick elephants. West Indians had long eaten certain species to relieve ptomaine poisoning from bad fish and used the pseudobulbs for pipes; Malaysians used dendrobiums to cure skin eruptions, dropsy, and headaches; Zulus used orchids as emetics; the Swagi people prescribed orchids for certain pediatric illnesses; in South America, *Cyrtopodium* orchids, known commonly as cigar orchids, were made into cobblers' glue and lubricant for violin strings. Nevertheless, in the early 1800s in England, orchids were brand-new. When the first tropical orchids appeared in England they were hardly more than curiosities. In 1813 the orchid collection at Kew consisted of only forty-six tropical species.

What changed was that in 1833 William Spencer Cavendish saw an oncidium at a small exhibition in London and decided to begin his own collection. Cavendish was the sixth duke of Devonshire. He was deaf and chronically depressed and was suspected of being a changeling because his father had lived with his wife and his wife's best friend and impregnated them both. Nonetheless Cavendish received the family title. He always lived alone and came to be known as the Bachelor Duke. Cavendish was an ardent and discriminating collector. He assembled a huge library and owned the first four Shakespeare folios and thirty-nine Shakespeare quartos. He loved plants, and in the 1820s he had served as the president of the Royal Horticultural Society. The duke's gardener was a farmer's son named Joseph Paxton who had been appointed head gardener at the duke's estate, Chatsworth, when he was only twenty-three. Paxton was a sort of genius at making things work. Soon after Cavendish hired him, he built a score of greenhouses at Chatsworth, including one called the Great Stove that was the biggest in the world—three hundred feet long and more than a hundred feet wide and heated by seven miles of pipes. In his spare time, Paxton invented a little mesh device called a strawberry crinoline, which was a sort of skirt for a strawberry plant that kept slugs from hopping onto the berries; in his honor, a popular strawberry species was named the Joseph Paxton and remained in cultivation as late as the 1950s. He named a species of dwarf banana *Musa cavendishii*. The Cavendish was such a successful banana that Paxton received a Royal Horticulture Society medal for it. Supposedly, Paxton had been inspired to work on breeding a dwarf banana after noticing some Chinese wallpaper at Chatsworth that had a tiny banana as part of its design. All British bananas today are descendants of Joseph Paxton's bananas.

Paxton was knighted after one of his most famous accomplishments, which involved a giant water lily discovered in 1837 in British Guiana. The lily was thought to be the biggest flowering plant in the world. A Victorian botanist described it as "a vegetable wonder." After it was discovered, all of horticultural England was competing to grow the first *Victoria amazonica* on British soil. Paxton won. His lily floated in a special pond at Chatsworth. It had leaves that were six feet in diameter and a flower that was bigger than a head of cabbage and it smelled like pineapple. The flowering of the plant was so momentous that Queen Victoria and Prince Albert came to Chatsworth to see it in flower. Once, just for fun, Paxton and the Bachelor Duke dressed Paxton's seven-year-old daughter, Annie, in a fairy costume and stood her up on one of the giant lily pads floating in the pond and took a picture. The image of Annie Paxton standing on the lily was a sensation. The writer Douglas Jerrold published a poem that began, "On unbent leaf in fairy guise/Reflected in the water/Beloved, admired by hearts and eyes/Stands Annie, Paxton's daughter." Water-lily motifs cropped up in wallpaper, china, fabrics, and chandeliers, and posing a child on a water-lily leaf became a photographic cliché. Paxton wasn't content to merely balance his daughter on the leaf. He found he could load the leaf with not just Annie but with *five* full-sized children or the equivalent of three hundred pounds of deadweight. After studying the leaf, he decided that it could support so much weight on account of its ribs, which formed a sort of cantilevered trussing. In 1850, Paxton designed a spectacular glass building, the Crystal Palace, for the first world's fair, the Great Exhibition of the Works of Industry of All Nations. He modeled the Crystal Palace on the giant weight-bearing water-lily pad. The Crystal Palace was an eighteen-acre exhibition hall constructed of crisscrossed iron girders that supported almost three hundred thousand panes of glass. Nothing like the Crystal Palace had ever been built before. It was the first major use of iron in architecture for aesthetic as well as structural purposes, and its great vault of glass was an engineering marvel. The exhibits it enclosed were impressive—a world-record *Grammatophyllum speciosum* orchid weighing two tons, the Koh-i-noor diamond displayed in a golden birdcage, statues of naked people, unusual pottery, clocks, fabrics, furniture, and a collection of German frogs that had been stuffed and arranged in human poses, which Queen Victoria reportedly loved. Some exhibits were practical—for instance, Francis Parkes unveiled his newly invented all-steel garden fork, which allowed farmers to turn soil easily—but most of the exhibits in the Crystal Palace were regarded by designers of the time as the most tasteless gathering of junk ever seen. On the other hand, Paxton's Crystal Palace itself was celebrated as a triumph of design. It became the consummate model for Victorian architects and engineers, and elements of its structure are still used in contemporary buildings. Without Paxton's study of the lily pad's cantilevered trussing, his glass-and-ironwork palace would never have been built.

Once the Bachelor Duke was smitten by the oncidium he devoted himself to orchids and instructed Paxton to develop a collection for him. Within ten years, Paxton had assembled the largest orchid collection in England. Paxton assigned a gardener on his staff to go orchid hunting. In 1837 the young gardener sent Paxton from Assam at least eighty or ninety species of plants never before seen in Europe, mostly orchids, but also an exceptional genus of Indian tree, *Amherstia nobilis*, from Calcutta. The duke's reaction to the *Amherstia* was so passionate that Paxton wrote to his wife: "Then came the solemn introduction of the duke to my long cherished love, the *Amherstia*. I cannot detail how this important introduction took place; suffice it to say that the duke ordered his breakfast to be brought into the Painted Hall where the plant stands, and he desired me to sit down and lavish my love upon the gem while he had his breakfast by it." Paxton built for the *Amherstia* a special greenhouse, where it flourished but never flowered. Nevertheless, Queen Victoria visited it in 1843. It must have been one of the most wonderful nights in the world. The queen and the prince drove their horse and carriage through the Bachelor Duke's Great Stove, which Paxton had illuminated for them with twelve thousand lights.

The Bachelor Duke's obsession ignited the fashion for orchids in English high society that continued for decades. Orchids were seen as the badge of wealth and refinement and worldliness; they implied mastery of the wilderness and of alien places; their preciousness made them the beautiful franchise of the upper class. So many new varieties were being found every day that no collector could ever rest—orchids were an endless preoccupation. Once the vogue for orchids began, the prices paid for the plants, the measures taken to obtain them, and the importance attached to them took on an air of madness. This Victorian obsession, this "orchidelirium," was a rapacious desire. In intensity, it was similar to the Dutch tulip mania of the 1630s, which reached its zenith in 1637, when the rights to a tulip bulb named Viceroy were sold at auction for a farm's worth of valuable goods including six loads of grain, four oxen, eight hogs, twelve sheep, wine, beer, and a thousand pounds of cheese. The most valued tulips were those with brilliant streaks and stripes of colors, then thought to be the mark of distinction, and now known by botanists to be the evidence of a devastating flower virus spread by aphids. The Dutch tulip market grew into something much more than gardening—it became a speculative, highly leveraged futures bubble, which soon burst.

An average Englishman couldn't afford an orchid collection or a greenhouse or a gardener or a professional hunter collecting for him. Owning orchids was the privilege of the rich, but the desire for orchids had no class distinction. Average Englishmen wanted orchids badly, too. In 1851 a man named Benjamin Williams wrote a series of articles advocating orchid ownership for everybody. The series was called "Orchids For the Millions." Eventually it was published as a book so popular that it had to be reprinted seven times.

———

The English were horrible orchid growers at first, and they usually killed every orchid they got their hands on. The di-

rector of the Royal Botanical Gardens at Kew in 1850 became so exasperated that he declared England "the grave of
all tropical orchids." Even if the great turn-of-the-century
nurseries like Black & Flory, Stuart Low & Co., Charles-
worth & Co., McBean's, and Sander & Son were graveyards,
they were magnificent graveyards, fitted with handblown
glass panels and lined with wrought-iron plant benches.
Toward the end of the 1800s orchid science progressed
enough to make cultivation more reliable and England's
greenhouses finally started to bloom. The plants were no
longer being potted in rotted wood and leaves, and instead
were put in a healthier growing medium. Joseph Paxton was
responsible for probably the most important advance: the
English believed that orchids thrived in jungle-like environments, so they kept their greenhouses—what they called
their "stoves"—suffocatingly steamy and hot. In fact most
orchids prefer temperate perches above the jungle floor, on
trees and rocks in the mountains. Until Paxton experimented
with cooler, drier greenhouses, English orchids were being
boiled to death. In 1856 the first artificial hybrid—a plant
made by intentionally cross-fertilizing different species—
bloomed. These early orchid "mules" were a botanical shock.
Upon seeing one, the orchid grower John Lindley is said to
have shouted, "My God! You will drive the botanists mad!"
The breeders, the botanists, the hunters, and the collectors
of orchids were all men. Victorian women were forbidden
from owning orchids because the shapes of the flowers were
considered too sexually suggestive for their shy constitutions,
and anyway the expense and danger and independence of
collecting in the tropics were beyond any Victorian woman's
ken. Englishwomen and orchids have for a long time had an
uneasy relationship; in 1912, in fact, suffragettes destroyed
most of the specimens at Kew Garden. Queen Victoria, how-

ever, was a passionate orchid fancier. She created the office of Royal Orchid Grower and appointed the celebrated grower Frederick Sander to it. For her Golden Jubilee, Sander presented her with an orchid bouquet that was seven feet high and five feet wide, and a collector named Loher named the newly discovered *Dendrobium victoria-regina* in her honor. Queen Victoria's affection for orchids added to their glamour in England and around the world. In 1883 Viscount Itsujin Fukuba built the first greenhouse in Asia. It was said to be as big as a mansion, and the viscount filled it with orchids that English growers, and particularly Frederick Sander, sent to him in Japan. In 1891 the Romanovs, who had built their enormous collection thanks to Sander, named him a baron of the Holy Russian Empire. Soon after, Sander awarded himself his own title. He began to refer to himself as the Orchid King.

———

In 1838 James Boott of London sent a tropical orchid to his brother John Wright Boott of Boston. John Boott liked the orchid so much that he asked his brother to send him more. His brother obliged, and over the next few years Boott built a substantial collection in his Boston home. When he died he willed his collection to John Amory Lowell of Roxbury, Massachusetts, who added even more plants to it, and then in 1853 Lowell sold the whole collection to the tenant in his country residence. The tenant let most of the orchids die. The few survivors were divided among a Miss Pratt of Watertown, Massachusetts, and a Boston man named Edward Rand, who expanded the collection once again, cultivated a cattleya reportedly as large as a small washtub, and then in 1865 sold his estate and donated the collection to Harvard College. This is how tropical orchids came to America. Right off the bat, they had admirers as zealous as their admirers in

Europe, and American collectors soon rivaled the English. A collector named Cornelius Van Voorst, of Jersey City, New Jersey, bought his first orchid in 1855, and by 1857 he had amassed almost three hundred species, including an *Ansellia africana* that was so large that two men could hardly lift it. General John Rathbone of Albany, New York, started his collection in 1866. He wrote to a friend in 1868: "I was so delighted with the plant and flowers that I caught the Orchid fever, which I am happy to say is now prevailing to considerable extent in this country, and which I trust will become epidemic. In 1867, so that I might successfully grow this charming family of plants, I built a house exclusively for Orchids."

In 1874 Miss Jane Kenniburgh of Carickfergus, Ireland, moved to Tallahassee, Florida. She brought with her a load of her favorite belongings, including her *Phaius grandfolius,* a variety of tropical orchid that is sometimes called "nun's lily." Before she died Miss Kenniburgh gave the plants to her friend Mrs. S. J. Douglas, the daughter of Florida's governor, and later Mrs. Douglas gave them to her daughter Mrs. George Lewis. Mrs. Lewis's orchids had a leisurely life. They lived in the Lewises' greenhouse in the winter and sunbathed under oak trees in the backyard during the summer. The Florida climate agreed with them and they thrived and multiplied. There is no record of what finally became of them, but Miss Kenniburgh's *Phaius* are recognized as the first greenhouse-cultivated orchids in Florida. More orchids followed. Orchid collectors sprang up in Miami, in Fort Lauderdale, in Naranja, in Homestead; the great estates of Palm Beach and Miami built orchid houses and hired resident orchid keepers; in 1886 Dr. Charles Torrey Simpson, the naturalist who later wrote the best-known guidebooks to Florida's animals and plants, bought a piece of jungle on Biscayne Bay and planted orchids on every other tree; commercial orchid nurseries like John Soar's of Little River popped up around the state. Businesses that rented blooming potted orchids for special occasions and took care of the plants when their owners were away were set up in society towns like Palm Beach.

———

Orchid hunting became known as terrible and romantic. A young preppie named Norman MacDonald wrote a book in 1939 called *The Orchid Hunters,* the story of how he and a college friend considered and rejected the idea of collecting monkeys, divi-divi, carnauba wax, and alligator hides, but then decided to go orchid hunting in South America. The book begins with the inscription: "Warning to the literal minded. Do not try to follow the trail of the orchid hunters on the [book's] map. In keeping with the close-lipped tradition of the profession, the real names of the towns and rivers have been deliberately changed. Not that you'd want to go there, but then . . ." and continues with this prologue: "The old orchid hunter lay back on his pillow, his body limp. . . . 'You'll curse the insects,' he said at last, 'and you'll curse the natives. . . . The sun will burn you by day and the cold will shrivel you by night. You'll be racked by fever and tormented by a hundred discomforts, but you'll go on. For when a man falls in love with orchids, he'll do anything to possess the one he wants. It's like chasing a green-eyed woman or taking cocaine. . . . it's a sort of madness. . . .' "

Men from Florida dominated American orchid hunting. They combed through Central America and South America and came back with shiploads. They dug around in the woods and swamps just a couple of miles from home. The Fakahatchee Strand was a plentiful place—long ago it was like an orchid supermarket. Hunters in the Fakahatchee hauled out thousands of orchids, piled them into horse-drawn flatbed carts, boxed them, shipped them, went back into the Fakahatchee again. In one shipment in 1890 two thousand butterfly orchids went by train from the Faka-hatchee to New York City, followed by trainloads of dollar or-chids, cow horn orchids, ladies' tresses. I came upon an old graying photograph of one of these shopping trips—two horses, four men in sun hats and short sleeves, two carts with wide-spoked wheels groaning with loads that look like brushy rubbish but were in fact stacks and stacks of orchid plants. Hunters in Florida found new species in their back-yards that they had expected to find in the Caribbean. Some of these species had probably traveled across the ocean by wind or bird or by some coincidental transport, and southern Florida was as far north as they could grow. In 1844 the botanist Jean-Jules Linden discovered an interesting snow-white orchid in Cuba. The plant was leafless and had a mass of roots, so he named it *Polyrrhiza lindenii*—"the many-rooted plant found by Linden." In 1880 a botanical explorer named A. H. Curtiss found the same Cuban species in Col-lier County, near the Fakahatchee Strand. It was definitely *Polyrrhiza lindenii*. After a while, the species acquired a com-mon name in Florida—it became known as the ghost.

———

One oven of a night while I was in Florida, the American Or-chid Society threw a black-tie gala to celebrate its seventy-fifth anniversary. The party was being held at the Flagler mansion in Palm Beach, just a couple of miles from the soci-ety's headquarters on the Vaughn estate in West Palm Beach and just a couple of miles from where I stayed most of the time when I was tagging along with Laroche. I assumed a lot of collectors would be coming to the party, so I wanted to go. It also meant that for the first time since coming to Florida I would have a chance to wear something other than swamp clothes—the clothes that I had to throw away as soon as they'd served their purpose—or plant-nursery clothes— baggy khakis, and T-shirts that were becoming permanently marked with dust and mulch. I had brought a black silk jacket and cocktail dress with me that I still hadn't even taken out of their dry-cleaning bags. I'm not sure what I had imagined my life in Florida was going to be like, but I guess I must have expected there might be more occasions that involved cocktails. It wasn't like that at all. I stayed at my parents' condominium in West Palm Beach—most of the time my parents weren't there—and every morning I'd get up, listen to the unvarying weather report, slap on some sunscreen, and then go down to Homestead or across to the Fakahatchee or over to Miami with a stop in Hollywood to talk to orchid growers and visit nurseries and see people at the Seminole reservation and take a walk in the woods. It felt as if I were driving a million miles every day. My right index finger got numb from pushing the scan button on the radio, and I started doing all those hot-weather traveling-salesman car things, like spreading a map across the dashboard whenever I parked and bending the sun visors at severe angles to get maximum shade and keeping a few changes of clothes in the car. My nose was always filled with the sugary smell of flowers and the bitter smell of fertilizer and the sour smell of tar melting on the road. At night I'd come back, usually muddy, to West Palm Beach, sometimes with a plant or two in the trunk that someone had pressed upon me, and first I'd look for someone to give the plant to and then I would go for a run on the golf course, watching for alligators and thinking over what I'd heard that day about plants and Florida and life and other things. Most of the restaurants in West Palm Beach stop serving early, so I had to really scamper to get food before everything was closed. The place open the latest was a sushi bar in a strip mall that was alongside an Australian steakhouse, an Italian café, and a Thai diner. A lot of the time I was in Florida I was in a bit of a daze, a kind of stranger's daze that comes on when you hear and see and smell and touch so many new things that they all start to smear together into one single feeling of newness and strangeness. I have friends and relatives in Florida, but I didn't see most of them while I was there; I felt as if I really was in some other exotic place where I didn't expect or want to recognize anything I'd see.

———

The American Orchid Society gala sounded as if it would be a rich business opportunity for Laroche, since these collectors were exactly who he expected would clamor for his homegrown ghost orchids someday, but I knew he wouldn't attend an event like this if you paid him a million dollars. I called and asked him to come with me anyway, just to get his goat. Also, I didn't really want to go all by myself. The day I called he was in an expansive mood. "Me at that party?" he said. "No fucking way. Those people hate me. They think I'm a criminal. They despise me. I'm bad news in the plant world." He sounded pleased. "They want me *dead*. I'm serious. You think I'm kidding? Well, I'm not. And to be honest, I feel the same way towards them."

"So you're not coming with me?"

He snorted and said absolutely nothing else, and after a moment he hung up the phone.

The Flagler mansion is a good place to have a gala. It was built in 1902 by Henry Flagler, the financier and oilman who was one of Miami's earliest developers, and it is an enormous place—even its wings have wings. Since 1959 it has been a historical museum, but you can still tell how nice it must have been when it was somebody's house. It is as square as a ship and its portico has six soaring columns. Inside, the rooms are large and the ceilings are high and heavy-beamed and everything in the house is twinkly—twinkly polished wood and twinkly polished silver and twinkly gilded curlicues on the walls and floors. For the party the front lawn of the mansion was dotted with winking yellow lights that looked bright and blurry in the night's wet heat. When I drove in, the mansion's half-moon driveway was filled with long, clean, twinkly cars and a half-dozen parking attendants wearing starched white shirts and bow ties who were sprinting back and forth from some faraway parking lot. I waited for my turn and watched each of the cars ahead of me pop out first a woman in a long gown with a stole around her shoulders and then a man in a crisp black tux. It was a luscious, moony night. Palm trees leaned over the driveway and cast shadows shaped like giant hands. The lawn was glittering with dew. Crickets hidden in the grass were chirping. Every now and then the door of the mansion would swing wide and let a blast of orchestra music out into the night air.

It was a little dazzling inside, too. A couple of hundred people were milling around in the entry hall, and more were inching through a receiving line where the Orchid Society's party chairmen were shaking hands and introducing the honorary chairmen from England—the earl and countess of Mansfield, Lord and Lady Skelmersdale, and the Honorable Alasdair Morrison and Mrs. Morrison. The Englishwomen were wearing beautiful poufy dresses in delicate colors and had upswept light-colored hair. There were sixty or seventy round dining tables arranged in the entry hall and along the balustrade overlooking the dance floor. Each table had a different arrangement of orchids at the center. The table orchids had been donated by growers from Florida and

California and Thailand and the Isle of Jersey and Hawaii and the Netherlands. In the entry hall there were three high platforms, about halfway to the ceiling, and on top of each platform was a brass bowl the size of a bathtub overfull with pink and ivory and pale green and lavender and lemon-orange and pure-white orchids. The orchids in the bowls had been flown in that morning from Singapore. Anywhere you stood the air smelled good. A waiter bobbed up and down through the crowd with tiny hors d'oeuvres on a silver platter that had orchids piled in the center. A woman I recognized from an orchid show grabbed my elbow and said hello and then whispered that she'd heard there were supposed to be pure chocolate orchids for dessert but they'd melted earlier in the day.

People had donated things to be auctioned after dinner—an antique slot machine, tickets to the Olympics, antique hand-painted orchid plates, six rare paphiopedilums, a portrait of a paphiopedilum by a famous paphiopedilum artist, a portrait of your favorite orchid painted for you by the official painter of the Royal Horticulture Society, the right to have a new orchid hybrid named for you or for whomever you chose. Elizabeth Taylor had donated six hundred bottles of her new perfume that were parceled out as little gifts for the guests. Next to the auction items a big portrait of her sat on an easel. The line to view the auction items was wide and long, so I could only peek over a shoulder here and there; I could see that someone had left a $575 bid for the orchid plates and $500 for the favorite-orchid portrait.

On my way to my table I saw the earl of Mansfield leaning against a wall. His wife had impressed me in the receiving line because she was so pretty and her hands felt like baby powder. The earl of Mansfield has a trim build, shiny white hair, black plastic eyeglasses, and an absentmindedly cheery aspect. He must have escaped from the receiving line. His head was now a little drooped. He was grimacing and rolling his shoulders but somehow managing not to spill his drink. I said hello, and he looked lively and said, "Nothing like a good American martini to make you feel well!" He invited me to lean against the wall with him. After a moment he said he'd just had a minor operation and was recuperating and had just finished a really delightful trip—he'd gone shooting with great friends in Spain and then shooting with great friends in Sweden and then visiting great friends in Italy and then visiting great friends in Barbados. He asked me what species I collected, and I admitted to him that I was just a spectator in the orchid world. He sighed and said his whole orchid obsession began innocently with a cymbidium from Harrods that was sent to him by a friend. "I'd never had anything to do with orchids before that. I put the cymbidium in my little greenhouse and I'm afraid to say it . . . *perished.* Then in 1971 I moved to Scotland and, oh, my, I started a collection. I had inherited an old gardener from my father who liked asparagus and tomatoes but didn't like orchids at all, so I had to keep after him."

The earl was now looking very perked up. He mentioned that he had his own little distillery that made Royal Lochnagar Special Reserve single-malt Scotch. A waiter was passing by, and the earl waved him over and traded his old martini for a new one. During the transaction the waiter stood stock-still and looked unaccountably bashful until the earl gave him a wink and then turned back to me. "Once we started with the orchids we've never looked back," he said. "I grew to be quite in love with them, you know. I like them because they're slightly evil and slightly mysterious, don't you think? In the early days I found it hard to make them flower, and when I did, it was a great, great triumph. They are a great, great challenge. They sulk, they pout, they ignore you. But it's been onward with the orchids! I've built a special orchid house on my estate, with three climates, all computer-controlled, so I can have species that don't tolerate one another's climates. I have all information about every single plant on the computer—where it came from, when it's flowered, all the particulars."

I asked Lord Mansfield what he did for a living. He said he'd been Margaret Thatcher's minister of state until 1981 and a member of the House of Lords. "Now I'm—I suppose you'd say I'm retired," he said. "I would spend every day in my orchid house if I could, but duty still beckons, doesn't it, though?" He gestured toward the receiving line and then made some comments about the flower arrangements in the entry hall. The rumble of the crowd was quieting and the orchestra was settling down, which meant it was getting to be time for dinner. The earl straightened up and then did that chicken-neck motion that men do to get their Adam's apple out of their collars. "You say you have no orchids at all?" he asked. "A young lady like you could start a collection now and by the time you were my age you'd have great, great results." His own collection was less than thirty years old and it was the largest one in Scotland.

"Do any of your kids have orchids?"

He laughed and said, "I have a son who is thirty-nine and I'm sure he wants to get his hands on my orchids. I think he's quite eagerly waiting for me to die."

Gorgeous

I called Laroche the next day to tell him about the gala and the flowers I'd seen and the people I'd met there. I had gotten to know him well enough by then to know exactly how he'd sound and what he'd say. No matter the time of day—that day I happened to be calling around noon—Laroche always answered the phone sounding as if he'd been woken up after falling asleep on a couch watching a game show. I don't think I ever actually woke him up. It was just his low, slushy voice and his manner—drowsy, cross, suspicious as a tax examiner's. Then, once he would establish that it was me on the phone, his voice would amplify in one blast and he would immediately start complaining that I had broken some promise to call him or see him or meet him somewhere. The complaints were never true. I had nothing *else* to do while I was in Florida except to follow him around, and besides the obvious fact that he was the whole point of my being in Florida I was very homesick a lot of the time and was always excited and conscientious when I had plans. In fact, Laroche was the one who was always leaving me in the lurch. When I first met him his accusations rattled me, but I had finally persuaded myself to ignore them. That day when I called he managed a muffled hello and then began chiding me for not calling earlier, and when he was done, I told him about the Orchid Society party, and when I was done, he cleared his throat and said, "I'm going to a little orchid show in Fort Lauderdale this afternoon, if you want to come. It's just a little show, but there will probably be some cute things there," and then he gave me directions to War Memorial Auditorium, where it was being held.

I always felt lucky when there was an orchid event being held while I was on one of my trips to Florida, but in truth there really isn't ever a time when there isn't some kind of plant show or garden meeting or plant lecture going on. The Miami paper always publishes a list of the week's upcoming plant events in the area. That week, for instance, there was going to be a Tropical Flowering Tree Society meeting; a South Florida Fern Society lecture ("How to Groom Ferns for Shows"); the Fort Lauderdale Orchid Society meeting; a Rare Fruit Council lecture ("Transplanting Mature Tropical Fruit Trees"); the Bromeliad Society of South Florida show and sale; meetings of the Gold Coast Orchid Society and the Florida Native Plant Society and the South Florida Orchid Society ("Orchid Trends in California") and the South Dade Garden Club and the Evening Garden Club of Fort Lauderdale. In Florida, plants are everywhere, like money. Plants *are* money. Wherever I drove, I passed greenhouses as long as train stations, and potted palms being sold out of the backs of rust-mottled pickup trucks, and Christmas tree farms, and orchid farms, and houseplant farms, and sod farms, and tree-moving companies (CALL US AT 930-TREE!), and signs on light posts saying PALMS CHEAP FOR SALE AHEAD or THIS WAY: MANGO AND BANANA TREES, and flatbed trucks loaded with palm trees stacked lengthwise, their trunks wrapped in wide white muslin strips so that they looked like racehorses' legs. If you didn't like plants you would be lonely here.

After I spoke to Laroche I got myself ready and then drove to the auditorium in Fort Lauderdale and waited for him. I didn't see him at first, so I wandered across the street to an antiques store that didn't have anything in it made any earlier than around 1968. Through the store's front window, I could see people hustling in and out of the auditorium. Everyone coming out was carrying a bag or a box with the top of a plant sticking out. At last I saw Laroche's van pull into the parking lot past the sign that said EXIT ONLY and past the orange cones marking the legitimate parking, and then it came to a stop in a shady spot. I left the store and crossed the street to meet him. When I got there he was leaning against the door of the van looking ashen-faced and skinny. I said hi and asked if he was feeling okay. "Of course I'm not," he said impatiently. "I'm fucking *dying*." He refused to specify what was killing him, so we just stood there quietly until he finished his cigarette and then walked to the auditorium entrance.

The tickets were six dollars. Laroche looked at me. "Can't you get these for free?" he asked.

"Free? How would I get them for free?" I said. Laroche frowned and then stepped in front of me and said to the man at the ticket table, "Hey, how about if you give us two tickets?" The ticket seller chuckled and stuck out his hand, palm up. "It's research," Laroche insisted. The man's hand didn't move. The door to the auditorium opened and a couple came through, leaving the show. The man was balancing a box full of plants on his hip. As they walked by he was saying, "I am

really not a cattleya person, Dee Dee!" and she was shaking
her head and saying, "Well, I am *really* not a paph person,
Phil!" A rush of warm air picked up one of the show programs sitting on the table and it went fluttering and landed
with a sigh on the floor. A fidgety line was forming behind us.
I counted out twelve dollars into the ticket man's hand.
Laroche dropped the stubs in the prize-drawing box and then
pushed through the door.

For the show, booths with orchids for sale were set up all
around the edge of the auditorium and in rows across the
middle. In the very center of the hall were two islands where
the dealers had arranged their displays. Laroche told me the
theme of the show had something to do with circuses, and
pointed to a display near us that had orchids set up on a
miniature Ferris wheel and grouped around toy clowns and
tableaux of circus animals. We started to circle clockwise.
The first booth we passed had a sign above it saying DANCIN'
DOLLS—PINK SHOWY BABY! FRAGRANT! and a long table
crowded with plastic pots. Most of the plants were tiny, just
squirts of foliage. One, toward the back, was tall with long,
arching leaves and a flower shaped like a little dustpan. The
leaves were blackish green and the flower itself was glossy
yellow, the yellow of a newly waxed taxi, and it was spattered
with hundreds and hundreds of burgundy flecks. The flecks
were slightly ovoid, and they were clustered in curving rows
so that they looked as if they had been painted on as the
flower spun around. Staring at the pattern of the flecks was
dizzying. Staring at it for a long time was hypnotizing. After a
while it made the muscles in the back of my eyes tingle.
Laroche leaned over and squinted at it. He moved the flower
from side to side. "These are as pretty as hell," he said at last.
"It's like an explosion in a paint factory. You know how this
happens? Its chromosomes are all fucked up. That's how you

get these nauseating patterns. The Japanese love that. This is probably a huge hit in Japan." He took a sharp breath. "If I could breed a black orchid with a purple lightning bolt across the petals, I'd never have to work again."

A woman wearing clingy pink shorts stopped at the table. She gaped at the flower Laroche was holding. "How do they *do* this?" she asked him. The dealer who was in charge of the booth came over. The woman said to him, "I have to ask you something. My orchids are wimps. Where did I go wrong? They're pathetic. I've been feeding them Bloom Booster and they're still wimpy."

The dealer said, "Don't give them too much food. It's like an eating disorder. It's like bingeing."

"But I thought Bloom Booster . . ."

The dealer scowled. "Well, people think Bloom Booster is a miracle and, honey, it's *not.*"

She pursed her lips. "I get it, I get it. Thanks. Now. Let's see. There's an orchid here *somewhere* that smells like chocolate that I want to go find."

Laroche tapped her shoulder. She turned around and he said, "It's none of my business but there's also one that smells like Grape Kool-Aid and you shouldn't miss that one, either."

They had fabulous, fantastic names: Golden Grail and Mama Cass and Markie Pooh and Golden Buddha Raspberry Delight and Dee Dee's Fat Lip. When orchids were first brought to England they were thought to be members of a very small and very unusual plant family. Then the number of newly discovered species reached the tens of thousands, and the nature of the orchid family was reconsidered. In fact, it became almost impossible to keep track of all the new orchids being discovered, so an official registry was established in 1895, which is now run by the Royal Horticultural Society, and has continued to be used by orchidists all over the world. New species were usually named by the person who discovered them or by the person who sponsored the person who actually discovered them or, in the case of hybrids, by the person who first created them. The International Orchid Register now lists the names, with explanations, for more than one hundred thousand species and hybrids:

"*Carteria:* Dedicated in 1910 to Mr. J. J. Carter of Pleasant Grove, who was the first one to lay eyes on it."

"*Hofmeistera:* I have dedicated the genus to a most friendly and distinguished man, W. Hofmeister, thinking that the plant both by its conspicuous pollen and all the beautiful coil-bearing little cells and the wonderful web of its perigonium exhibiting so many microscopic virtues is properly and appropriately dedicated to Hofmeister, a microscopist."

"*Robiquetia:* In honor of M. Pierre Robiquet, French chemist, for his numerous important discoveries, including caffeine and morphine."

"*Orleanesia:* In honor of Prince Gaston d'Orleans, Comte d'Eu, distinguished amateur and patron of floriculture in Brazil."

Some orchids have been named for their appearances. The ghost orchid has many roots; its official genus name is *Polyrrhiza*, which is Greek for many roots. A genus with a droopy head and floppy petals was named *Corybas*, which is the Greek name for the attendants of the goddess Cybele, who accompanied her in wild dances and orgies. Some orchids have been named for revenge. In the late 1960s, two species of *Oncidium* were discovered in Brazil by an American whom I will call John Smith. One species was big and beautiful; one was measly. Smith persuaded a Brazilian man to collect the plants for him and to make the difficult trip with them to port by promising to name one of the orchids in his honor. He did, but the one he named in honor of his Brazilian porter was the measly *Oncidium*, not the showy one. A few years later, Brazilian orchid breeders used Smith's big, beautiful *Oncidium* to make hybrids; the first two were given the names Greedy Gringo and Very Bad John.

Commercial growers often name new hybrids after friends or good customers or favorite famous people. Chadwick & Son, a Virginia nursery, recently registered a hybrid named Hillary Rodham Clinton 'First Lady.' In honor of Elizabeth Taylor, the chairwoman of the American Orchid Society's seventy-fifth anniversary gala, there is a *Laelia anceps* cultivar named 'Elizabeth's Eyes.' The 'Jackie Kennedy' orchid is snow-white with purple trim; the 'Richard Nixon' is the color of putty with brown speckles. There is a 'Nancy Reagan' orchid and an orchid hybrid named for the daughter of writer Joan Didion and an orchid hybrid named Rajah's Ruby 'Babe's Baby,' named by Brooklyn Dodger Babe Herman, who bred it. An Illinois orchid breeder named a new *Phalaenopsis* hybrid after Shinichi Suzuki, the Japanese violinist who developed a method for teaching music to tiny children. I met many people in Florida who had orchids named for them by Florida nurserymen Bob Fuchs and Martin Motes. Once, I was at a show with an orchid judge named Howard Bronstein, who pointed at one of the plants and exclaimed, "My God, what a *terrific* 'Howard Bronstein'!" In fact, Howard Bronstein said it was one of the best 'Howard Bronstein's he'd ever seen. He had seen a lot of them, because the plant is a popular hybrid that had been created and named for him by his friend Bob Fuchs.

———

Laroche narrated for me as we walked through the show. "I used to be dearly in love with these. They're *Oncidium papilio* . . . butterfly orchids. I used to love the hell out of them. . . . That's a clamshell orchid, it's a miserable little thing. . . . Look at this rigid, blackish one, it's a *Paphiopedilum*. Can you imagine if you lived in Victorian England where the idea of a flower was a daisy, and you instead had this black, rubbery, hooded thing in your house? You would rule. . . . Oh, someone's got some ferns. Isn't that gorgeous? That's gorgeous. I collected ferns for a while. They're hard to grow. They like to die. That's what they like to do the most. 'What should we do today? Hey, let's die!' There are a lot of great ferns on the Seminoles' land. I want some for the nursery. I think we could make a dollar. . . . Do you like this? My ex-wife used to grow these, so every time I see them I get kind of nauseous. Why did we break up? Hell if I know. Why does anyone break up? Actually, we broke up because she could sit through an entire side of a Grateful Dead album and I couldn't. . . . Quick! What's this? I just showed you this. Clamshell orchid. Easy, look at the little shell shape of the petal. . . . Here's a weird shape. Look at this long tube. A moth uses its big-ass tongue to get this guy pollinated. It's just like the ghost orchid. They get pollinated by this huge hawk wing moth. They're *huge* moths. One time when I was in the Fakahatchee one of them flew out of nowhere and hit me in the face and I started screaming like a little girl." We stopped in front of an orchid that had a rounded top petal and a bulbous pouch and a long skinny petal on either side that curled in a corkscrew and stood straight out. Each piece of the flower was a different color—cocoa, rust, gold. To me it had the face and silhouette of a poodle riding in a car with the windows open so its ears were blown back from its face. Laroche ran his finger along one of the curly ears and said, "Imagine you're this plant. Why do you have petals that do this? It has some purpose, everything has some purpose. I believe in botany by imagination. I try to put myself in the

plant's point of view and try to figure them out. The only
ones with features that have no real purpose are the hybrids,
because someone put them together and came up with an
unnatural thing. That's the cool thing with hybridizing. You
are God. You do the plant sex. It's a man-made hobby."

"Are there any hybrids that occur naturally?"

"Hardly any," he said.

"Why?"

He snorted. "Well, you wouldn't, even in a fit of boredom,
decide to have sex with a gorilla, right?"

—

We were in a hall of clones, Laroche said, a room full of artificially made genetic copies. Some of the orchids we were
looking at were grown from seed or taken as cuttings, but
most of them were made in labs. Cloning plants is now com-
monplace, but the method has existed only since the late
1950s, when a French botanist named Georges Morel developed it while trying to figure out how to grow virus-free potatoes. Morel discovered that if he placed a few cells from the
most actively growing part of a potato plant into a growing
medium and provided hormonal and chemical stimulation,
the cells would multiply. Plant cells are undifferentiated
until they orient themselves to the earth and the sun by de-
tecting the force of gravity and warmth; as soon as they get
oriented, some of the cells evolve into roots and others into
leaves and others into stems. Morel realized that if he kept
agitating and twirling the culture dishes, the cells would divide but remain undifferentiated—they kept splitting into
more basic cells rather than developing into plants. He let
the cells divide into thousands of basic cells and then he
stopped shaking the dishes, separated the cells into smaller
clumps, and placed the small clumps in another growing
medium in motionless culture dishes. In a while the clumps

matured into thousands of plants, and each one was an exact genetic copy—a clone—of the original plant. Morel had a number of graduate students assisting him with the potato-cloning experiments. One of them was a young man named Walter Bertsch, who happened to be an orchid fancier and also happened to be dating a girl who worked at a famous French orchid company. Bertsch tried applying Morel's cloning technique to orchids and discovered that many species responded well. This is how orchids came to be the first ornamental plant to be cloned on a large scale.

Before cloning, propagating orchids required a lot of patience. Orchids grown from seed took forever because the plants so rarely form seedpods, and then the seeds take seven years to mature. Orchids could also be divided—that is, one plant could be divided into two or, at the very most, three—but the rate of increase was unimpressive. The science of cloning remade the nature of orchid collecting. It became possible to reproduce most species quickly and in large quantities and with perfect genetic uniformity, and that in turn made it possible to sell the plants at a reasonable price. Orchids used to live only in the wild or in millionaires' hothouses. With cloning, they could be almost as common as daisies. The finest orchids do still cost a fortune. A show-quality *Phragmipedium besseae* is worth five thousand dollars or more, and species like lady's slipper orchids that resist cloning are still rare and cost a ransom. Many species, though, can be created in a lab—created in tremendous quantities with absolute uniformity. An orchid breeder can be a sort of sorcerer's apprentice, multiplying one plant into hundreds or thousands or even more. In theory there is no limit to the number of copies you can create. One beautiful plant could be cloned and turned into a million.

—

The door prize ticket was drawn and announced. We didn't win. "There really is an orchid that smells like Grape Kool-Aid," Laroche said, "and I would really like to find that son of a bitch." He went booth by booth. Stewart Orchids. The Orchid Man. Mountain View Orchids. Orchids by Alexandra. Gold Country Orchids, "Our First Release of This Wonderful Orange Brassia!" A grower from Hawaii, whose sign said ALL PLANTS 30% OFF. I DON'T WANT TO TAKE THEM HOME! A grower from Venezuela with hundred-dollar cattleyas, who was saying, "These flowers are poetic. They hold themselves horizontally because they want to go back to Venezuela." Swirls of people around the booths, stroking stems, leaves, petals, pushing money and credit cards across the tables, pointing at plants and saying "Covet, covet, covet!" and "Don't let me even *look* at that," and "I should wear a straitjacket to these shows"; they were old and young and middle-aged; couples whispering to one another with their eyes fixed on a plant and mothers with strollers that they leaned across to see the plants on the tables; they were dressed in white windbreakers and good shoes, or cardigans with orchid patterns, or silk ties printed with a hundred little cattleyas, or silver filigreed orchid earrings and pins, and shorts and T-shirts with orchids silk-screened across the fronts. They examined the plants up close, with one eye shut, the way a jeweler examines a stone, and then they stepped back and cocked their heads and had a second look, the way a curator studies a painting, and then they paid and walked off wearing the crazy grin of prizewinners.

Laroche stopped at a small booth in a corner. "Here's a weird-ass thing," he said to me. He pointed to a row of tiny clay pots, thumb-sized maybe, and in each tiny pot was a clump of scaly gray-green roots. No leaves, no flowers. Laroche glanced at me and said, "Isn't it beautiful?" He was,

I think, kidding. The little roots of the plant quivered when he picked up the pot and held it up to me. "It's an Asian ghost orchid. Pitiful-looking but rare and therefore desirable. You get so obsessed with these goddamn orchids that they all start to look beautiful," he said. "It's part of the sickness."

A young blond woman wearing a baby on her back stopped at the booth and stood next to Laroche, scanning the table of plants.

"Look," he said to her, holding out one of the pots, "isn't this beautiful?"

"It's gorgeous," she said.

In a loud voice, Laroche pointed to the ghost orchids and said, "Oh, these plants look awful. They must be dying!" The dealer had been ringing up someone's order at the other end of the sales table. He snapped his head around and glared at Laroche.

Laroche raised his eyebrows and said, "Sorry, dude."

The young woman turned the plant around and around in her hands and ran her finger down the roots and then pulled them apart a little so she could see if there was more to it inside the pot.

Laroche watched her. Then he asked, "Do you love it?"

"I do love it," she said. She hesitated. "I mean . . . it's . . . it's a little . . . *unusual*. But I do love it."

"You love it even though it's an ugly little runt," Laroche said. "It has no flower, it has no foliage, it probably looks just like it does now when it blooms." His voice was warm. She nodded. "I know why you love it," he said. "It's just part of the sickness."

It was illuminating to be with Laroche in a place like this. People noticed him. In appearance he was arresting. He had possibly the most untanned complexion in the state of Florida, and his thinness made his body look as if it stuck in

more than out. At the Fort Lauderdale show he was wearing
overalls faded almost white that hung off him like laundry on
a line. His nearly colorless eyes and toothlessness made him
look spectral. People seemed to take to him anyway. He chatted his way around the auditorium. Some people recognized
him from the photograph that ran with the story I wrote
about him in *The New Yorker*, so they approached him and
said something friendly about it, which pleased him—he'd
answer, "Yep, that *was* me, I'm the one who stole all those orchids," and talk proudly about the case. Or he'd volunteer
comments to the dealers or the spectators, or declare something loudly and profanely, which always got him a look and
usually started a conversation. He talked constantly, he knew
something about everything or he was very good at faking
that he did, he reeled off Latin names and botanical facts
and took professorial interest in my learning as we went
along. He was an endless puzzlement. I was always surprised
by how much people liked him. They liked him in spite of the
fact that he is a confirmed misanthrope, and that he has
none of the usual traits of popularity—conventional good
looks, smooth manners, an agreeable temperament—and
that he has a challenging, slightly obscene sense of humor
and the habit of lateness and that he constantly over-
promises. They liked him, I think, because he could be as
earnest about their concerns as he was about his own, and
because his self-confidence was contagious—he made people feel that they were innately able to do the right thing. He
could even persuade you that the wrong thing was the right
thing if it was the only option you had. A few weeks before
the Fort Lauderdale show I was staying in West Palm Beach
at my parents' condominium and wanted to talk to Laroche,
so we arranged to meet halfway between West Palm and his
house in North Miami. I told him I had to meet early be-

cause my mother was in Florida with me and I needed to borrow her car and didn't want to leave her stranded for the day. Laroche insisted that he was always up at dawn and could meet me at 7:30 A.M. or so. He also promised that he would figure out an easy place for our rendezvous and call me in the morning with directions. He even offered to give me a wakeup call. I woke up on my own at 6:30 A.M. and went for a short run around the golf course. I came back and showered and got dressed. At 10:00 A.M. I still hadn't heard from him, so I finally called his house. His dad answered and said John was sleeping and would probably be mad if he woke him up. By the time Laroche called me back it was almost 11:00. Before I had a chance to bawl him out, he announced that he had decided that getting together wasn't a good idea since I was visiting with my mom. "I mean, she's your mom and all that," he said. "I mean, that's *important*. You don't see your mom every day, you know? Look, look, here's what we'll do. I think you should go hang out with your mom, take her out for a nice lunch or brunch, enjoy the day, you call me tomorrow, I'll let you know what's going on, we'll talk, everything will be fine." He was so sure it was the right plan that he convinced me that it was the right plan and probably what I'd wanted to do all along.

As we walked around the Fort Lauderdale show he said the most awful things—for instance, I asked him what his current girlfriend did and he said, "She's a bitch"—and then a minute later he bragged that she was incredibly smart and had been in medical school before she took her current sales position at Miami Subs. As usual he was sarcastic about everyone and everything, but then he would become lyrical and sad as he described a trip he took into the Fakahatchee with his late mother, when they had hiked to a clearing and suddenly the swamp opened onto this: a pond filled with bright yellow water lilies, an otter, a piliated woodpecker, and a scarlet ibis staring into the pond. I was getting used to his contrariness but he still puzzled me. He was always daring me to mistrust him, and then surprising me by being reliable, and he was always daring me to think he was a creep, and then he would unveil something that belied any creepiness. When I first met him, he told me he had found the only gem-grade fossil pearl in existence, a boast so specific that I couldn't resist investigating it, and no one I talked to ever confirmed that such a thing could be true. I really wanted to confront him about it, but when he brought it up another time and I was about to challenge him, he said, "You know why I love that pearl so much? Because as long as I have it, I still sort of have the moment when I got it. The place I got it was wild when I was there, and it's gone now, it's all developed and the woods are just *gone*. And I was with my wife when I found it, she's my ex-wife now, and I was with my mom, and my mom's dead now. But having that pearl is like still having that moment, my mom is alive and I'm still happily married and the place I found it is still gorgeous." I never brought up the question of the pearl again. I'm not a sucker. It's just that questioning whether it really is the only gem-grade fossil pearl in existence felt piddling compared to what he said it meant to him—it would have felt like telling someone deeply in love that the beloved one was ugly and short.

———

I had to take a break from the flowers. My eyes were tired. I had a tendency to look too hard into the flowers' centers, because I kept seeing faces in the crinkles and spikes—little tongues, blind eyes, puffy lips, pugilists' squashed noses, a lobster, a caterpillar with a grin. When I saw a face I would stare at it and try to remember who or what it reminded me of until my eyes twinged. Also there was something bottomless about the colors and patterns that drew me, so I stared and stared until Laroche would get impatient and pry me away. After an hour or so I suggested that we take a recess, so we walked over to the auditorium snack bar and sat down at a tipsy linoleum table. I drank sour brown coffee and Laroche ate a hot dog, and we both breathed greasy snack-bar air. "You want to know how much a dealer can make at a show like this?" Laroche asked me when he was finished eating. "You can make a *shitload* of money. There's a lot of money in plants. Plants are a commodity, just like pork bellies. Here's an example. There are eight million dollars' worth of palm trees in the Fakahatchee and Collier-Seminole State Park—*eight million dollars' worth.* One royal palm sells for four thousand dollars. Landscapers love them. I was thinking the other day that if you stole one palm a week, you could make fifty thousand dollars a year." I asked if he was considering becoming a palm rustler. "Of course not," he said peevishly. "It'd be a great little business, but bottom line, I'm on the side of the plants. See, with the ghost orchids, I wanted to make a dollar but I really want the plants to be saved from extinction. And even then, when we were taking them out of the Fakahatchee, in my own sick little morality I felt kind of guilty." He stood up and fished around in his pockets for cigarettes. "People get crazy for plants. I took this woman once to the Fakahatchee, she wanted to see—oh, it was a ghost orchid, as a matter of fact. She had been having *dreams* about this plant. I knew where one was that was blooming, so we go to the swamp, walk in for two miles through the nastiest stuff, she's practically running to get there, and I see something that I don't like, so I'm saying, 'Oh, *Baaaarbra,* you might want to slow down,' because right in front of her is a six-foot-long rattlesnake. She freezes, I chop it with the machete, I'm ready to, oh fuck, I'd had enough, and she's just off and running again. She just couldn't wait to go on to see the damn flower. She reminded me of a friend of mine who found this great weird orchid in Ecuador. What he didn't realize was that he was on military land. So he gets stopped by the military police and they are *really* pissed, and they want him to hand over his bag of plants. So he says, 'Go ahead, shoot me. I'm not leaving without this plant. I'd rather that you shoot me,' and they look at him like he's totally insane. Which he is."

The Good Life

Some of the stolen orchids died. The rest had been glued onto trees in the Fakahatchee.

The rangers at the Fakahatchee had put the orchids they'd confiscated from Laroche back into the woods and were waiting to see if they would survive. This was not the first time I had heard of gluing orchids onto trees. On my first trip to Florida after Laroche's arrest I met a naturalist named Roger Hammer who had hiked through the Fakahatchee after Hurricane Andrew and whenever he found orchids that had been blown down in the storm he glued them onto standing trees with a few squeezes of an adhesive called Liquid Nails. The orchids tolerated the glue. In general, orchids are tougher than you expect them to be. They look as fragile as glass but they aren't. Baby orchids are shipped around the world stuffed into boxes, matted, squashed, jostled, and suffocated, and yet most of the time when the boxes are opened and the little plants are untangled and dusted off they're fine. The first time I saw an orchid grower open a shipment he'd gotten from Singapore I took one look at the mess of seedlings and figured the grower would sue. Instead he pulled a few out and admired them and said, "Well, hello, babies!" Wild orchids can take a lot of punishment too. After Hurricane Andrew, people found trees that had been slammed down and were dead as doornails and yet orchids on them were still flourishing. Laroche told me that he and his ex-wife used to drive around on orchid-rescue missions all the time. At construction sites they would hunt through the rubbish to look for orchids on trees that had been plowed down and pitched aside. If Laroche could get to the flowers without getting in trouble, he'd pry them off and take them to some nearby woods and attach them to an upright tree.

You could write a book about the invincible plants of Florida. I was once introduced to some in the Loxahatchee Refuge in Palm Beach County. The refuge is marshy and level and most of its vegetation is either bushes or cattails or hip-high grass or clumps of cypresses, all low as the horizon, except for three skinny Australian pine trees in the middle of the marsh. The trees aren't especially tall, but in that level world they stick up like skyscrapers. Whenever there is lightning in the area, it automatically gravitates to these trees, and since there is lightning all the time in south Florida the trees are hit over and over again. By now their branches are partly stripped and their insides are probably toasted, but somehow they have managed to remain standing and to still be living trees. There is even a grand champion of Florida's deathless plants. It is the melaleuca, a homely tree from Australia that was brought to the state in 1906 as an ornamental landscaping plant. Melaleucas grow to be fifty feet tall and have spongy white bark and look a little like a eucalyptus tree with long hair. They drink so much water that they can dry out an acre of wetlands a day, so they were also used to help drain what was then considered Florida's useless swampland. In the 1930s real estate developers had melaleuca seeds scattered over the Everglades by plane. Melaleucas love living in Florida. Since their introduction they have multiplied by the thousands. They spread at the rate of fifty acres a day. They have parched and then taken over a half million of the Everglades' 7.6 million acres. Melaleuca leaves are oily and burn intensely. A melaleuca-leaf fire in 1985 left two million people in Florida without electricity because the fueled-up flames reached as high as the main power-transmission lines. No one has any sentimental feelings about the species, and most people now consider them a spreading evil. The problem is that melaleucas hate to die. If a melaleuca tree is frozen or starved or chopped or poisoned or broken or burned, it will release twenty million seeds right before it dies and resow itself in every direction, so in a sense it ends up more alive than dead. The trick is to kill the tree gradually, because the shock of dying is what causes it to shoot out its seeds. The ranger who led me on my first walk in the Fakahatchee was a melaleuca-murder expert. He said that a tiny, pudgy Australian weevil known as the snout beetle lives on melaleuca leaves and flower buds, and that three hundred of them had been imported and released in the Everglades in hopes of paring down the melaleuca population. He said that, otherwise, the only way to kill the trees in an unshocking way is a method called hack-and-squirt—you hack a little bit of the tree, squirt in just a little bit of herbicide, come back after a while and hack and squirt again, and keep hacking and squirting until the tree languidly dies.

Foreigners in general do well in Florida. Twenty-five percent of all the plants in the state are aliens. The most common orchid in Florida, the little lawn orchid, is a native of

India. Its seeds had been mixed in sacks of grass seed by accident and then shipped to Miami and sown unwittingly in thousands of lawns. Brazilian pepper trees are all over; like melaleucas, they were imported as landscape plants but then escaped and took hold in the wild, and like melaleucas they hate to die and will reseed themselves if they are burned or cut down or pulled up. They are so at home in the Everglades that they have taken over huge tracts, and botanists have concluded that the only way to get rid of them is to scrape away the entire surface layer of dirt they are growing in. Common Asian cogon grass entered Florida as seeds stuck in the tire treads of road-building equipment and in packing material. Noxious alligator weed has been a runaway success since it sneaked into Florida from its native South America. The day I decided to go to the Fakahatchee to check on the poached orchids I saw an article in the Miami paper reporting that Vietnamese farmers were being ordered to destroy their Chinese water-spinach crops. The spinach is common in Asia. The Vietnamese farmers were new to Florida and so was the spinach. The article didn't mention how the farmers were faring, but the spinach had certainly done well, and in fact it was now growing so ferociously that it was plugging up local waterways. A few weeks later I saw a story about another overly successful immigrant, a species of poisonous South American toad that had been introduced to Florida to eat sugarcane pests. They are now growing as long as seven inches and weighing in at more than three pounds. Recently they have been accused of killing house pets with their poison and scaring tourists with their monstrous pimply looks.

—

There are two ways to get from my quarters in West Palm Beach to the Fakahatchee Strand, which is diagonally across from West Palm on the other side of the state. One way is to drive west on Alligator Alley. I preferred going the other way, zigzagging across Palm Beach County and Hendry County, rounding the bottom of Lake Okeechobee, then cutting across the Everglades and along the edges of the sugar farms and through the Seminole reservation near Immokalee, past the ghostly signs for long-gone tourist stops like Gatorama and Native Village, on the small state roads that go off at right angles every few miles as if they had been drawn by a box cutter. It is slow going but broadening. The day I went to see the glued-on orchids I knew I should get to the swamp early before it got intolerably hot, but I liked the small roads too much to take the faster route. It was a windy morning, and all the palm trees had their fronds tossed forward like models' hair in a fashion shoot. There was no one walking on any block I drove past. Just outside Palm Beach I finally saw some people, a lot of people marching single file on the shoulder of the road carrying banners with nothing written on them and long poles with bird feathers tied to the tops. I rolled down my window as I drove by to see if they were chanting or saying anything that would explain what they were doing, but they were absolutely quiet, and all I heard was the sound of forty pairs of feet crunching the sand on the side of the road. I passed the entrance to Lion Country Safari and then I was alongside sugarcane fields that were miles long and miles wide, covered with cane as high as my head or cane cut down to dry stubble. A few trucks pulled in and out of field roads. Now and again there were houses far off the road so miniaturized by the distance that they looked like toys, but I didn't see a human being in any direction. The sugar fields went on forever. With miles of sugar behind me and miles more to go, I stopped at a gas station and went inside to buy a Diet Coke, but there was not a single artificially sweetened soft drink in the place.

Near the high, humpy levee of Lake Okeechobee I saw a sign for a picnic area at something called John Stretch Park. I pulled in so I could climb up the levee to take a look at the lake. There were six yellow taxicabs in the John Stretch parking lot. Three stout women in rich-colored saris were inching up the trail that led to the top of the levee, and in an open-sided pavilion across from the taxis there were about twenty other adults and a bunch of kids running around. A few men were tending barbecue grills and a few women were setting the picnic tables. The whole park smelled like cumin. I climbed to the top of the levee and looked at the big blue lake. The three stout women were already at the top and then two women climbed up behind me, holding their saris high to keep them out of the dirt, and each time the skirts rippled in the wind the sequins on them threw brilliant dime-sized dots of light. Everyone nodded and gazed at the blue blob of lake, and then we all walked down together and I followed them into the pavilion. One of the men tending the grills told me that they were members of a large Pakistani family from Fort Lauderdale and that they'd gathered at the park for a picnic. Several of the men were taxicab drivers in Fort Lauderdale; the cabs in the parking lot were theirs. The man at the grill was wearing dress trousers and a starchy white shirt and large and glittering jewelry. As he was talking he flipped patties that were sputtering on the grill. "Lamb and chili patties," he explained, pointing with his spatula. "Pakistani burgers. You've ever had them?"

"I don't think so."

"We have plenty, you know," he said. "You should sit with us and eat."

I told him I couldn't stay because I was late as it was. He looked deflated. "I understand," he said. "A lot of people in Florida are afraid of our food."

Past John Stretch Park the roads bent through towns called
Devil's Garden and Bean City and Citrus Center and Harlem
and Flag Hole and around wetlands called Telegraph Swamp
and Corkscrew Swamp and Grassy Marsh and Graham
Marsh. The land was marble-smooth and it rolled without a
pucker to the horizon. My eyes grazed across the green band
of ground and the blue bowl of sky and then lingered on a
dead tire, a bird in flight, an old fence, a rusted barrel.
Hardly any cars came toward me, and I saw no one in the
rearview mirror the entire time. I passed so many vacant
acres and looked past them to so many more vacant acres
and looked ahead and behind at the empty road and up at the
empty sky; the sheer bigness of the world made me feel
lonely to the bone. The world is so huge that people are always getting lost in it. There are too many ideas and things
and people, too many directions to go. I was starting to believe that the reason it matters to care passionately about
something is that it whittles the world down to a more man-
ageable size. It makes the world seem not huge and empty
but full of possibility. If I had been an orchid hunter I
wouldn't have seen this space as sad-making and vacant—I
think I would have seen it as acres of opportunity where the
things I loved were waiting to be found.

All along the roads there were shallow trenches filled with
black muck and brown water and green snarls of weeds. They
looked like somewhere an alligator might like to loaf around.
Near one of the trenches a billboard for an old tourist attraction promised in giant black letters GATOR GUARAN-
TEED!!! It wasn't a very daring guarantee, because in Florida
alligators are as common as crickets. In fact, every county in
the state has an official Nuisance Alligator Rustler who is on

call to remove excess or inappropriate reptiles. On my last trip to the Fakahatchee I stopped at a gas station, and as I was squeegeeing the bugs off my windshield, four baby alligators scooted from one trench to another, about six inches away from my feet. At that particular moment I was wearing sandals. About one second later I changed into regular shoes.

Before I got to the road that leads into the Fakahatchee, I stopped at a fork to read another sign. I was heading to the right. The sign was pointing to the left: BIG CYPRESS SEMINOLE INDIAN RESERVATION. RECREATIONAL AREA. BILLIE SWAMP SAFARI. AIRBOAT RIDES! WILD BOAR HUNTS! ECO-TOURS! BIG CYPRESS RODEO! The Billie of the this Billie Swamp Safari was Chief James E. Billie, whose acquittal on the Florida panther case had been a great inspiration to Laroche. The Seminoles set up the safari after Chief Billie visited a private exotic big-game preserve in Texas and had such a good time that he thought the tribe should set one up, too. A two-thousand-acre site on the Big Cypress reservation was stocked with European fallow deer, black buck antelope from India, sika deer from China, Corsican sheep from the Mediterranean, and scimitar-horned oryx from Africa. For a fee of one thousand dollars, tourists were guided through the safari and could take home whatever they killed. The outcry was speedy and loud. Chief Billie told a reporter that Seminole kids were even being taunted in school as Bambi killers. Moreover, the tribe had to construct big, expensive fences around the safari—not to keep the imported animals in but to keep native animals out, because Florida panthers and alligators had discovered a taste for exotic meat and had killed dozens of the safari animals within the first few weeks. Finally Billie conceded that the safari wasn't worth the trouble it was causing, and it was repackaged as a photographic hunting ground. Laroche and Chief Billie had never met, but there was an echo in their personal stories: both were men who seemed to thrive on controversy and have a preternatural talent for landing on their feet.

State Road 29 went through the town of Immokalee, past a Kuntry Kubbard and a Melon-Pac factory, past a Citrus Belle packing plant and Brahma cattle ranches, past orange groves and the Hendry Correctional Institution; beyond Hendry it was nearly wild except for traffic signs warning of panther crossings and a couple of bungalows and the small buildings that made up Copeland Road Prison Number 27. Near the prison was a small store that looked abandoned, but a man was in front of it, sweeping the dirt driveway, so I decided to take a chance. It had been eighty-one degrees when I left Palm Beach. Now it was at least fifteen degrees warmer, and I was desperate for something to drink. The store's door was stiff and made a horrible sound when I pushed it open. Inside it was nearly lightless. The wooden floors sloped and buckled. The shelves were set at funny angles and the refrigerator cases had almost nothing in them except some sticky cans of soda and dusty brown bottles of beer. Two stocky women were sitting behind the cash register with tart expressions on their faces. I bought a Coke and went outside to drink it, but it tasted weird and for a moment I entertained the thought that it might be poisoned, so I poured it out and went back to get something else. I didn't see anything I wanted to drink, but I did notice a plastic container of raspberry Jell-O that appealed to me. The women had been following me with their eyes the whole time. Neither of them moved when I put the Jell-O down and took out my wallet. Finally the bigger one picked up the Jell-O and twirled it around in her hand for a moment and said at last, "Nope, miss. This one's not for sale."

"Fakahatchee" is a Seminole word that means "forked river" or "hunting river" or "river of vines" or "river of clay" or "muddy creek." "Strand" is local slang for any long, narrow swamp forest. The Fakahatchee Strand is a wedge of land containing dozens of smaller strands and a chain of sinkhole lakes connected by natural channels cut into the south Florida limestone floor that are watered by a sixty-mile-long drainage that starts to the north at the Okaloacoochee Slough and the Caloosahatchee River. The Fakahatchee has an exceptional character. Some of its sinkholes are nearly a hundred feet deep. Otherwise the land is so level that wherever there is even just an inch or two of elevation the habitat completely changes. Elevated land shifts from mushy marsh to crumbly soil. On these elevated inches trees have taken hold and formed clusters—cypress islands, oak heads, pine islands, royal palm hammocks. The rise determines what kind of trees congregate on the rises, depending on how much water they need. A few inches can make the difference between a mangrove clump and a buttonwood hammock. Some of these clusters have only a dozen trees, but others have thousands of trees. More than half of the Fakahatchee's trees are tropical, but it is essentially a temperate forest. The two coexisting environments mean there are things living within the Fakahatchee that aren't usually found together— for instance, it is the only place in the world where royal palm trees, which are tropical, and cypress trees, which are found in temperate regions, live side by side. The Faka- hatchee's central royal palm hammock has three thousand trees and is the biggest, healthiest such hammock in the world. The royal palms are one of the treasures of the Faka- hatchee. They are a rare sort of palm with a monumental cement-gray trunk and a tuft of slim green leaves—the form of a hundred-foot-tall feather duster. Royal palms are related to a Cuban palm and are accustomed to warm weather; the Fakahatchee is about as far north as they can grow. Explorers remarked on the swamp's royal palms as early as 1860, but the palms didn't become famous until the 1920s, when the owners of Hialeah Race Track in Miami transplanted some from the Fakahatchee to the infield of the race track. Bromeliads also flourish in the Fakahatchee. In some of the deep sloughs, every tree is weighed down with *Guzmania monostachia*—huge, flaring bromeliads in green and brown and red. More different kinds of native North American orchids grow in the Fakahatchee than anywhere else, and eleven species in the Fakahatchee are found nowhere else in North America.

The Fakahatchee looks utterly wild, but it is in fact a corrupted wilderness. It has been meddled with and invaded. For a while, people cleared and plowed parcels of its wet prairies and tried to grow oranges, grapefruits, tangerines, tomatoes, mangoes, and winter vegetables. The swamp made for lousy farming. The farmers eventually left, but their produce lingered. Even now you can still see crop rows under the native grass and a few weather-beaten citrus trees amid the palm and cypress. Melaleucas and Brazilian peppers and Australian pine trees, non-natives, have roamed into the strand and multiplied. So have walking catfish, who swam in through the sinkhole lakes and stayed. And so have armadillos, the offspring of armadillos used in leprosy experiments in a Jacksonville hospital that managed to get away. And so for a while did wild cows, who were normal cows that escaped nearby ranches and lived comfortably in the swamp until the state of Florida hired marksmen in 1948 to do away with them. The biggest unnatural success in the Fakahatchee has been pigs. Hunting clubs used to raise and fatten ordinary pigs on local farms and then let them loose in the swamp so the club members could then have fun tracking them down and shooting them. Some of the pigs didn't get shot, and some of those adapted to swamp living. Their offspring are now thriving in the Fakahatchee and have been transformed from mild barnyard animals into gigantic, nasty swamp pigs who are totally mad and totally wild.

The Fakahatchee would be inaccessible if it weren't for the Tamiami Trail, the road that runs from Fort Meyers to Miami and crosses the southern end of the preserve. Before the trail was built, a trip across the Fakahatchee was an obstacle course. In 1908 a traveler described such a trip: "We began the trip in canoes, but ended it in an oxcart. We paddled and wallowed through two hundred miles of flower clad lakes and boggy, moccasin-infested trails, zigzagging from border to border of the Florida Everglades, and were hauled for five days on pine-covered stretches of sand, across submerged prairies, and through sloughs of the Big Cypress Country, but we failed to reach the big lake by twenty five miles."

It took three tries to build the Tamiami Trail. The first attempt was in 1915, when a road crew tried to cut through the slough and failed. In 1923 a group calling itself the Trail Blazers set out from Fort Meyers vowing they'd get through. Most of the twenty-five Trail Blazers were Florida businessmen who hoped that a good road to Miami would make the southwestern coast less of a businessless hinterland. They expected the trip to take three days. After two days they vanished. It was assumed they had been captured by the Miccosukee Indians who lived in the swamp and considered the Trail Blazers intruders. Almost a month later the worn-out Trail Blazers showed up near Miami. It was five more years before a real road crew made it through.

In 1947 the Lee Tidewater Cypress Company began logging the Fakahatchee for cypress. To penetrate the strands, the company built dozens of tramways, each exactly 1,650 feet from the next. The tramways had to be elevated. Dirt was scooped out and piled into a bank and the tracks laid on top of that, which meant that every elevated tramway created a carved-out trench beside it. Every trench filled with water. Some of it was collected rainwater, but most was surrounding swamp water that drained into the trenches. After the tramways were built and the trenches filled up, the water level in the Fakahatchee dropped by more than two feet. Crews rode in on cabbagehead locomotives that ran back and forth along the tramways. Once a mature cypress tree was sighted, it was grooved, sawed, dragged down, and hauled out by chains to a double-saw mill in Perry, Florida, where it was cut up for paneling, shingles, caskets, and pickle tanks. The timber cruisers and groovers and sawyers and dragline operators and skidder crews lived in tent villages on the edge of the swamp. The groovers were mostly Seminoles. The other workers were black and white and had a tendency to get into fights. Some of the workers didn't like the quality of life in the swamp. Several of the sawyers claimed they kept coming across skeletons in the woods, and a few even quit because they said it gave them the creeps, even though at a wage of eight hundred dollars a month, sawing down the Fakahatchee was a lucrative job. Anyhow, the work got done: Lee Tidewater took one million board feet of cypress out of the Fakahatchee every year.

By 1952 the Fakahatchee's cypress was almost entirely logged out, so Lee Tidewater closed up its operation and left the area. In the five years of logging the tramways had cut up the woods; the trenches had drained it; the falling timber had pulled down brush; the logs that were dragged out had gouged long deep channels into the swamp floor. After Lee Tidewater left, surveyors described the Fakahatchee as looking like "a green Hell."

In 1966 Lee Tidewater sold seventy-five thousand acres of

the Fakahatchee and the surrounding land. The purchasers were two brothers, Julius and Leonard Rosen, who called their company Gulf American Corporation. The Rosens were born in Baltimore and had begun their business lives selling pots and pans. In the late forties they concocted a home-made shampoo and named it Formula Number 9 and claimed it could restore hair to bald men. They advertised Formula Number 9 on television with ads that lasted any-where from five minutes to thirty minutes; it was one of the first television ads of all time. The main ingredient of the shampoo was lanolin. Most of the ads began with Leonard Rosen extolling the virtues of lanolin, saying, "Have you ever seen a bald-headed sheep?" The Rosens made a fortune from Formula Number 9 and, more important, discovered how easy it was to mass-market anything. Eventually they hooked up with a real estate salesman named Milt Mendelsohn, who convinced them that land could be marketed just like bald-ness shampoo. Like the Rosens, Mendelsohn was an innova-tor—he had dotted Florida with billboards that said FLORIDA LAND: $10 DOWN AND $10 A MONTH and had sold hundreds of overpriced parcels on the strength of that pitch. The Rosens wanted to join Mendelsohn in a similar venture, so Leonard Rosen and Mendelsohn flew together over south Florida looking for pieces of vacant land they could buy and sell. Their first project was Cape Coral, a 114-square-mile penin-sula bordered by the Gulf of Mexico and the Caloosahatchee River. They platted 138,000 lots and paved 1,700 miles of roads but made no provisions for schools, shopping, water, sewer, or landfills, although they did build Cape Coral Gar-dens, a tourist attraction featuring a Porpoise Pool, a Garden of the Patriots with busts of every American president, and a fountain called Waltzing Waters with jets of water that shot eighty-five feet into the air.

During the Rosens' ownership, only 25 percent of the
Cape Coral lots were ever sold, and Cape Coral Gardens was
soon abandoned and reduced to a pile of dirt, but the brothers had managed to make a fortune and wanted to market
even more Florida land. They worked out a deal with Lee
Tidewater Cypress Co. and set out to develop the deserted
area on the southwest coast that included the Lee Tidewater
property and what is now the Big Cypress Swamp. The Rosens
never actually bought most of the land they were selling—they
just bought a little and then took out options on the rest—but
their sales brochure nonetheless described Gulf American as
"the largest marketer of land of its kind in the world."

Gulf American drained the land by building two hundred
miles of canals. It was hard going; unlike Cape Coral, which
was mostly sandbar, the Lee Tidewater property was low
swamp underlaid with a layer of solid rock that wouldn't
budge unless it was dynamited. Then the land was platted
and subdivided and surveyed and overlaid with a grid of three
hundred miles of roads on top of the dried-out swamp. The
water table dropped fourteen feet. Emptied of water, the
swamp transformed from grass plains and cypress strands
into an upland ecosystem of underbrush and trashy trees and
tough invaders like Brazilian pepper. The Rosens named one
section of the property Golden Gate Estates and another Remuda Ranch Grants. Near Golden Gate, Gulf American built
a two-hundred-room hotel and an airplane landing strip. No
houses were put up in either Golden Gate Estates or Remuda Ranch Grants, although if you had read their sales
brochure you would have gotten a different impression:

Wherever one goes in this vast Gulf American Country, he
finds atmosphere, appeal, and delights of a rich man's paradise, yet within the financial reach of almost everyone.

Beautiful homes set back from the wide streets and boulevards. Impressive is the fact that Golden Gate homes, just as the community of Golden Gate itself, were created and built to fit the incomes of people of average means.

At Golden Gate one may visit and relax at the Golden Gate Country Club . . . one of the finest, with a professional golf course, scene of important tournaments. One may dine at the Country Squire or at the elegant Le Petit Gourmet— have cocktails at the intimate Beau Brummel Room. He may stay at the Golden Gate Inn, a handsome hostelry. There are opportunities to swim, boat, fish, play tennis and take part in a wide variety of social events. An entirely new and wonderful way of life at Golden Gate is offered.

—

Remuda Ranch Grants features elegant Mediterranean-styled buildings towering over the horizon like Spanish castles . . . but nowhere in Spain, not even on that famous plain, will be found such an abundance of good living!

Golden Gate Estates was the bigger of the two properties. If it had ever been developed by Gulf American, it would have been the largest subdivision in the world.

The Gulf American land was offered in five-acre lots that were priced at $1,250 and could be paid off at a rate of ten dollars a month. The lots were advertised as waterfront property with boating access to the Gulf of Mexico—which it wasn't, unless you planned to paddle to the Gulf by way of the drainage canals. The Rosens wanted to attract people who had little opportunity to inspect the property before they bought it so that they wouldn't have an opportunity to raise issues like how close to the water the land actually was. Gulf American pictured its perfect customers as people without much money who lived far from Florida or were members of the armed forces who were heading home from overseas and could get mortgages through the GI Bill or were just big dreamers. To attract those kinds of customers Gulf American had a battery of different sales tactics. They gave away houses on *The Price Is Right*. They set up sales offices around the country and sent out millions of invitations to "friendly dinners," which often featured a local sports star or celebrity. Some invitations suggested that the dinner was a celebration of the recipient's anniversary or birthday or promotion. The invitations sent to enlisted men stated that Gulf American was affiliated with the U.S. armed forces. The sales dinners usually began with a movie about the beauty and affordability of Golden Gate Estates and suggested that the smart customer would buy one of the lots for his dream house and then several more lots as an investment. According to Gulf American, the land's value was about to fly, thanks to Disney World and proposed airports and highways in the area, so in a few years the customer certainly could sell his extra lots at a huge profit. Gulf American provided instructional booklets for the more ambitious customers called *How to Make Money from Florida Acreage* and *Your Golden Gate Way to a Prosperous Future.*

After dinner, salesmen sat down with each customer and started to work with an air of urgency. According to the salesmen, land prices were creeping upward and very soon land in Florida would be unaffordable. Gulf American pledged that anyone who bought land at the dinner would be flown to Florida for free and put up with all expenses paid in the Gulf American hotel. When a customer at one of these dinners did decide to buy, the salesman assigned to him would jump up and shout, "Lot Number Twenty-three is sold!" Or ringers hired by the company would jump up now and then and shout, "I bought one!" If a customer was interested in a parcel of land but was wavering, his salesman would offer to put the parcel on hold while the customer was considering it. A few minutes later the manager would jump up and shout, "I can't keep this on hold much longer!" and force the customer into a decision on the spot.

Not every buyer took the free flight to Florida. Some buyers were satisfied enough with having seen the movie of the property, so they just signed a contract and probably decided it would be soon enough to see their lot when they were ready to retire to it. Anyone who did take the free Florida trip was flown over the swamp in a little buzz plane, and his salesman would lean out of the plane and drop a ten-pound sack of flour to mark the customer's lot. If the client saw other pieces of property he liked, the salesman would drop more sacks of flour on those, too. Some salesmen would drive the prospective buyer miles out in the far swampy ends of the property and then suggest that he either sign the land contract or walk back on his own. The rooms at the Gulf American hotel were bugged so salesmen could listen in on hesitant customers and adapt their sales pitch to each customer's specific concerns. Gulf American marketed its land from the mid-1950s until 1970. The cheapness of the land and the prospect of living in warm Florida and the promise of the good life to be found there turned out to be enthralling. More than forty-six thousand people flew over the swamp and dropped a flour bag on their favorite acre; more than 470,000 acres of land were sold. The Rosens' initial investment in Florida, at Cape Coral, had been $125,000. In a few years the value of their company was $450 million.

No elegant Mediterranean buildings were ever built, no Golden Gate Inn, no Le Petit Gourmet; maybe thirty houses. The land was waterlogged, inaccessible, unserviced by telephones and electricity, buggy, sandy, unfriendly. The nearest

convenience store was ten miles away and the nearest hospital was twenty. In spite of the drainage canals, most of the
land was still underwater six or eight months a year, and
when it was dry it was so dry that it would burst into flame as
if it were paper. Golden Gate was sort of the end of the
world, gloomy and remote, a checkerboard of roads that went
nowhere and houses that were never built. In a 1970 lawsuit
brought against Gulf American, a disgruntled customer
claimed that Gulf American had told him that the land he'd
bought was in the path of development of the city of Naples,
and that meant its value would soar and he would be able to
sell it in a few years and "make a fortune." In his opinion, the
presiding judge wrote: "In fact, the land is not in the path of
development of Naples and is, instead, in The Big Cypress
Swamp." According to the Federal Trade Commission con-
sent order in 1974: "Golden Gate is not a developed community. Golden Gate consists primarily of vacant land, and
has shopping facilities which are incomplete and inadequate,
and resort facilities which are incomplete. There are few
amenities and public services available."

—

Florida land is unusually fertile. One thing that has always
grown well on it is real estate schemes. Until the mid-1950s
the state didn't even regulate large-scale land sales. The
Florida land scam is generally thought to have been inaugu-
rated in 1824. That year General Lafayette was given a tract
near Tallahassee in appreciation of his help in the Revolution. Everyone assumed he would sell it back to local farmers, and indeed he did, but he demanded a price that was at
least twice the land's actual value. In the 1830s a New Yorker
named Peter Sken touted land near St. Augustine "covered
with genuine Florida crabgrass." He was able to make crabgrass sound so rare and wonderful that he managed to sell

hundreds of crabgrassy acres even though he didn't happen to own the land he was selling. Then came John Whitney, who sold swamp lots to Northerners after assuring them that in Florida "insects are neither numerous nor troublesome"; and Hamilton Disston, who in the 1880s sold underwater lots in the Everglades and then, when his scheme fell apart, committed suicide by shooting himself in his bathtub; and Richard Bolles, who marketed his underwater lots at the turn of the century with the slogan "A good investment beats a lifetime of labor"; and Barron Collier, who took a million acres of marshy scrubland near the Fakahatchee and set out to build a replica of Paris; and Charles Rodes, who felt there wasn't enough premium-priced waterfront property to sell, so in the 1920s he built narrow banks of land out into lakes and sold it as waterfront property, and then he dug wide canals and sold the land adjacent to the boggy canals as waterfront property too—a practice that became known as "finger-islanding"; and of course Carl Fisher, a Detroit automobile mogul who came to Florida right after World War I and poured three million cubic yards of sand onto an expanse of mangrove swamp and created Miami Beach.

Scams and real estate schemes flourish because land in Florida is not like land anywhere else in the country. For one thing, Florida land is elastic. You can make more of it. The Florida peninsula is the last part of the continental United States to have emerged from the ocean; most of it is just settling in, and some of it—the swamps and marshes and wetlands—is still only half emerged. With a load of soil and a few canals you can dry out a half-emerged swamp and make a new piece of land. You really can turn a Florida swamp into real estate. A lot of the state *is* man-made. In 1850 a state survey estimated that two thirds of Florida was wetlands that were unfit for development or cultivation. Since then the water has been drawn off more than 75 percent of those wet-lands and most of the newly created land is already built up or is marked for development. There are more vacant zoned lots in Florida than in any other state. Currently there are two million vacant lots in twenty-six hundred subdivisions, most of them on land that hadn't even *been* land until some-one drained and filled it. If every one of those available lots were developed, the state's population could reach ninety-one million.

What is compelling about Florida is not just its ever-expanding quantity of land—it is the qualities that the land has come to represent. In the 1800s, agriculture was domi-nant in American life, and Florida was the American farmer's dream because of its cheap acreage and a ten-month growing season. By the 1900s, American ambitions shifted from good farming to "the good life," and Florida shifted with it—it still represented the farmer's dream, but it now also represented the middle-class dream of a place you could find health and warmth and leisure. Florida wasn't grimy or industrial or hidebound or ingrown. It wasn't seared and dry like the desert—it was luscious and fruitful. It felt new and it looked new, with all its newly minted land and all the billboards pointing to new developments and the bright new sand that had been dredged up and added to the beach. Florida was to Americans what America had always been to the rest of the world—a fresh, free, unspoiled start.

Florida is a wet, warm, tropical place, essentially feature-less and infinitely transformable. It is as suggestible as someone under hypnosis. Its essential character can be re-peatedly reimagined. The Everglades soil that is contami-nated by intractable Brazilian pepper trees is now being scraped up in order to kill the invader trees, and then the sterilized soil is going to be piled high, covered with plastic snow, and turned into a ski resort. Any dank Florida cypress swamp can be drained and remade as a subdivision, and that subdivision can be made to look like a Tuscan village or a New England town, and the imitation Tuscan village or Vermont town can be filled with people from New York or Chicago or Haiti who have remade themselves into Floridians. The flat plainness of Florida doesn't impose itself on you, so you can impose upon it your own kind of dream.

—

In 1967 Gulf American pleaded guilty to using "false, misleading, deceptive, and unfair practices" to sell its Florida land. The next year Leonard Rosen sold Gulf American to a Pennsylvania finance company called GAC Corporation; he and his brother each received stock in GAC worth $63 million. Leonard eventually started up another land company that marketed desert wasteland in Nevada to German investors. In 1977 he was indicted for tax fraud, and a grand jury investigated secret offshore bank accounts that he controlled; he pleaded no contest and received a $5,000 fine and three years' probation.

GAC had given the Rosens stock worth almost $115 million in exchange for Gulf American. GAC marketed the Gulf American property until 1975. By then GAC was $350 million in debt. The subsequent bankruptcy took thirteen years to settle and is considered the biggest and most complex reorganization in Florida's corporate history, involving more than nine thousand creditors, twenty-seven thousand lot owners, and five hundred thousand acres of land. After the bankruptcy, the Gulf American hotel was sold to a group of chiropractors, who soon went bankrupt themselves. Then it was sold to a South American company called International Wholesale Products of Hollywood whose security guards used the hotel to store bales of marijuana. The Gulf Ameri-

can airport where planes carrying prospective customers
landed was used as a landing strip for cargo planes that were
transporting drugs.

As part of a settlement over the wetlands it destroyed at
Cape Coral, GAC donated almost ten thousand acres in the
Fakahatchee to the state of Florida; the state then began
buying up the privately held Gulf American lots, acre by acre.
This land eventually became the Fakahatchee Strand State
Preserve. There are still thousands and thousands of inhold-
ings within the preserve that the state continues to buy, but
since most of the lots are less than two acres, there are thousands of individual owners, and each purchase means a slow
negotiation with an individual owner who often lives far
away. The acquisition project is the most complex, controversial, and litigious of Florida's land-conservation program.
One hundred families did eventually move into Golden Gate
Estates. They live in isolated houses without telephones or
electricity or city water supplies, and the vacant lots all
around them are slowly reverting back to swamp. Many people who bought land in Golden Gate probably never even visited it, and most of them have been happy to sell as soon as
the government has offered to buy. Living in Golden Gate appeals to a highly independent individual. Many independent
individuals in Golden Gate have mightily resisted the government's acquisition plans. A while ago, one homesteader
declared himself chairman and director of research of the
East Collier County Landowners Improvement Committee.
The committee's slogan was "God promises to kill with the
sword government men which take the land from widows
and fatherless children."

The grid of Golden Gate streets is still in place. People
drag-race on them now and dump trash on them and land
airplanes carrying drugs on them and stash smuggled goods

alongside them, and now that the swamp is repossessing the
land they also chase bears and panthers across them and go
fishing for snapper and needlefish in the drainage canals.
Half of the emergency calls to the Collier County fire department are reporting fires on the old Gulf American land.
Some of the fires are caused by lightning strikes. The rest are
what is called "hunters' lightning." These are fires set by deer
hunters to burn out a section of woods so that in a few weeks
there will be tender new growth on the burned land and the
hunters know that new growth is a sure way to attract deer.
The only way into the area from the highway is a barely
marked road called Miller Road Extension. Collier County
doesn't maintain Miller Road Extension, and left alone the
road would be quickly overgrown by weeds and bushes or
buried under accumulated trash. But, for years now, some
unknown person comes with a bulldozer or a road grader
every month or so and clears the road, smashing plants that
have crept across it and nosing trash off to the side of the
road. The anonymous bulldozer has been nicknamed the
Ghost Grader. The property the Ghost Grader clears is no
longer known as Golden Gate Estates or Remuda Ranch
Grants. Officially, it is now referred to as Collier County Parcel 197, and the people who live nearby just call it the
Blocks.

———

A ranger named Mike Owen met me at the Fakahatchee
Strand headquarters, and before we went to see the stolen
orchids we went for a drive around the Blocks. The roads
were chalky and heat-beaten, and hip-high weeds knit an
edge along them that shut off almost anything other than a
straight-ahead view. The blocks were straight and squared,
like blocks in a real suburb, and the roads were wide and
white, like suburban streets, and some of the intersections

had street signs with ordinary-sounding street names and
stop signs that jutted up out of a mesh of wild pine and salt
grass and poison ivy. Driving around the Blocks wasn't like
driving through a jungle—it was like driving through a suburb that had had all its houses and people erased. Every once
in a while we passed a shaved-down patch in the thick
growth, probably the start of what would have been a driveway that would have led to what would have been somebody's
home. Some of these clearings were dotted with piles of
junk—old rusted-out refrigerators missing their doors, a
black heap of tires, a lawn chair. In one clearing I saw a
pickup truck that looked as if it was operational. The bed of
the truck was loaded with a dozen beekeeper boxes, but there
was no beekeeper around. Far ahead, on the horizon, miles
down the road, I noticed a shimmer, and then the shimmer
became a blot and then the blot became a bigger blot and
then it became a black sedan that looked as if it was growing
rather than moving. In an instant it was in front of us and
then in an instant it whooshed past and the road was blank
again. It was spooky not to see any other cars or people but it
was almost spookier to finally see one—it was like an intruder intruding on an intruder. I opened my window and
stuck my head out. There were only a few sounds, and each
of them was amplified—the thunking of the ranger's car, the
whirring and whining of invisible insects, the whistle of a
bird. It was a weird unquiet stillness, and yet the place had a
weird overfull emptiness. It was more ghostly than a ghost
town. In a ghost town only the people are missing. Here the
buildings were missing, too. It didn't seem like a peaceful
place where nothing ever happened—it was full of the feeling of a million things planned on and never done.

On a culvert over a drainage canal a man was lining up
fishing rods and a little boy crouching beside him had his

arm wrist-deep in a bucket of bait. The ranger slowed his car down as we passed them and opened his window. "Hot out here," he said to the man. Watery waves of heat rippled up from the hood of the car.

"Hot, yes, sir," the man said, nodding. The little boy stood up and waved at us with a hand full of worms.

The ranger turned at the next corner so we could start back to headquarters. Every stop sign we passed was punched with dozens of buckshot holes. After a couple of blocks we came upon a Ford Bronco. The driver was a large man with a long black beard. He stopped his Bronco and waved the ranger over. The bearded man was wearing khaki pants and a belt with a shiny buckle but no shirt at all. He was sweating on his forehead and along his collarbone, and his chest looked like damp rising dough. He told the ranger he had just passed a black bear that was being chased across a street by two hound dogs and a man carrying an assault rifle. The ranger had his hand on his gun the whole time the bearded man was talking. He took some notes and then said to the man, "Now, where did you say you saw the bear?"

The man pulled his beard and screwed up his face. After a minute he said, "Honest, sir, it's kind of hard to describe in this jungle, but I think he was near the intersection of Stewart and De Soto." It was odd to hear someone using street names to describe a place in a swamp that a bear would run past. It was odder to realize that years ago it was going to be someone's address.

———

We went back to the preserve headquarters and I got myself ready to go into the swamp on foot. When I'd first walked into the Fakahatchee I hadn't known what to wear; I just knew that I wanted to cover as much of my body as I could but still avoid getting parboiled. Finally I settled on a long-sleeved shirt, a pair of cotton and Lycra leggings, some tube socks and a pair of cheap sneakers. The outfit actually worked pretty well but it didn't last long. When I got back to the ranger station at the end of that hike, I grabbed some spare clothes out of my car, ran to the restroom and washed my face for about ten minutes straight, and then stripped off every piece of my swamp outfit and threw it all out. My shirt was soaked with bug repellent and sunscreen, and my leggings were stiff with mud, and my shoes and socks were blackened by the silt I'd walked through in the sinkholes. Anyway, I was so happy to get out of them that I couldn't think of anything I wanted more than to pull everything off and stuff it into the wastebasket. On my way back to my hotel I stopped at a Kmart and stocked up on cheap long-sleeved shirts and leggings and sneakers to use on future walks in the swamp. When I got back to New York everyone I talked to about the hike asked what I wore, and they seemed surprised when I described my outfit. I suppose they expected that I would have worn something more heavy-duty and protective. It would be great if you could walk in a swamp wearing something secure-feeling like chest-high waders or a head-to-toe wet suit, but if you did you would die of heat prostration, and if your waders filled with water you would die of heat prostration and on top of that you would drown. Some of the Fakahatchee rangers wear their Park Service uniforms and regular leather boots in the swamp. I preferred wearing sneakers rather than boots, because even though boots feel safer and more substantial I thought that wearing sneakers would allow me to feel around on the bottom of the sinkholes to see if there were alligators in them or not. This was something Laroche had advised me to do, but when I came upon my first sinkhole I realized that he had never told me what to do if I thought I *had* found an alligator. The fact is that the swamp is so grabby that even though I was covered from neck to foot I felt stark naked. The water was freezing cold, and mosquitoes sneaked in and out of my shirt by way of my collar and sleeves, and every plant with prickers snatched at my leggings, and the gritty sinkhole muck passed right through my socks and sneakers and stained my ankles and toes. I had mosquito bites on my stomach and my face, and toward the end of that first hike I got so nervous and exhausted that I broke out in hives for the first time in my life.

Mike Owens, the ranger who drove me through the Blocks, was going to drop me off near the big sinkhole lake where some of Laroche's orchids had been wired up. He said that he was not going to go into the swamp with me—he was going to leave me there because he had some other things to do, and Katherine, the other ranger, was already out near the lake and would walk me in. He mentioned that Katherine might have a few volunteer workers with her who would join us so they could see the stolen orchids too. After I changed into my swamp clothes we drove a couple of miles down the Fakahatchee's only road. Every mile looked like every other mile to me—profuse and green and impenetrable. After a few minutes we pulled over and parked at a profuse, green, impenetrable-looking spot, and in a moment Katherine emerged from the woods. She was solidly built and had flushed cheeks and curly brown hair that had frizzed into a nimbus around her head. Her ranger uniform was soaking wet up to her waist. Behind her were two huge men, the biggest men I have ever seen, as big as sides of beef, shoulders like sirloin roasts. I had once read that the Skunk Man who supposedly lives in the Fakahatchee is seven feet tall and weighs seven hundred pounds. These huge men were dressed in shapeless pastel prison uniforms and they had rags wrapped jauntily around their hair. "Come on in," the ranger said, waving to me. Mike Owens said he'd see me later and got back into his car and drove away.

I stepped off the shoulder of the road into the swamp without looking; if I had looked, I might not have done it, since stepping off a high bank into deep black water is something I can do only if I don't think about it too much. I sank up to my knees and then over my knees. Bladderwort and pennywort floating on the water surface looped around my legs. The muck on the bottom was soft, but not soft in a pleasant way—it was mushy-soft, like cereal that had been sitting too long in milk. The ranger set off at a clip, and we waded after her in a line—first me, then Giant #1 and then, a few feet behind him, Giant #2. The ranger mentioned the orchids were in a swamp lake that we would be able to walk through because it was deep but not as deep as some lakes in the Fakahatchee. Deep Lake, for instance, drops ninety-seven feet into the ground. We walked for about ten minutes to a spot where the underbrush opened and you couldn't see through the water to the floor of the swamp. This was the lake. In the middle of the lake were a few pond apple trees, and the ranger beckoned me over so I could see the orchids that she had attached to them. There were several sawed-off sections of logs attached to branches by baling wire. Laroche had removed the orchids by sawing off sections of the tree limbs they had been attached to because he didn't want to risk hurting them by prying them off the limbs. The rangers got the orchids back after they had been photographed for evidence, and they left them on their limbs and wired the limbs onto pond apple trees. They'd put them in several locations around the swamp. Here there were two clamshell orchids and one butterfly orchid and one ghost. None of the plants were in bloom—they were just small knots of roots and almond-shaped pseudobulbs, and all but the leafless ghost orchids had light-green tapering leaves. The baling wire was wrapped a couple of times around the trees to hold the limbs securely. It was a crazy-looking concoction, but so far the orchids hadn't died.

To get a good look at the orchids we had to walk from thigh-high water into waist-high and deeper. It was a good time for me to recite to myself the section of the Faka-hatchee Strategic Plan that states, "The preserve attracts visitors with an affinity for totally undeveloped areas, who enjoy strenuous hikes and have no aversion to wading hip-deep in a swamp." When the four of us were gathered by the tree, the ranger finally introduced me to the giants and said they were in the inmate work-release program of Copeland Road Prison, just down the road from the Fakahatchee—I had passed it on my way in. Both of the men were bashful and spoke in tiny, mumbly voices. After we were introduced I noticed that both of them were carrying three-foot-long machetes. I'm not sure how I hadn't seen the machetes before that, but maybe it was because the men had been wading behind me most of the way. I hate hiking with convicts carrying machetes. We stood in the lake for a while and every now and then one or the other or both of them would raise their machetes and then smash them into the water with a frightful, squeamish look on their faces. The speed of their swings was ferocious, and the machetes smashing against the water sounded like someone getting spanked. The ranger leaned over and whispered to me that she had given the men the machetes because they were both terrified of snakes and had refused to get into the swamp without some protection. After she gave them the machetes they had agreed to get in, but even heavily armed they were as jumpy as rabbits and stood holding their hands stiff and high above the water. Every time a bubble would rise to the surface of the lake or a tree would drop a leaf or a bird would peep, the giants and I would panic. When I panicked I froze. When one of the giants panicked he would pop up nervously and then the other one would pop up nervously too, and the water displaced by their combined weight rolled in silky waves across the lake. The cold black water slapped at my belly button every time they would pop up and down. The swamp was hot and hushed except for all the splashing and the smack of the giants' machetes against the water. You could disappear in a place like this, really disappear, into one of these inky sinkholes or in the warm muck under the thick brush. No one could find you in a place like this once you sank in. Just then I got extremely curious but decided to wait until we were out of the swamp and in a secure government vehicle before I asked the giants what they were in prison for.

Anyone Can Grow Orchids

 I told a famous Florida orchid man I'd met named Tom Fennell about Laroche's plan to make and sell millions of ghost orchids. Tom said he thought Laroche's idea was insane. "Ghost orchids are sure death," he said. "You can't grow them. They've reduced themselves through reverse evolution into nothing but roots and flowers, and they can only survive in a perfect microclimate that you just can't reproduce." I told him Laroche believed that the ghost orchid would make him a millionaire. "That's crazy too," he said. "There might be a hundred real nuts in the United States who would want a ghost orchid. Other than that I don't think you could sell one at a Food Fair for more than a dime." As it happened, Tom Fennell was himself a millionaire, although not on account of his orchids. In 1994, right before I met him, he and his wife, Trudy, had won $6.76 million in the Florida state lottery. Two weeks later they closed Orchid Jungle, which the Fennell family had operated near Homestead for more than thirty years.

Orchid Jungle was a plot of hardwood hammock that Tom's grandfather bought in 1923. He built a house and an orchid nursery on the property, and then in the remaining jungle he wired tropical orchids onto the trees. He meant for the jungle to just be an oversized and unusual family garden, but in 1926 *The Miami Herald* ran an article about the place and nearly two thousand curious visitors showed up the very next day. Eventually the Fennells turned Orchid Jungle into a tourist attraction. In its prime it attracted fifty thousand people a season and the nursery sold sixty thousand plants a year. But by the time Tom and Trudy won the lottery the Jungle was in trouble. Hurricane Andrew had blown up all thirteen of their greenhouses and blown down half the trees in the jungle part of Orchid Jungle, and the tourists who used to come by the busload for package tours of the local attractions like Orchid Jungle and Monkey Jungle and the Coral Castle just didn't come to Homestead anymore.

I did go to Homestead one hot day after my hike with the convicts when Tom invited me to see what remained of the Jungle and to visit some of his orchid-growing neighbors. He also wanted me to meet Snake Boy, the young guy who rented a cottage on the Fennells' property, but the day I was going to come over, Snake Boy wasn't around. Tom said that Snake Boy had filled the cottage with interesting reptiles and spiders he had collected. As impressive as Tom made this sound, I was only partly sorry we wouldn't be able to stop by. I wasn't crazy about a cottage full of reptiles and spiders, but the part of me that was sorry was the part that was beginning to understand where Laroche fit in the universe. When I had first heard about Laroche I had thought of him as an extremist, a madman with a passion for orchids that was far removed from the average way that people feel about plants, about *anything*. Then I met more and more orchid people in

Florida who were utterly devoted to, utterly engrossed in, their plants. Then I heard about people like Snake Boy, who lives in his little shack with his snakes and bugs, and the old man out on the Tamiami Trail who has a private museum of cypress knees, and the Miami drug dealer named Mario Tabraue, who had been collecting specimens of every endangered plant and animal species in the world. Tabraue had a company called Zoological Imports Unlimited through which he acquired a giraffe, two cheetahs, a two-headed python named Medusa, and dozens of rare birds, as well as $79 million worth of cocaine and marijuana. I wanted to talk to Mr. Tabraue about his enthusiasm for rare creatures, but shortly before I went down to Florida, he had chopped a government drug informant into little pieces and then barbecued him on a backyard grill and consequently was sent to jail for a hundred years for murder and racketeering. I wrote to him in prison but I never heard back. Later I did hear that Tabraue had gotten good-behavior points for testifying against a prominent parrot expert and endangered-animal activist named Tony Silva, who had partnered with his mother to smuggle inside perforated plastic pipes hundreds of very rare hyacinth macaws from Brazil to the United States. It seemed as if there were hundreds and hundreds of people who were wrapped up in their special passion for the natural world. I still considered Laroche and his schemes exceptional—actually, something *beyond* exceptional—but he had started to seem more like the endpoint in a continuum. He was the oddball ultimate of those people who are enthralled by non-human living things and who pursue them like lovers.

—

The Fennells' house and what is left of Orchid Jungle are on a quiet road in Homestead with no sidewalks. The house is low and wide. Even though the hurricane had swept so much of the jungle away, everything around the house was still bushy and green and crowding forward toward the street. All the plants were supersized. Giant palm fronds formed a curtain around the house. The foliage plants in the front yard had leaves four feet long and as wide as my thighs. As you come up the Fennells' driveway it looks as if the jungle is about to gift-wrap the house. Tom met me at the door and led me inside. He is the tallest or second-tallest orchid man I met while I was in Florida, and he has excellent posture and a sort of patrician bearing that makes him look even taller. He is sixtyish and has a forthright jaw and a flurry of thick white hair and an unhurried manner of speech. Since becoming millionaires, he and Trudy have traveled a lot and bought good paintings for their house and forever given up the painful practice of raising a plant and bringing it to its best only to see it carted away by a customer. There were times when pre-millionaire Tom couldn't afford to be picky, but he couldn't bear seeing a favorite plant sold to an unfavorite customer, so he would decide at the last minute that the plant was no longer for sale and turn the customer away. It was a practice that horrified his children; his son told me that as soon as he opened his own nursery he established an unsentimental "all plants for sale always to anyone" policy, the single exception being a cattleya his grandfather had collected decades ago in South America.

Before we went for our drive Tom showed me around the house and pointed out some of his finest plants and told me the Fennell family history. The story begins in Kentucky after the Civil War, where Tom's great-grandfather was in the horse-harness business. In addition, his great-grandfather was an inventor—twenty of the twenty-two patented styles of horse boots are his inventions, and so is the Fennell tail set, a harness contraption used to hold up a horse's tail. Most of his inventions are still in use. Great-grandmother Fennell tended her large rose pit, a conservatory, some rare plants from Mexico, and an orchid a missionary friend had sent to her from Madagascar. When he was growing up, their son Lee (Tom's grandfather) gardened a little. Then he developed tuberculosis and was told to spend more time in moist places like greenhouses, so he started gardening a lot. He eventually opened his own nursery in Cynthiana, a town in the Bluegrass region of Kentucky. He favored orchids and became the first commercial orchid grower west of the Alleghenies. When Lee Fennell opened his business in 1888 an orchid nurseryman couldn't place orders for plants—he had to go to the jungle and collect them. Lee took an orchid-collecting trip to Colombia and Venezuela in 1888 and brought back over a thousand cattleyas. He went back again in 1891. He also hired English and German orchid hunters to collect for him in jungles around the world. On his trips to South America he discovered a number of new species but refused to list them with England's Royal Horticultural Society's official orchid registry because he was Irish and spurned any association with the English.

The Fennell Orchid Company greenhouses were on the South Fork of the Licking River in Cynthiana and were damaged badly by floods several times. After one especially devastating flood, Lee had to declare bankruptcy. In 1922 he decided to move himself, his family, and his orchids and bromeliads to Florida. He converted three trucks into orchid moving vans and made two round trips from Kentucky to Florida to bring all his flowers south. When Lee bought the land that became Orchid Jungle, South Dade County was still wild. Lee cut a clearing in the thick of it and built a house and a nursery and a plant lab. In his lab he worked on techniques for germinating orchid seeds and eventually developed the now-famous Cake-Pan Method and the Turkish Towel Method. (The Fennells are an inventive family. Years after great-grandfather's horse boots and Lee's Cake-Pan Method, Lee's son Thomas Sr. developed the Butterball Turkey.) In 1926 a huge hurricane blew through the Homestead area, battering Lee's house and vacuuming the jungle. The family waited out the storm safely in their Studebaker convertible. Then *The Miami Herald* ran its article and Orchid Jungle was stormed again, this time by thousands of plant lovers. In 1941 Lee Fennell died. His widow, Dorothy, was convinced he had buried money throughout Orchid Jungle, so she spent the next decade digging holes in the property trying to find the hidden treasure. Dorothy and Lee's son Thomas Sr., who at the time was working in Haiti for the U.S. Department of Agriculture, was convinced that there was no money at all in Orchid Jungle, underground or otherwise, and proposed that the family sell it. At the time, Thomas Sr.'s son Tom—the Tom I was visiting that day in Homestead—was an undergraduate at Harvard. On a visit home he realized he couldn't stand the thought of selling Orchid Jungle, so he dropped out of college for a few years to help his mother run it. When he went back to Harvard he switched his major from government to biology. In 1949 he came back to Orchid Jungle full-time.

Tom's return happened at the same moment Americans were becoming enchanted with orchids. Soldiers saw fantastic tropical species growing in the Pacific, and many of them received an orchid lei in Hawaii on their way home from the war. Rex Stout was publishing his popular mysteries starring the brilliant detective Nero Wolfe, an orchid fancier who visited the ten thousand orchids he kept on the roof of his New York brownstone twice a day, two hours at a time, accompanied by Theodore Horstmann, his personal botanist. In 1951

The Saturday Evening Post ran an article by Philip Wylie called "Anyone Can Raise Orchids." In the story, Wylie wrote about visiting "the overwhelming spectacle" of Orchid Jungle and then described Fennell's easy and inexpensive Cake-Pan Method of orchid cultivation, which made the high-priced hobby available to anyone. At the time, an article saying that orchid growing wasn't the exclusive province of the rich must have been as startling as an article titled "Anyone Can Raise Polo Ponies" would be. Wylie wrote: "Fennell's ideas are regarded as heresy. . . . Even the average amateur goes about the business of cultivating orchids with more and costlier equipment than is required for the raising of the average American baby." The magazine got more responses to Wylie's story than anything except an earlier article about Pearl Harbor. The Fennells got so many letters after the story ran that they had to hire three secretaries to answer them all. "Everyone wanted to know how to get orchids and how to come to the Jungle," Tom said. "About a third of the letters actually had blank signed checks in them and just a little note attached saying 'Please send me some orchids, anything at all.' "

———

Tom said he wanted to first introduce me to his neighbors and save my tour of Orchid Jungle for the end of the day. We walked through the front yard to his car. It's funny to even call it a front yard—it was just an open spot in the midst of opulent growth, a bald spot in a carpet. And even the bald spot wasn't entirely bald. Here and there those incredible foliage plants had sneaked onto the mowed grass. They were so huge that they were like science-fiction plants with monstrous leaves. When Tom wasn't looking I tried wrapping myself in one. Snake Boy's dog was bouncing around in the driveway, so as we were leaving Tom pulled up by the cottage to see if Snake Boy might actually be home. Snake Boy wasn't Tom's son, but there was something fatherly about Tom's regard for him. There are many fathers and sons in the plant world, and some surrogate fathers and sons, too. Maybe the reason the passion for orchids lasted within a family for generations was that the fathers instilled in the sons their love of orchids, or maybe there was some instinct about plants that was passed down through a family, like folktales. Tom Fennell was the son and the grandson and the great-grandson of orchid men, and his own son Tom III was now an orchid man as well. Snake Boy, with his crazy congeniality with insects and plants, almost seemed like a family member, too. The cottage appeared shut tight, so after a moment Tom shrugged and pulled away.

Everyone drives everywhere in Florida, and if you are an orchid man you do an extra share of driving. Tom used to go to dozens of orchid shows around the country every year. "One year I did *seventeen* shows," he said. "I needed two trailers for all the orchids and the display material. I don't mean little trailers—I mean big ones about sixteen feet long. I drove one and Trudy drove one, and we drove all day and night without stopping because if you stopped, the trailers would get too hot and the orchids would die. And my displays were really something. Now you're supposed to limit your display to a hundred square feet although no one *really* does, but back then you could do whatever you wanted. One year I had a six-hundred-square-foot exhibit with a three-level waterfall and dozens of my best plants. One of them had sixteen hundred blooms on it at one of the shows." I asked what display he was most proud of. He tapped the steering wheel for a minute and then said, "I did a fantastic display one year with a Jack-in-the-Beanstalk theme. I carved Jack out of Styrofoam and dressed him in my son Tommy's clothes. It was quite impressive."

The signs flashed past us: NATIVE TREE NURSERY; HANCK WHOLESALE FOLIAGE; KERRY'S BROMELIADS; GOD (HOLY) SIN—REPENTANCE—THE ONLY CHOICE. Every inch of land was swollen with something—with grass, with fruit trees, with shaggy bushes, with anonymous spikes of green. We drove alongside acres of ficus trees planted in rows like corn. Little plants I usually see in florist shops were growing in columns of hundreds, and each was a hundred times bigger than the ones I usually see. At a sign that said MOTES ORCHIDS Tom drove in. "I want you to meet Martin Motes," he said. "He's a very, very good vanda man. He has his own ideas. Some of them are quite controversial and he's a little bit of a . . . *hippie,* but I'm very fond of him." Motes Orchids was a complex of slightly seedy shadehouses and little outbuildings and Martin's slightly shambling house. In the yard two large mud-colored dogs were lounging around. In the driveway there was a late-model BMW with the license plate VANDA 1. Standing beside it I could see a swath of fuchsia and lavender and white behind the flapping shade cloths. After a moment Martin Motes came out of the shadehouse. He looked about fifty and had a lean, jaunty build and a close-shaven beard and the kind of tan that looks as if it will never go away. Everything he was wearing was baggy and soil-colored, and he had soil from his fingertips to his elbows. "Senor Fennell!" he said cheerfully. "You have caught me in the middle of my ruminations." He looked at me and said, "My dear, I am working on a twenty- to thirty-year botanical plan to break the teeth of time."

Tom rummaged around in his pocket. "Seedpod for you, Martin," he said, pulling out a brown sickle-shaped thing. "Lee Moore brought this for you from Peru. I also wanted to bring you something Snake Boy found, but he wasn't home." Just then, a truck drove in and grumbled to a stop behind

Tom's car. The driver climbed out and started unloading boxes from the back of the truck. Martin glanced over and said, "Aaahhh, the jewels have arrived." I said that I'd never heard anyone greet a truck so ceremoniously. "I must inform you that I am a recovering academic," Martin said. "I'm still fighting off the effects of a doctorate in twentieth-century poetry." He started reciting some early Yeats and then broke off in the middle of a couplet to open one of the boxes. Inside were a half-dozen orchid plants with sickly-looking leaves. Martin said they were from Peru, and like many plants coming in from abroad they had been in the USDA quarantine in Miami for twenty-one days. Once plants finish their quarantine they are fumigated and released. Martin resumed the Yeats couplet and then stopped and said to the truck driver, "Tell your guy that this is not the way I like my plants to look after fumigation. I'm sure he'll be, uh, most appreciative upon receiving that news." The driver shrugged and handed Martin a clipboard and a pen and said, "Yep. Now sign."

Martin's shadehouses were filled with vandas, an orchid genus with rounded petals and a wide, open face and foliage that looks like the top of a pineapple. Vandas have a benign aspect and a lip that isn't as pouchy or weird as that of other species. They come in every color in the world and with leaves that can be freckled or veiny or unmarked. That day it happened that a lot of Martin's plants were blooming. Most were in shades of purple or pink, and in the dim shadehouse they looked illuminated. Martin said most of his imported plants were from Thailand. In his lab he was working on some new hybrids that he would germinate and grow himself. Hybridizing is a tricky part of the orchid business. The goal is to cross-pollinate two plants with good qualities and end up with a hybrid that has the best qualities of each of its parents. There are more than sixty thousand orchid species

and at least sixty thousand registered hybrids, all one hundred twenty thousand of which can be crossed with natural
species or with other hybrids—in other words, you would
need a calculator to figure out how many possible hybrid
crossings there are. Some crosses produce weaklings or mutants that have no redeeming features. Others produce wonderful new flowers with, say, the rich color of one parent and
the fine shape and hardiness of the other. It's impossible to
know in advance which crosses will work and which won't. A
successful hybridizer has to have good instincts, good luck, a
lot of knowledge about each parent he plans to use, and a lot
of time, since a new cross won't have its first flower for about
seven years.

If an orchid breeder can come up with a good cross, he will
have a flower that people will want and will have to come to
him to buy. Anyone can then duplicate the same cross on his
own because the parentage isn't kept a secret, but he will
have to wait seven years to get a bloom. In other words, a
grower with a new hybrid has in effect a seven-year copyright
on the flower. For those seven years, he has the monopoly on
its commercial value. For those seven years, he also has monopoly on the status creating a new hybrid confers—he can
register it with the name of his nursery and enter it in American Orchid Society competitions and get attention for his
cultivation skills. He can even influence the future of the
flower. He can hybridize with a particular characteristic in
mind, and if his hybrids become popular and award-winning,
other growers will probably start working on hybrids with the
same traits. Martin, for instance, wants to breed vandas that
look more the way vandas did when the Victorian orchid
hunter Carl Roebelin first found *Vanda sanderiana* in the
rubble of an earthquake in the Philippines. Other growers
want to move the species in the opposite direction, and their
hybrids are bigger, more sculpted, more vivid, and more ex-

treme. Whoever has more success in orchid shows and among the orchid opinion makers will set the fashion for the vanda of the future.

Coming up with a good hybrid is as troublesome as inventing a new recipe. A lot of orchid growers don't bother with it at all and instead specialize in growing the finest specimens of orchids that already exist. Martin told me that he thought a lot of breeders who claim to have produced new hybrids have actually bought them from a nursery in Taiwan and Thailand and take credit for it themselves. "I am absolutely certain that some of the hybrids you hear about have been spirited away from distant points," Martin said. "There are too many occasions when some breeder in Florida announces a hybrid cross he claims to have just made and *coincidentally* you will see the exact same cross at a nursery in Thailand. Just think about it. There are untold millions and billions of possible orchid crosses you can come up with. Either the American breeder is buying the new Thai hybrid and claiming it as his own or this is the most remarkable coincidence in the history of human creativity." He said many orchid people want to have new plants to market and want the prestige of creating something but are really too busy or lazy to work on their own. "It's a falling-off of the basic sense of honor," he said. "It's conceptual theft. The guy who came up with the hybrid in Thailand is probably a Buddhist and therefore is nonconfrontational. For a Buddhist it would be spiritually incorrect to protest about intellectual pirating, so whatever breeder here buys it can claim it as his own and never worry about being contradicted."

As we walked through the shadehouse, Martin and Tom traded orchid stories and debated the botanical advantages of pollination by pseudoantagonism versus pseudocopulation. I walked a few feet behind, listening, and then stopped by a sexy pink flower and sniffed it. It smelled like lemon sponge cake. "That's a nice flower," Martin said. "That goes for about a thousand dollars." We passed a table of small pots of little bloomless plants. Martin picked up one of the pots, poked his finger into the soil, and then shook his head. Tom raised his eyebrows and asked, "What have you got here?"

"Here we have a failed experiment," Martin said. "And Dr. Martin Motes made an executive decision the other night that we have a hell of a lot of those, man."

——

Sophisticated shoppers stop at Motes Orchids all the time. That afternoon two shoppers happened to arrive while Martin was showing us around. Their names were Richard Fulford and Denise McConnell, and both were elegant and polished Jamaicans who were regulars at Martin's and had extensive orchid collections of their own. Richard was a businessman in Miami. Denise was just visiting. She said she lived on a gigantic estate in Jamaica called Bog Walk. Martin had been expecting them, so when he heard Richard's car he hollered a few lines from *Romeo and Juliet* and then gestured for them to join us in the shadehouse. They hopped out of the car, raced up the driveway, ducked under the piece of green cloth at the entry of the shadehouse, and then slowed to a halting, window-shopping pace. They dawdled toward us past a group of plants with purple blooms the size of coffee cups. Above the purple plants hung slatted wooden baskets with plants blooming in bright white and pink. When Richard and Denise finally reached us they both had the same dazed look on their faces. "God, I feel like I might go crazy," Denise said. She sighed. "Richard," she said, "help me contain myself." She told Martin she had promised her husband that she would exercise restraint. Her husband was also in Miami, but he didn't want to come out to Martin's. "Not an orchid man," Martin explained to me.

"No, it's not his hobby," Denise said. "His hobby is eating."

"Denise already got a box of plants today," Richard said.

Denise waved her hand and said, "Oh, those were just babies in that box. Maybe four or five thousand but they're just little babies."

"Oh, my," Martin said. Richard and Denise began inching away from us, toward a table with dappled yellow flowers. "Too many beautiful things, Martin," Denise said.

"I spent a decade to get that one," Martin said. He pointed at one of the yellow flowers that was brighter and bigger than the others. "A decade of a man's life."

"And just look at that lip," Richard said. Everyone stood silently. A bumblebee floated by, listing from side to side like a drunk. It bumped into the yellow flower and ricocheted off it and bumped into another one. The flower quivered from the impact of the fat bee. "Denise," Martin said, "you should own this plant. A woman of your discriminating taste! 'Present mirth hath present laughter, every wise man's son doth know.' You owe it to yourself to own this."

"It's definitely pulling me," she said.

"Do you need something suitable to put in a suitcase and smuggle back to Jamaica?" Martin said. He was joking. He winked at her. "Because, my dear, if you do, here's a delicious little miniature." He reached for a pot that held the cutest plant in the world. I had vowed that I would acquire not even a single orchid on any of my trips down here, but I thought I might die if I couldn't have this one. The background of the petals was the beigey yellow of a legal pad, and over the yellow background was a spray of hot-pink pinpoint dots, and the flower was attached to the plant by a stem that was twisted like a stick of licorice. The petals were plump and supple and pleasant to touch. The center of the flower looked like the face of a piglet. I felt as if the plant was looking at me as much as I was looking at it. The flower wasn't beautiful—it was absorbing. I felt that I could stare into the center of the flower for hours.

"Oh, Martin, I don't need to smuggle, Martin," Denise said. Her rolling accent gave his name a romantic sound. "I don't have to shop to fit my suitcase. I have a permit." She and Richard headed toward the back of the shadehouse. One of them spotted a cream-and-pink flower and pointed to it. They both gasped. "What is this, Martin?" Denise called out. "I'm going *wild*, Martin."

He looked over to see what she and Richard were pointing at. "Oh, yes. Ain't that a caution!" he drawled. "Bless its little heart." Then he pretended to get busy with something. Denise gave Richard a look and said quietly, "It must be some special cross. He isn't going to tell us what it is."

"Tsk, tsk," Martin said without looking up. "Thou shalt not covet."

Just then one of Martin's long-legged mud-colored dogs trotted into the shadehouse and bit me really hard. I made enough noise that everyone noticed immediately. Martin grabbed the dog and started discussing how interesting this was because the dog had never bitten anyone before. I thought the conversation was rather academic, so after listening for a second I limped over to the house and went to find some rabies medicine. By the time I came out Denise had assembled about forty plants that she wanted to buy. Martin was writing a receipt for her. "Let's see, Denise," he said, squinting at the receipt. "Have we spent all your money yet?"

She groaned. "Oh, Martin, unfortunately we have got to go."

"Oh, well," he said. "All right. Now, my dear, I have an announcement to make. Dr. Motes has decided to throw in one

of those mysterious pink vandas that you had your eye on."
He grinned. "I believe in the Eleventh Commandment: Thou
shalt not withhold gorgeous new vandas from thy dearest
customers and friends." He went over to the table with the
anonymous flower. Denise and Richard followed him with
their eyes. Denise looked as if she was holding her breath. As
Martin lifted one of the pots he turned to us and said,
"Dearly beloved, have I shared my views on organized religion with you yet?"

———

The day had slipped into that yellowy hour when the sun is
lingering on the horizon still hoping to burn you to death.
Tom said we ought to move on, so I said good-bye to Martin
and arranged to see him again in a day or two. When we got
back into the car, Tom sat and pondered for a few minutes
about where we should go next. There were orchid growers
in every direction. Within a mile radius of Martin's driveway
there probably were a billion orchids. It was a fact I never got
used to in Florida, the fact of seeing so many and so much of
something as exotic and precious as orchids, and seeing
them without ceremony, lined up on long factory benches in
toss-away pots. It didn't make the orchids seem like ordinary
merchandise—it reminded me more of the time I toured
Harry Winston's jewelry workshop and saw about two hundred thousand dollars' worth of pear-shaped diamonds
heaped in an old cigar box. It was actually more amazing
than seeing them upstairs in a display case lined with red velvet. Tom said he wanted to take me to the ultimate of botanical superabundance, a place called Kerry's Bromeliads.
Kerry's consisted of 329,000 square feet of greenhouses. In
the 329,000 square feet of greenhouses there were 3.6 million orchids and 1.4 million bromeliads. "It's a big place,"
Tom said, as we drove toward it. "It's really bigger than big."

The original Kerry's Bromeliads had been swept away by Hurricane Andrew, so it was actually a brand-new bigger-than-big place with milk-white sheet-metal buildings and white golf carts zipping back and forth. There really is a Kerry, but when Tom and I arrived he was occupied with a new shipment of one million *Phalaenopsis,* so the nursery foreman offered to take us around instead. Kerry's Bromeliads was not the sort of place you *walked* around. It was the sort of place you had to ride around in one of those golf carts and you talked to people by walkie-talkie and you identified by sector and subsector. The foreman's name was Mike. He was a young guy, good-looking, and dressed in a beige polo shirt and shorts. He climbed into a golf cart and told Tom and me to sit in back, and then the cart lurched forward and we puttered toward one of the mammoth greenhouses.

He said he would start by showing us some of the bromeliads. "What exactly?" Tom asked.

"*Neoregelia* 'Fireball,'" Mike said. "We've got about an acre of them here." He steered into the greenhouse and drove down one of the rows. Each row had a bench on each side. The benches were about hip-high and a few feet wide, and the rows were as long as three tennis courts, and the greenhouse had dozens and dozens of rows, and the benches held thousands and thousands of plants. On this stainless, quiet, orderly grid of metal benches there was a wild-looking miniature jungle. Mike stopped the cart beside one of the benches. The plants on it had rigid red center spikes and stiff green leaves that peeled away from the stalks like the skin of a banana. These were the *Neoregelia* 'Fireball.' There were hundreds of thousands of them in the greenhouse. They were about to be packed and shipped to Home Depots and garden centers and Kmarts all over the country.

"Let me tell you a story," Tom said. "Do you know where these neoregelias came from? Well, there was this little old

The Orchid Thief 🌺 151

fellow who lived in a trailer park right near here in Goulds. He lived alone—well, as a matter of fact, he lived in his trailer with a dog and a pony. It was really something. One day he found a little mysterious seedling on an orchid he'd gotten. He stuck the seedling in a hollowed-out coconut shell and grew it up, and it was this good-looking bromeliad. He set up his own little nursery and sold nothing but pups from that bromeliad. He must have made fifty thousand dollars on it. He lived off that one plant for *years*. That was his life, his livelihood, that one bromeliad he just stumbled upon."

"Amazing," Mike said. He idly picked dead leaves off a plant near the cart.

"You know, when the old fellow was retiring, I went and bought that original plant from him," Tom said. "The plant was enormous by then. After I bought it I dug around and cut it back, and wouldn't you know it, it was still growing in that same hollow coconut shell."

Mike started the cart and we rolled slowly down the row, brushing by leaves that hung over the edge of the bench. One bench was stacked high with small plastic pots. The plants inside them were withered and droopy. The other benches in the greenhouse were as ordered as checkerboards, but this one was a jumbled mess. Mike nodded toward it and said, "Failed *Antherium* project."

"What was it?" Tom asked. He reached for one of the pots and sifted the dirt in it with his finger.

"Elaine," Mike said. "A species called Elaine. It was created by irradiation. We took the germinating material and radiated it. We hoped to get some interesting mutations, but it didn't work out that way."

I asked him what they were going to do with all the loser Elaines. "Take all ten thousand of them and toss them in the Dumpster," he said.

I wondered if it ever made him sad, to take thousands of plants and throw them away. I wasn't being sentimental. I just wondered how it felt to create ten thousand new life forms and pitch the whole load into the garbage. Mike pursed his lips and squinted at me with one eye. Finally he said, "Well, of course it makes me sad. Really sad. I hate to see all that money down the drain."

It had gotten too late that day for me to hike around Orchid Jungle with Tom, so he offered to have me come back in a couple of days. When I did, I took a meandering route through Homestead just to drive by the nurseries again. It occurred to me when I passed by Kerry's that the Elaines were probably gone by then.

Plant Crimes

Plants disappear all the time in south Florida. So do most other living things. One day after my trip to Kerry's Bromeliads, after all the Elaines had disappeared, *The Miami Herald* reported that frog poachers were hard at work in the Big Cypress Swamp near the Fakahatchee, and that they were poaching two tons of Everglades pig frogs out of the swamp every month. This would yield approximately one and a half tons of legs for cooking. A few of the poachers were interviewed while they sat in their frogging camp one night skinning their catch. They said that except for all the slime involved, frog hunting was a good way to make a living. On the other hand, bell peppers are not a good way to make a living—a neighbor of Tom Fennell's had twenty thousand dollars' worth of them stolen out of his fields. He was so incensed that he pulled up every last one of his remaining peppers and said he would never grow them again.

Laroche had a lot of company as a plant poacher. In fact, plant crimes showed up all the time in the

Miami police blotter between the usual reports of assaults and stickups and stolen vehicles. That winter, instead of collecting plants, I began to collect news of plant crimes:

FEBRUARY 6, 1992 — Burglars attempted to enter a home in the 6500 block of West 27th Court sometime over the weekend but couldn't open the front door. Instead, they cut open a rear screen and stole eight orchids.

APRIL 30, 1992 — Someone jumped the fence of a home in the 700 block of East 43rd Street Saturday and stole several orchids. The plants were valued at more than $1,000.

JULY 18, 1985 — Frank Labate had $1,800 worth of plants stolen from the patio of his home. Labate said he lost an eight-foot-tall palm tree, a six-foot white bird of paradise, a fern, six orchids, and two bonsai plants.

SEPTEMBER 2, 1984 — More than $2,000 worth of plants and patio furniture were taken from the backyard of Barry Burak. Burak reported 35 orchids totaling $1,400, a $200 staghorn fern, 10 hanging plants totaling $150, five potted plants totaling $200, and three metal patio chairs totaling $150 missing.

MAY 6, 1984 — A seven-foot alligator meandered into the parking lot of the Venice Gardens apartments. When police arrived they found the gray gator trying to bite a man who attempted to get a rope around the reptile's neck while another man held its tail.

MAY 6, 1984 — Six show orchids, worth more than $700, were stolen from the backyard of Barbara Carter's house.

JANUARY 10, 1991 — A dwarf palm tree was dug up and removed from Ron Prekup's front yard. A witness told police that two men dug up the tree, placed it in their pickup and left.

JANUARY 10, 1991 — TREE MISSING.

FEBRUARY 12, 1995 — A $250 palm tree was stolen from a yard. Someone dug up the tree, filled the hole and left with the fifteen-foot palm.

JULY 27, 1991 — ORCHIDS STOLEN.

MAY 16, 1991 — ORCHIDS STOLEN.

MARCH 10, 1991 — ORCHIDS STOLEN.

JANUARY 31, 1991 — ORCHIDS STOLEN.

SEPTEMBER 20, 1990 — ORCHIDS STOLEN.

JANUARY 5, 1995 — A palm tree and an electric meter were stolen from outside a home in the 200 block of S.W. 22nd Avenue. The owner peeked outside his house in the morning and noticed the items gone.

AUGUST 20, 1994 — A thief stole a potted pygmy palm tree from the front yard.

MAY 6, 1991 — The sago palm tree has become the hottest target of trendy thieves in the DeLand area. So far this year, as many as four hundred sago palms have been dug up in the middle of the night from yards throughout west Volusia County. Two were taken from the DeLand post office.

JULY 20, 1997 — The Polk County sheriff's office is investigating the theft of more than thirty orchids during two separate burglaries at Starr Lake Nursery near Lake Wales. Sheriff officials believe the burglaries occurred between 9 P.M. on July 20 and 6 A.M. on July 21. The nursery was also burglarized during the early morning of July 26.

APRIL 21, 1994 — Police saw a man pushing a shopping cart with a big palm tree in it about 10:45 P.M. Saturday. When they approached him the man abandoned the cart and tried to hide behind a van. When police found him, he told them he stole the palm tree from a house and was going to sell it to buy crack.

I sometimes collected international plant crimes, too. The English have especially felonious urges toward orchids. Kew Gardens has to display its orchids behind shatterproof glass and surrounded by surveillance cameras the way Tiffany's displays its jewels. In 1993 a rare six-foot-tall monkey orchid with light pink flowers bloomed near London, and the Naturalists' Trust had to hire two security guards to stand watch and protect the plant from collectors. The one extraterrestrial orchid crime I read about took place in the Soviet Union:

MOSCOW, April 1988 — Police arrested an amateur biologist who flower-napped "Cosmonaut," the only orchid ever grown in outer space, and planned to sell it on the black market to an orchid collector, a Soviet newspaper said yesterday. "Cosmonaut," which was grown aboard the Salyut 6 space station and returned to Earth in 1980, died during the bungled flower-napping, Socialist Industry newspaper said. "Cosmonaut" was considered priceless because of its space origin.

Police arrested Vladimir Tyurin, 36, a down-on-his-luck amateur biologist. Tyurin, who once worked on the cleanup detail at the Chernobyl nuclear power station, was the gardener at the Academy of Sciences botanical garden in Kiev. It appeared he had a Moscow buyer all lined up for "Cosmonaut" when police raided his apartment only to find the unique orchid limp and dying. The flower died before experts arrived, the newspaper said.

—

As far as plant crimes on earth are concerned, Laroche's acquisitiveness was exceptional but not unrivaled. The Fakahatchee, the Everglades, the Big Cypress, and the Loxahatchee have been plundered since the day they were discovered. Sometimes, when the swamps were first being explored, orchid hunters would refuse to say where they'd found new species in hopes of protecting the plants. Fred Fuchs, Jr., a Fakahatchee regular, discovered *Bulbophyllum pachyrhachis* in Pond Apple Slough in 1956 but tried to keep the location secret. Eventually collectors figured out where the cache was, and by 1962 they'd swept it clean. It is illegal to take any plant or animal out of state or federal preserves, but plants and animals get taken anyway. Every day, casual visitors to Florida's protected areas yank air plants off easy-to-reach trees—as a result, there are no longer any bromeliads left on the trees that are within an arm's length from the Fakahatchee's boardwalk. Lately there has been a great enthusiasm for a particularly rare Fakahatchee fern called a hand fern, which looks exactly like a filmy green human hand and has its spores grow out of its filmy green wrist. Hand ferns grow in the boot of cabbage palms—the crotch where the fronds attach to the trunk of the tree—and they are more abundant in the Fakahatchee than anywhere else in the United States. Laroche told me he knew where there were thousands of hand ferns on the Seminole reservation and that when he got around to it he was going to get a hand-fern marketing program under way. Hand ferns are hard to collect because they die when they are relocated, so the only way to possess them is to collect and cultivate their spores. The rangers in the Fakahatchee pay special attention to their hand ferns. A week or so after Laroche was arrested with his orchids, two clumps of ferns that were about to release their spores disappeared.

In the Big Cypress Swamp, dwarf cypresses are regularly stolen and sold as bonsai trees. In 1970, a champion mahogany tree on Key Largo was chopped down by someone who wanted to get to the dollar orchids growing on the top branches. Poachers have been caught with every kind of fern, with azalea bushes, with every species of palm, with cactus, with coontie plants. A man was caught in the Fakahatchee with twenty paurotis palms in his truck that were destined for a shopping mall where they would be stripped of their fronds, be refitted with artificial fronds made of silk, and then be arranged in the middle of a food court or in front of a boutique. Two men were caught in the Big Cypress with 110 pounds of goldfoot ferns that were bound for their Santeria store in Miami, where they would be used for medicinal tea that supposedly cures prostate problems. It seems as if everything in the woods gets stalked because so many things in the woods have a price. In 1993 three poachers were arrested in the Everglades with a haul of Alpine Silk butterflies, a species that has sold for thirty-seven thousand dollars a pair in Japan. In the Fakahatchee, rangers are kept busy arresting hunters for a "gun-and-light"—for hunting deer illegally at night, using a stunning floodlight. Alligators vanish all the time. Recently, two men were arrested in the Loxahatchee for killing an alligator. They'd shot it dead, cut off a twenty-nine-inch-long piece of its tail, loaded it into a canoe, then somehow capsized their canoe and got into a fight over which of them had caused the canoe to tip over. When rangers arrested them, they were still in the middle of the fight.

—

A couple of nights after I met Martin Motes, I went to a meeting of the Orchid Society of the Palm Beaches to hear him give a lecture. The meeting was a mile or so from the West Palm greyhound racetrack in an odd squat building that was in the direct landing path of the West Palm Beach airport. When I arrived, people were already milling around the room trading plants and eating cookies. The society's president was standing at the podium. "Did someone park a white Honda with a little raccoon in it?" he called out. "Whoever you are, your windows are open." A few minutes later he banged the podium with his fist and said, "As soon as you will take your seats I will present the only English professor/orchidologist who quotes Milton to his plants." Before Martin began the lecture, he took me around and introduced me to a funeral home director/orchid collector, and a seventy-five-year old man who first bragged to me about his mini-cattleyas and then about his thirty-year-old girlfriend, and then a woman named Savilla Quick, who was famous for having a lucky touch with ghost orchids. Savilla had long Cleopatra eyes and a button nose and a drawly voice. She told me she was a farmer's daughter and had grown up west of Miami, when west of Miami was still nothing but cypress stands and acres of saw grass and one vast spread called Flying Cow Ranch. On Sundays she used to go riding around the swamps looking for interesting things, especially orchids, and in particular the leafless species like the clamshells and the ghosts. At the time, it was still legal to collect wild orchids. Whenever Savilla spotted something she wanted, she'd stand up in her saddle and reach. "The horses *knew* what I was doing," she said to me. "They'd stand perfectly still while I was balancing up there. There was only one exception, my palomino stallion. He always got a little wiggly whenever I stood up." She would bring the wild plants home and attach them to trees in her yard. This was decades ago. Since then, the woods west of Miami have disappeared, and Savilla has grown up, married twice, moved several times, had children, and retired from her job, but the orchids she collected when she was young are still growing in her backyard.

Savilla said I could come over to her house in Boynton Beach to see her old ghost orchids. She said I had to come the next day, because she and her husband, Bob, were packing to go to Arkansas for the summer, but I was so excited to finally see a ghost orchid that I wouldn't have waited a minute longer. The next day I even got to Savilla's early, which might have been the first time in my life I've ever gotten anywhere ahead of time. Savilla was busy on the phone trying to arrange for summer homes for her orchids when I arrived. Her husband met me at the door and deposited me at the dining room table, and then went into another room and came out a few minutes later to show me some pens he had carved out of exotic wood. When I wasn't admiring the pens, I glanced out the dining room window into Savilla's shadehouse, trying to see if I could catch a glimpse of her ghosts. The shadehouse was about the size of a tractor-trailer and bristling with plants. A little wind was pushing the hanging baskets around and rustling the green shade cloth and making pieces of a wind chime click against one another with a lazy sound.

When Savilla got off the phone, she rushed into the dining room and perched on the edge of a chair, lacing and unlacing her fingers and giving me a sideways look. "So, you want to know about the ghost orchids?" she asked. "Oh, I don't know! Should I really tell you my secrets? Oh, I suppose I should. It's good for the orchids, isn't it? Everybody's always trying to get my secrets out of me, because I'm one of the only ones who seem to be able to grow them."

Bob was packing up his exotic-wood pens. "Sugar, I don't know what it is that you do, but you do have your way."

"The secret I've discovered is that the ghost orchids love a mango tree," Savilla went on. "You put the little babies on a mango tree right where the sprinkler hits it, and they love it. And whenever I get some pollen from one of them I put it right into the refrigerator. Then there's a wonderful gal in Jupiter who germinates the seeds for me. The little ghosts also love a pond apple tree. Right now I'm growing a pond apple tree in a pot to take with me to Arkansas. It's not ready yet. When it's big enough, I'll train the ghosts onto it, and then we can take it in the car with us when we leave for Arkansas."

Many people in the orchid world knew about Savilla's success with ghost orchids, and she got calls all the time from people who wanted to buy one. That week she had already gotten a call from Tampa and a call from California. The woman in California had told Savilla that she was desperate for a ghost orchid and asked how much Savilla wanted for one of hers. "I told her a hundred dollars," Savilla said. "Honestly, I could have said a thousand dollars! She had gobs of money! She said she was *desperate*! But I could tell she wanted it only so she could brag about it. I think it was just a statusy thing for her." I asked her what she had decided to do. She frowned and said, "I told her I'd call her if I had some seeds. I'll probably do that, but I bet a nickel I never give her one. I can tell she was one of those people who would love the orchid for a minute and end up letting it die."

Sometimes Bob and Savilla sell their surplus orchids at plant shows. A while ago at one of the shows a man lingered at the Quicks' table and then struck up a conversation with Savilla. Maybe they talked about ghost orchids and maybe they didn't. Maybe he said he had a friend who wanted to buy one and maybe he didn't. The one certainty is that the man bought one little orchid from the Quicks and left. Two days later the man called Savilla at home and said he wanted a few more orchids. She agreed to let him see her collection. "He'd been so sweet and so nice and so this and so that," she said. "That's why I let him come over, even though he'd only bought one little bitty orchid at the sale." The man was especially curious about her ghost orchids, so when he came over she took him around the side of the house and showed him the cluster of them on her mango tree. Most of them weren't blooming at the time, but one of the plants had started forming two seedpods. That evening the man called Savilla and offered her a hundred dollars for one of those pods. She couldn't decide whether she should sell one, but the next day she called him back and said she'd decided that she would, and then she explained that the pods weren't ready to pick, so he couldn't have it quite yet. She said she would call him when his pod was ready. She had his business card, which had only a beeper number on it instead of a regular phone number, and a post office box instead of a regular address.

A few days later Savilla decided to check on the progress of the ghost orchid seedpods, so she walked over to the mango tree and bent down to take a look. The pods were gone. One was missing altogether. The other was broken in two. Half of the broken one was still attached to the roots and the other half was lying in the grass around the bottom of the tree. Savilla describes herself as an extremely emotional person. She says that she now wishes she hadn't let herself get so upset about the seedpods, but she did. She went berserk. She stormed around her yard and her house. Then she gathered the pieces of the broken pod and took them to Nancy Preiss, her seed germinator in Jupiter. Nancy looked at the pods and said they were ruined, but Savilla wouldn't leave until Nancy agreed to examine them in the lab and see if they could be saved. When Savilla got home, she called the curious man for some sympathy. She told him what happened and reminded him that he had said that he was buying the pod for a friend of his. She asked him if he thought that his friend might have gotten impatient and didn't want to wait any longer to get the seedpod. The curious man said he was awfully sorry about the pods but that she'd misremembered—he hadn't been buying the pod for a friend, he wanted it for himself. He said some other ghost orchid fancier must have heard that Savilla had seedpods and had stolen them.

Right after the pod theft, someone broke into the Quicks' shadehouse and stole almost three hundred plants, including twenty-three of a variety that is more valuable than it is beautiful—something only an orchid person could love. The Quicks installed video cameras in the shadehouse and an alarm system in the yard. Sometime later Savilla spotted the curious man at a plant show. It was the first time she'd seen him since the pods disappeared. She hardly recognized him because he had completely changed his looks. "When I first

met him, he was blondy-headed. Now his hair was dark,"
Savilla said. "When I met him, he was wearing glasses, and
now he had gone to contact lenses. And even his clothes had
changed! He had been real casual when I met him, and when
I saw him again he was in this sort of macho attire." They
didn't speak; in fact, the curious man went out of his way to
not even show Savilla his face.

Savilla interrupted herself and said we should take a walk
in the shadehouse. It was boiling outside. Savilla mentioned
that her daughter had moved away from Florida and now
lives in Anchorage, Alaska. We walked between the benches
of plants, ducking to miss the hanging baskets of orchids. A
turtledove was nesting in one of the baskets and watched us
with its calm round eye, purring like a cat. The bird's tail had
a neon-orange stripe on it that looked unnatural. "I did that,"
Savilla said, pointing to the bird. "I spray-painted the stripe
on her when she first came to nest, because I want to keep
track of the bird and see if she returns to her basket. With
her stripe now I won't mix her up with any other little bird."
We dallied. Savilla pointed out things she wanted me to
see—a champion *Vanda*, an iridescent fern, a frizzy little orchid she'd collected as a teenager. I loved all of them. The
leaves on her plants were glossy and full, as if they'd been
shampooed and conditioned. The late-day light made the
pink and purple blooms look incandescent and the red ones
look like emergency flares. Savilla said we should go peek at
the ghost orchid, and I got so eager I thought I would burst.
We walked under the purring turtledove and around the side
of the house to the mango tree. There, I expected to finally
see my first ghost orchid flower. The plant's green roots
were spread on the trunk in the kind of starry web pattern
that forms when you throw a rock through a window. I could
see right away that none of the plants were flowering, and I

felt the air leak out of me in disappointment. One clump of roots did have a tiny raised pale-green bump that Savilla said would become a flower in a month or two. I ran my fingers up and down the smooth, rubbery orchid roots and up and down the nubbly mango bark, and then we went back in the house. Savilla opened a small file box and pulled out the index cards on which she records information about all the wild plants she's collected. She handed me two cards. One said "Tiny Ghost *Harrisella porrecta* Collected 5/89 Big Cypress" and the other said "*Polyrrhiza lindenii* 5/89 Collected Big Cypress." These were the plants that were on her mango tree.

She put the index cards away and said there was one last chapter in the story of the seedpod. It takes about eight months for orchid seeds to germinate, and eight months after her seedpods were stolen Savilla received a letter from the curious man. "It was around Christmas time," she said. "But it wasn't a Christmas card, it was just a note. I first thought it was awful strange not even to say Merry Christmas. It just said, 'Dear Savilla, I hope you've gotten over the tragic loss of your seedpod. Call me when there's another.' Isn't that peculiar?" Her theory is that since she had hesitated before she agreed to sell the man a pod he had suspected that she would change her mind again, so he had decided to steal a pod before that happened. She figures that he had sneaked into her yard one night, stolen one pod and accidentally broken the other, then had tried to germinate the seeds, waited eight months, realized that the seeds weren't going to grow, and so he had written Savilla a note just to seem friendly and also to con her for another seedpod. She never called him after she got the letter, but she still keeps his business card taped to one of her kitchen cabinet doors. She has asked around about him, and none of the orchid people she knows have ever heard of the man. She assumes that she will never hear from him again.

—

One of the most notorious plant crimes in Florida took place in the spring of 1990, when someone broke into a shadehouse at R. F. Orchids and stole $150,000 worth of prizewinning orchids. Many of the stolen orchids were irreplaceable. Many were show plants that had won the American Orchid Society's highest honors and were used as stud plants—big, vigorous specimens with deluxe pedigrees used for breeding and cloning. The break-in was big news among orchid growers and collectors because it was probably the biggest-ever orchid theft in Florida and maybe the biggest-ever in the United States, and it was definitely the biggest-ever theft of such special plants. The fact that it happened at R. F. Orchids made it even more newsworthy, because R. F. Orchids is one of the best and most successful nurseries in south Florida, and its owner, Robert Fuchs, is a grower everybody seems to know.

Bob Fuchs has been a full-time commercial grower only since 1985, but the Fuchs family has been involved with plants for three generations. The first Fuchs to come to Florida was Bob's great-grandfather Charles, who had been a baker in Milan, Tennessee. In 1912, when Charles was forty-eight, he developed malaria. His doctor advised him to move south. A friend of Charles's happened to be on his way to look at land in south Florida and invited Charles to come along, but he declined because the circus was in Milan that week and he didn't want to miss it. A few weeks later he changed his mind and caught up with his friend in Homestead, Florida. In 1912 Homestead was not particularly developed. There were hardly any houses, no restaurants, no refrigerators, only a couple of telephones, and whatever telephone wires there were had been strung up on pine trees. Charles and his friend decided to go for a walk around the area. The walk lasted ten days, and they never stepped out of piney woods the entire time. Charles fell in love with the land, so he mailed his family in Tennessee a box of Florida kumquats to show them his enthusiasm. No one in the Fuchs family had ever seen kumquats before, so they thought Charles had sent them strange little oranges. When Charles got back to Tennessee, he and his wife sold most of their belongings and their bakery business and arrived in Miami with just their children, their clothing, and two live chickens. Charles had bought a house for them in Homestead while he was on his trip. When the family arrived they found the house rough, dark, and filled with ants and fleas. The roads around the house were bumpy and narrow. After the family settled in, Charles's oldest sons, Charlie and Fred, would ride their motorcycles to market every Sunday and go shopping. One time the boys bought some coconuts at the market and were carrying them tucked under their shirts so they could have both hands free to steer their motorcycles. On the ride home they hit some wild coconuts that were lying on the road. They were thrown off their bikes and sustained injuries from the store-bought coconuts under their shirts. Charles tried to make a living as a farmer when they first got to Florida, but the soil in Homestead was just a thin crust of sandy soil on top of hard coral rock. To plant something, you had to first blast a hole in the ground with dynamite. Charles finally gave up farming. He went back to baking and soon developed a recipe for a soft white sandwich loaf he named Cream Bread. Cream Bread became the most popular bread in Florida, and the Fuchs bakery eventually grew into a prosperous national business called Holsum Bakery.

In the 1920s, when Charles's son Fred—Bob Fuchs's grandfather—was first on his own, life in much of America was starting to look modern, but south Florida was still wild, even wilder than the West. It was unexplored and choked with jungle. The minutes of the American Orchid Society's trustee meeting in 1921 note that a few trustees "gave some interesting accounts of their efforts to locate native orchids [in Florida] and the difficulties in trying to get them out of the dense woods—in some cases far removed from the hearts of men." Even they regarded the Florida swamp with dread, as if it were an animal that could eat you alive. Only twenty years earlier it was considered reckless to try to cross south Florida. When an adventurer named Hugh Willoughby crossed the Everglades in a canoe in 1898, he was regarded with stupefaction. In his journal Willoughby wrote that he dined on fried blue herons and lobsters and cabbage-palm salads accompanied by the bacon, lemonade, and chewing gum he had brought along. He had planned to sleep on an air mattress, but it didn't work out. "The experiment was a failure, and ended by my sleeping on [the mattress] without blowing it up, as whenever I would turn over it would roar like an alligator, and it bulged so in the middle that I would constantly fall off." That he made it out alive at all astonished Willoughby's friends. "Since returning home I have frequently been asked, Did you not suffer fever? Were you not made ill by your exposure in that terrible, malarious swamp? I reply that during the entire winter I did not have a single ache or pain, with the exception of an accident which befell me on the Florida Reefs, in which the bone of my nose was half cut through."

Florida was a different kind of wild than Western wild. The pioneers out west were crossing wide plains and mountain ranges that were too open and endless for one set of eyes to take in. Traveling west across those vacant and monumental spaces made human beings look lonely and puny, like doodles on a blank page. The pioneer-adventurers in south Florida were traveling *inward,* into a place as dark and dense as steel wool, a place that already held an overabundance of living things. The Florida pioneers had to confront what a dark, dense, overabundant place might have hidden in it. To explore such a place you had to vanish into it. I would argue that it might be easier to endure loneliness than to endure the idea that you might disappear.

—

Fred Fuchs was as good a baker as his father and occasionally helped out at Holsum, but he really preferred to work outside. As soon as he was on his own he became a farmer and an outdoorsman. He raised hogs and grew okra and developed a hardy and delicious species of avocado called the Fuchs Avocado. He liked to hunt in the Everglades with the Seminoles who lived nearby. He was big and strong and fond of eating raw deer meat. He and a few other men—Tom Fennell, Sr., Bill Osment, Captain C. C. von Paulsen, Raleigh Burney—were the great swamp explorers of their generation and the last generation to have so much of south Florida left to penetrate. Now, especially when I am sitting in line at a tollbooth on the Florida Turnpike, and the tile-roofed town houses spread in every direction look like the world's biggest casserole of scalloped potatoes, I am astounded by the lives of Fred Fuchs and his fellow adventurers—that they had lives in which they slept on regular mattresses, had cars, and went to the movies, and yet still could walk just a few miles into the swamps behind their houses and find things never before seen or imagined. In the swamps Fred found many unusual things. In the Fakahatchee he found the cannonball that supposedly killed Chief Tallahassee. In the Everglades he found a recording of "Yes, We Have No Bananas" in an old Indian camp in an abandoned grove of sugarcane and banana trees. He began collecting orchids around 1935 and took probably tens of thousands from the swamps, including fifteen or twenty new species. He found and named dozens of new air plant species. He also collected tree snails and trees. He was particularly impressed by royal palm trees, the Fakahatchee's tufty-topped palm that is seen in this country only in south Florida. Because royal palms hardly ever fall down, Fred decided to plant a row of fourteen on his property. In the hurricane of 1945 most of Fred's farm was blown away. He and his wife survived by tying themselves to one of those royal palm trees. In 1947, which came to be known in south Florida as the Year It Wouldn't Stop Raining, gallons of rain fell and washed his farm clean, but Fred didn't lose a single tree.

Fred's son Freddie—Bob Fuchs's father—also had a knack for discovery. He once tumbled into a deep hole in Sykes Hammock, a hardwood forest that had sprung up when primeval oceans first retreated and exposed south Florida twelve thousand years ago. While Freddie was stuck in the hole he noticed a rare fern that was thought to have become extinct since Dr. Charles Torrey Simpson last sighted it in 1903. Freddie went orchid hunting with his father, Fred, as soon as he was able to walk. Usually Fred would tie a rope around Freddie's waist so he wouldn't lose him in the mud. When Freddie was a teenager he helped out on the family farm by stuffing ground pork into sausage casings. When he grew up, he became the postmaster of Naranja, the town next to Homestead, and ran an orchid business on the side. By that time much of the Homestead area had been cleared and cultivated and you couldn't even *dream* anymore about walking ten days through unbroken pine woods. Orchid hunters who came to south Florida had to pierce deeper and deeper into the woods to find anything unusual. Freddie was tall and strapping and adventurous. He was happy to tramp through the inner acres of the Fakahatchee, the Big Cypress, and the Everglades to find orchids, and he later went orchid hunting in almost every single country in South America and the West Indies.

Bob Fuchs, Freddie's son, is now fifty years old. He started with plants when he was little—he had his own bench of orchids in his father Freddie's greenhouse and his own collection of African violets. When Bob was thirteen, he went on his first international orchid-hunting trip with Freddie in the Dominican Republic. The trip was supposed to begin in Santo Domingo, but their plane ran low on fuel and landed in Santiago instead. Authorities were suspicious of this unplanned landing, so they sent fully armed soldiers to meet the plane. When the Fuches climbed down to the tarmac, Freddie offered the soldiers a bucket of Kentucky Fried Chicken as a goodwill gesture. This apparently pleased them because they allowed Freddie and Bob to stay and collect for three days. When Bob was nineteen he discovered a new species in Nicaragua, which he registered as *Schomburgkia fuchsii* with the Royal Horticultural Society. His parents gave him a greenhouse as a high school graduation gift. Bob didn't go directly into the orchid business. Instead he went to college, got an art degree, and became a junior high school art teacher in Homestead. In 1970, while he was still teaching, he set up a small orchid business in Naranja on his grandparents' property. He called it R. F. Orchids, because his father, Freddie, was still operating his business, Fuchs Orchids. In 1984, a flower of Bob's called *Vanda* Deva 'Robert' won the grand champion award at the Miami World Orchid

Conference and brought him fame in the orchid world. After that victory Bob retired from teaching and went into the orchid business full-time.

The first time I met Bob was the night before the annual South Florida Orchid Show was going to open at the Miami Convention Center. Exhibitors build their displays the night before the show opens, and I was at the Convention Center with Martin watching him put together the Motes Orchids display. Martin and Bob Fuchs don't like each other, largely because both are vanda men and they have very different philosophies about petal shape and size and because businessmen are naturally competitive, and because they just don't like each other. Nonetheless Martin said I should meet Bob because Bob is an important orchid person. During a break, Martin led me over to the R.F. display and made the introductions. Bob turned out to be a striking person. He looked as if he was at least six feet tall and had a fit, husky, high school linebacker's build. He was absolutely, completely not tan. His hair was peach-colored and brushy, and he had a fluffy mustache and squinty blue eyes. He was the only person in the south Florida orchid world who was regularly described to me as being very handsome.

Just then, in fact, several women were twittering around trying and failing to get his attention. One of them was saying, "Bob, Bob, did you know the word 'fuchsia' came from the name of your family?" and another one was calling out, "Bob, Bob, I need to ask you about that vanda. . . ." Bob ignored them because he was watching his mother, who was heading toward us dragging a three-foot-long piece of driftwood that he wanted to add to his display. The women kept chattering. He kept ignoring them and instead turned and pointed to the side of the display and said, "Mother, *please*. I want the driftwood *here*."

Everyone I met in the orchid world knew of Bob Fuchs. Some raved about him and said they considered him the king of the orchid world. Other people I asked would take deep breaths and release the air very slowly and then say that Bob was controversial. After a while I began to see this as a polite way to say that these people hated him, or at the very least that he made them unhappily jealous. I figured out right away why some people hated him—he is brassy and opinionated and has at times gone out of his way to be argumentative, and apparently his philosophy about orchid breeding is not everyone's cup of tea. The list of what is jealous-making about him is also long—that he is from a family of Florida orchid aristocracy, that his business is very successful, that he wins a lot of awards, that the public loves his flowers and loves his displays, that he knows how to cultivate customers almost as well as he cultivates orchids. Or just go to his house! If you like flowers, or fluorescent-feathered exotic birds, or a perfect turquoise swimming pool with a vanda orchid mosaic in the middle, or a coral-rock pond with a waterfall and a special kind of dappled fish that flash to the surface of the pond when you feed them, or a beautiful wooden grandstand where you can sit and watch the waterfall and the fish, or a dramatic, airy house filled with antique Limoges and Royal Worcester orchid porcelains and fine furniture and trophy heads of African game and a Fabergé egg of gold and rubies with a tiny jeweled orchid sculpture for its yolk, or a front yard that opens onto a path leading to a spick-and-span nursery of seven greenhouses filled with a hundred thousand candy-colored flowers, you would probably like his house. One afternoon after the Miami show I went out to Bob's, and after he showed me around he led me over to a grassy patch beside one of the shadehouses where there was a huge chikee hut—the hut must have been the size of four hotel rooms—and we sat down at some kind of lovely table on some lovely chairs, and beside us were terra-cotta pots of 'Miss Joaquin' orchids with their pencil-thin leaves, and above us were a couple of ceiling fans going *chuk-chuk-chuk* as the blades flicked around, and the ice in our lemonade was clicking and sparkling, and behind Bob was a flow of green grass and green palm fronds and the blur of green in his shadehouses and above all that green was the blank blue Homestead sky, and from the west a breeze lifted and dropped pieces of Bob's blond hair like an idle shopper, and from behind us came the sound of cars rumbling over the gravel of his driveway and then sighing to a stop, and then came the clunk of an expensive car door opening and shutting, and then, not too long after, the tweeting of a cash register inside the shop, and for a long time I didn't want to say anything—I just wanted to sink into the greenness and the accidental melodies and the rich, hot laziness of the day. Bob finally started talking, and said he didn't know what made people so jealous of him, but at that moment, in that big breezy chikee hut, with that green plushness all around us, I did.

———

Bob Fuchs's fame peaked at the World Orchid Conference that was held in Miami in 1984. World conferences are held in a different city once every three years. They have been held in Glasgow, Tokyo, Honolulu, St. Louis, Singapore, and Long Beach. Miami hosted it only once, in 1984, and drew a record number of exhibitors from Florida and from all over the world. Scores of awards are given out at an orchid conference, but the one an orchid person would really dream about is the award given to the single best orchid in the show. To win that award at the world's biggest show, especially in Miami—arguably the capital of American orchid growing and collecting—would be the equivalent of winning a gold medal at the orchid Olympics. The award for the best orchid at the 1984 World Orchid Conference in Miami went to *Vanda* Deva 'Robert,' owned by Bob Fuchs. *Vanda* Deva 'Robert' is a brilliant red orchid with a small blackish lip and a speck of yellow in the center and large petals that are tessellated with blood-colored veins. The flower is full and round. Its deep color is luscious and sexy, but at the same time there is something about its shape and aspect that makes it look a little like a teddy bear. 'Robert' is unforgettable because it is extremely pretty, and because it won the biggest award at the biggest show in the world when the show was last held in this country, and because after it won it was used to breed thousands of other extremely pretty orchids, and because it made Bob Fuchs a star. It is also unforgettable because the success of *Vanda* Deva 'Robert' probably marks the moment when ill will between Bob Fuchs and another grower named Frank Smith began.

Frank Smith is a man about Bob's age who owns his own well-known and successful Florida nursery, Krull-Smith Orchids, which is in Apopka, near Disney World. Frank Smith is an accredited orchid judge and has also won many awards for his plants at shows. He and Bob Fuchs are competitors, but the ill will between them was more than ordinary competition. What had happened after the World Orchid Conference was that Bob had his spectacular win with *Vanda* Deva 'Robert' and decided to quit teaching junior high and go into the orchid business full-time. From the beginning he seemed to have a way of getting on some people's nerves. An elderly female orchid judge once sued him for a million dollars, asserting that he had defamed her in a South Florida Orchid Society memo. People took heightened delight in beating him at shows. One man whose orchid had triumphed over him at a show came up to Bob later and said, "Fuchs, do you know how *long* I've been waiting to kick your fucking ass?" Before he was growing orchids full-time, Bob had been studying to become an accredited show judge in the south Florida region. Getting accredited is a long process that involves studying and student judging for as many as six years. It is a valued position because judges are respected as great orchid authorities and through their choices they can influence trends in orchid breeding. A judge who favors small round petals, for instance, can give his awards to plants with small, round petals, and that in turn will encourage breeders to aim for small, round-petaled plants as well as increasing the commercial value of the ones that have been winners. In 1983 when Bob finished his requirements, he applied to the American Orchid Society's judging committee for his accreditation in the south Florida region. His application was rejected. He was told that someone had sent a letter to the committee claiming that Bob had tried to bribe show judges by offering them cuttings from his best plants. The letter was written by Frank Smith. In his letter Frank said he knew exactly what he was talking about because he was one of the judges Bob had tried to bribe.

In 1990 the big robbery took place at R. F. Orchids. The police investigated, but because there were no witnesses and few clues they told Bob that it was unlikely that the orchids or the thief would ever be found. About two days after the break-in, an orchid hobbyist named Robert Perry was touring Florida orchid nurseries with his wife. They stopped at Krull-Smith Orchids, and while they were looking around, Robert Perry noticed a bunch of exceptional-looking plants piled haphazardly in the back of a secluded shadehouse. Among them was a plant Perry fell in love with—a silvery-gray flower with a reddish-purple lip. Because of the way the plants were piled up, Perry couldn't reach the silvery orchid, but he could see it well enough to know he had never seen anything like it. On the way out he asked a nursery worker if he could buy a pup—an orchid baby—from the plant, but the worker told him that none of the plants in the pile were for sale. A month later Perry was browsing through an old orchid magazine and saw an R. F. Orchids ad featuring a picture of a silvery flower that looked to him exactly like the flower he had swooned over at Krull-Smith. He believed that an orchid that special was unlikely to be found at more than one nursery. He remembered having heard something or other about a robbery at R. F. Orchids. Perry had never met Bob Fuchs but he decided to call him and tell him he'd seen that same rare orchid at Krull-Smith. A few days later a sheriff, Bob Fuchs, Robert Perry, and Bob's partner, Mike Coronado, drove to Krull-Smith Orchids in the middle of the night. Perry led the men to the secluded shadehouse. It was now empty. The stack of plants, including that silvery one, was gone. Perry was dumbfounded. As the men were leaving, Mike Coronado wandered into another shadehouse. A moment later he ran back to show the sheriff a plant tag from Fuchs Orchids that he said he had found lying on the floor. The sheriff recorded all the information, but in the end there was not enough to charge anyone with anything.

There have always been a lot of theories about what had happened to the stolen orchids. Plenty of people thought that maybe Robert Perry's memory wasn't entirely reliable and that even though the orchids had disappeared from R. F. Orchids, they had never reappeared at Krull-Smith. Some people thought that someone had stolen them and that Frank Smith might have bought them without realizing they were stolen. Perhaps the tag Mike Coronado found had nothing to do with any stolen plants at all—it might have been a tag from an old plant that Frank Smith bought legitimately from Bob's father's nursery, which is why it was a Fuchs Orchids tag rather than a R. F. Orchids tag. Frank Smith even speculated in his testimony that he might have been "set up" by Fuchs because he wanted to pay him back for blocking Bob's application to be an orchid judge.

During the fall and winter after the possible reappearance and disappearance of the stolen plants at Krull-Smith, someone started making threatening phone calls to several south Florida orchid growers. Frank Smith got a few of the calls over the course of several weeks. On the morning of February 20, 1991, he received two of the calls in one hour. The first call was answered by a friend of Frank's named Jane Daugherty who was at Krull-Smith office that morning feeding pet birds belonging to her and Frank. According to her later testimony, the man on the phone told Jane Daugherty that if she cared about Frank Smith at all, she should stop him from going to the 1991 South Florida Orchid Society show, which was being held in Miami the following week. Then, she testified, the caller identified himself as Bob Fuchs. The next time the phone rang at Krull-Smith, Frank himself answered and later testified that he recognized Bob's voice and that the caller had said, "Well, it's like this: if you come to the Miami show you'll get fucked up." Smith said the call scared him because he knew that Bob was angry about the critical letter he had written to the judging committee that might have wrecked Bob's chances of becoming an accredited south Florida judge, and he also knew that Bob was still suspicious about the stolen plants that supposedly spent time in the Krull-Smith greenhouses. Even though the phone calls scared him, Frank was determined to attend the four-day-long orchid show, so he hired two bodyguards to accompany him. Another nursery owner who said she'd also

gotten threatening calls came to the show that year with
bodyguards, too.

In Florida the felony of telephone harassment is defined as
more than one call placed in one day specifically to "annoy,
abuse, threaten or harass any person." Frank Smith alleged
that he had received two calls that day in February, so he was
entitled to press charges. Depositions were taken that July.
Bob Fuchs was charged with felony harassment by telephone, and on August 27, 1991, Judge Theotis Bronson and
a twelve-member jury heard the matter of *State of Florida v.
Robert Fuchs*. No one likes to talk about the case these days,
so to learn more about it I had to listen to a tape of the trial
proceedings. It made better listening than most trials because it was only a little bit about phone harassment and
business competition and a lot more about passion and
memorable flowers and secret love affairs. The trial began
with Bob Fuchs's lawyer questioning Frank Smith's friend
Jane Daugherty about the orchid show that launched *Vanda
Deva* 'Robert':

DEFENSE COUNSEL: Now, Miss Daugherty, you say you first
became acquainted with Mr. Fuchs at the World Orchid
Conference in Miami in 1984?
JANE DAUGHERTY: Yes.
COUNSEL: This is the grand conference of all in the world?
DAUGHERTY: Yes sir.

———

COUNSEL: In fact, wasn't Mr. Fuchs' orchid the . . . what do
you call it . . . the . . . the . . . *champion* of show? The top
orchid of show?
DAUGHERTY: I don't remember.
COUNSEL: You don't *remember* that his orchid was the grand
champion?

DAUGHERTY: He had an orchid that won. I thought you meant his exhibit.

COUNSEL: *An* orchid, that was biggest, best orchid in the whole show? Right? And boy, that got everybody's nose out of joint, now, didn't it? Wasn't there jealousy?

PROSECUTOR: Objection!

JUDGE: Sustained.

COUNSEL: Miss Daugherty, was Frank Smith jealous because Bob Fuchs—who in 1984 was not even a judge yet—that *Bob Fuchs'* orchid was the best orchid in the world?

DAUGHERTY: His orchid was the best one in that particular show.

COUNSEL: Which *was* the *worldwide* show. And it kind of catapulted Bob Fuchs to everybody's attention, didn't it?

DAUGHERTY: He was already *in* everybody's attention at that point.

Jane Daugherty had been feeding pet birds at Krull-Smith the morning of the phone calls. Some of the birds belonged to Frank, and the rest were hers. The defense counsel tried to suggest that Daugherty was an unreliable witness who was biased in favor of Frank Smith, since they were so intimate that they even commingled their birds:

COUNSEL: How long have you been a friend of Frank Smith?

DAUGHERTY: Nine years.

COUNSEL: Would it be fair to say you *love* Frank Smith?

DAUGHERTY: No sir, I'm a friend.

COUNSEL: No, you do not?

DAUGHERTY: I'm a good friend.

COUNSEL: A good friend. And you have no romantic connection to him whatsoever?

DAUGHERTY: No, sir.

COUNSEL: You don't travel with him?

DAUGHERTY: I help him put in orchid exhibits but I do not *travel* with him.

COUNSEL: Uh-*huh*. Well, how long has this . . . this mutual bird . . . *hobby* been going on?

DAUGHERTY: About six years.

COUNSEL: And you keep *your* birds at *his* place?

DAUGHERTY: I keep some of my birds at his place.

COUNSEL: Well, how many birds do you keep at his place?

DAUGHERTY: Approximately twenty-five of the English budgies are mine.

COUNSEL: You keep twenty-five of your *personal* birds at his place! Is this a business that you and he are in together?

DAUGHERTY: No, sir. This is a hobby.

COUNSEL: So you have a hobby, a mutual hobby with him that you devote . . . twenty-five of these birds that you keep with him, and you're *just friends*?

From there, the trial became a speculative romance free-for-all. The prosecutor tried to show that Mike Coronado was in love with Bob Fuchs, his partner, and therefore could not be trusted as a witness; Coronado dismissed the suggestion. Then Fuchs's attorney tried to show that not only was Jane Daugherty too enamored of Frank Smith to be a fair witness, *another* one of the state's witnesses was also in love with Frank and therefore also unreliable. The prosecutor countered by saying that a witness who claimed he had been at R. F. Orchids the day of the phone calls and was Bob's alibi was "very close" with Bob and therefore should be disregarded, and also that the college administrator who testified that Frank confessed to her that he didn't think Bob was making the calls was also partial to Bob and thus one more biased witness. No one ever explained why Robert

Perry, the man who'd seen the silvery flower at Krull-Smith, had gotten himself involved—whether he was motivated by being in love with anything other than the silvery flower or anyone other than his wife. Bob Fuchs didn't testify. In closing arguments, both his attorney and the prosecutor admitted wearily that the history of suspicion between the two men was so enmeshed in enmity that it was hard to draw out any individual thread. Did Bob threaten Frank Smith because he was convinced Smith had robbed his nursery? Did Frank Smith interfere with Bob's application to be an orchid judge out of jealousy or because he really knew Bob to be dishonest? Did Bob actually try to frame Smith for the robbery as revenge for his rejection by the judging committee?

The jury found Bob Fuchs not guilty on all counts of felony harassment. The verdict meant that Bob Fuchs would not spend the growing season in jail. Besides that, the verdict made nothing else clear. It is impossible to know whether the jurors voted for acquittal because they didn't believe Bob Fuchs had made threatening phone calls or because they believed he did make the calls but that the calls simply didn't fit Florida's narrow definition of harassment. And certainly nothing in the verdict helped solve the mystery of the stolen orchids. That night when I first met Bob Fuchs, I also met Frank Smith. He seemed pleasant and polite, but when I asked him to talk about the trial he looked at me as if my hair were on fire. He said he didn't want to talk to me and he didn't want to discuss the case at all, ever. He said the whole thing had come about because he'd been "talked into something" and that he had been "misled," and anyhow, it was way in the past and everything was now all patched up. He agreed to talk to me about orchids sometime if I promised I wouldn't ask him about the case.

The war between Fuchs and Smith lasted more than a decade. Probably no one except Frank and Bob will ever know what really happened, and it's possible that even they don't know exactly what had gone on. Bob is now an accredited judge in a different region of the country, and both he and Frank are continuing to do well in orchid shows. All of the R.F. orchids that disappeared, including the unforgettable silvery one, have still never been found.

Barbecued Doves

Things disappear all the time in Florida, but they show up all the time, too. Florida is powerfully attractive. It is less like a state than a sponge. People are drawn to it. When white settlers arrived, they filled up the hospitable corners of the state and then they even filled up what was thought to be uninhabitable, including the "terrible strip of grass" of the Everglades, and they have never stopped coming. These days, in Collier County, where the Fakahatchee lies, a hundred newcomers set up households every single day, and urban planners say that there will be no more room in Naples—no room *at all*—in only eight more years. Exotic plants and animals are drawn to Florida, too. Many come in naturally—they swim ashore or are blown in on the wind—or are carried inadvertently on cargo boats or brought in legally for commerce, but a great number of the animals and plants that are brought to Florida are illegal to collect, transport, and trade. The Port of Miami is one of the biggest points of entry for smug-

gled plants and animals in the country. The chief of environ-
mental enforcement in Miami told me that it was especially
popular with the sort of guys who might wake up one morning and say to themselves, "Boy, wouldn't it be nice to have a
pair of reticulated boa constrictors?" In 1996, for instance, a
total of seven hundred thousand iguanas were smuggled into
the United States through Miami. The devices smugglers use
are manifold. In recent years, customs inspectors in Miami
arrested a woman trying to smuggle in a rare woolly monkey
by hiding it in her blouse, and a man wearing a vest with special pockets to carry his Australian palm cockatoo eggs, and
a man carrying a toy teddy bear stuffed with live tortoises,
and a man with a live boa constrictor under his shirt, and a
man with pygmy marmosets in his fanny pack. They arrested
a man who was trying to sneak a gibbon in by having the animal hug him around the middle and then hiding the bulge
by wearing a very loose shirt. Inspectors have found falcons
hidden in milk cartons, parakeets tucked in hair curlers,
monkeys under people's hats. They arrested a man named
Lenin Oviedo, of Caracus, Venezuela, whose suitcase was
packed with forty-seven rainbow boas, eleven redtail boas,
forty-four red-footed tortoises, twenty-seven Amazon turtles,
twenty-seven river turtles, and twelve pit vipers. Recently,
they arrested another Venezuelan smuggler. This man had a
bird-eating tarantula spider, two hundred baby tarantulas,
and three hundred thumb-sized poison-arrow frogs in his
carry-on bag. He also had fourteen juvenile boa constrictors
in his pants.

Plant smuggling in general and orchid smuggling in particular are dynamic worldwide enterprises. They have gotten
even more so since the Convention on International Trade in
Endangered Species of Wild Fauna and Flora—now known

as CITES—by which more than one hundred nations have agreed to ban or restrict international trade in all wild things. The degree of restriction varies depending on the species. Orchids fall into two categories. Species that are considered rare and endangered fall under the stricter Appendix I of CITES, which forbids all collecting and trade of those plants. Every other orchid species on earth falls under Appendix II, which allows limited commercial and personal trade if the country of export issues a permit to the collector.

CITES is not universally admired. Many orchid people told me they think CITES is too broad because the real threat to endangered plants is not collectors but rather the loss of wild habitat. Collectors complain that developing countries are plowing down forests as fast as they can, destroying rare plants in the process, and collectors who will retrieve plants out of these areas are the only chance to preserve species that otherwise might vanish forever—the plants could then be cultivated and multiplied, the way endangered animals are put in breeding programs in zoos. In 1992 the International Orchid Seed Bank was established to preserve rare seeds. Orchid seeds can live for thirty-five years, so they can be preserved in the Seed Bank and someday be germinated and perhaps reestablished in the wild. The Seed Bank has storage facilities in Texas and California—according to the director, they need to spread the seeds among several locations in case one is sabotaged by, I guess, anyone on a mission to destroy orchid seeds. CITES has many supporters among orchid people, too, who argue that throughout history collectors have stripped the woods bare whenever they've had the chance, and orchids are so valuable that they have to be guarded against people motivated by profit rather than conservation. When I first heard impassioned speeches deriding CITES in my journeys in the or-

chid world, I was shocked that any orchid lovers would op-
pose an environmentally protective treaty. Then I heard story
after story of collectors who said they watched forests in
places like Java and Belize burned down to make way for
farmland, and rather than let the collectors go in and retrieve
the orchids first, the CITES enforcers ordered that they
stand back and watch the plants go up in smoke.

Hot orchids have gotten higher-priced and harder to find
all over the world since CITES was established. Henry
Azadehdel, an Armenian plant fanatic and UFO scholar who
moved to England in 1979, claimed recently that in one year
he made more than four hundred thousand dollars dealing in
black-market orchids. He sold one Rothschild's lady's slipper,
poached in Borneo, for nineteen thousand dollars. He sold
several specimens of another lady's slipper species for six
thousand dollars per plant and boasted that he'd bought
them from locals for just two dollars a piece. These facts and
figures emerged when Azadehdel pleaded guilty in 1989 to
four counts of "smuggling, harboring, and selling endangered orchids." Before his sentencing, Azadehdel declared, "I
have been shipwrecked, chased by drug traffickers, and fed
by the chief of a clan of head hunters. I've been to places
where no white man has ever been. I'm proud to have ex-
tended the boundaries of science." His defense lawyer argued that Azadehdel's "life-long hobby of orchids has
ceased. . . . He no longer has a collection and has no desire
to collect," but Azadehdel was nevertheless fined thirty thousand dollars and sent to jail for a year. After his release he
disappeared. His lawyer insisted that he had professed that
he never wanted to see another orchid as long as he lived.
Since then Azadehdel has adopted several pseudonyms, including Dr. Armen Victorian, Dr. Alan Jones, and Kasaba
Ntumba, is promoting a UFO conspiracy theory involving an

alien spacecraft landing in South Africa, and is said to be continuing his quest for new species.

An especially spectacular bust took place a few years ago at the Japan Grand Prix in Tokyo, an orchid show that attracts more than a half-million visitors. The flower in question was one of the lost orchids, a North Vietnamese species that had been discovered in the early 1900s and had then become extinct in the wild. Just a few years ago, orchid hunters rediscovered the plant and smuggled thousands of them to Hong Kong and Taiwan and Japan—more particularly, to several high-ranking judges at the Tokyo Grand Prix. It was a worldwide orchid scandal. The smugglers were caught; the plants were confiscated, the judges resigned in disgrace. In 1990 Belgian authorities launched Operation Nero Wolfe, in which they seized thousands of smuggled orchids from Thailand. Recently, the forestry department in Thailand estimated that nearly six hundred thousand wild orchids are illegally exported each year, mainly to Japan and Europe. Soon after, Suman Sahai, an Indian environmentalist, called for India to patent its native flora and fauna because "India's biological wealth is being plundered . . . whether it is seeds of special varieties of rice going to American seed companies or orchids from which European firms are earning millions." Internationally plundered orchids often make their way to the United States. Houston customs agents recently apprehended two men who each had sixteen orchids, worth ten thousand dollars apiece, wired onto various parts of their bodies. One of the most famous American orchid-smuggling arrests took place in 1994, when a twenty-eight-year-old man named Harto Kolopaking sold 216 rare lady's slipper orchids to a U.S. Fish and Wildlife undercover agent for nearly thirteen thousand dollars. Kolopaking had been shipping the orchids to California since 1993 in packages that he marked "Sample Material." In court, he admitted that in 1992 he had smuggled in another thousand orchids to a wholesaler in Malibu. Kolopaking was well known in the orchid world. His family owns a distinguished nursery in East Java, and *Paphiopedilum kolopakingii* is named for his father. Kolopaking was the first person in the United States to face a jail term for smuggling orchids. In a San Francisco courtroom, he pleaded guilty to all charges and was sentenced to five months in federal prison.

Just before I first met Laroche, federal agents had landed a catch of two thousand rare lady's slipper orchids being smuggled into Miami from China. The orchids were exceptionally desirable. The federal government donated the seized orchids to Selby Botanical Gardens in Sarasota, and after the plants arrived, the director of Selby installed new locks and a security system in the orchid compound. A few weeks later I went to a hearing at the federal courthouse in West Palm Beach in *United States v. Michael Cohen*, a case against an exotic plant dealer in Lake Worth accused of smuggling in carnivorous pitcher plants from Malaysia. Cohen had labeled the plants as something common and unprotected, but a government plant inspector identified them as rare pitcher plants and intercepted a fax Cohen had sent to his Malaysian supplier saying: "Remember, we are not going to identify them correctly." Mr. Cohen looked a little depressed at the hearing, which began with the judge saying, "Mr. Cohen, are you under the influence of any drugs?" I assume it is a standard question a judge asks before accepting a defendant's plea, but I found myself thinking that the passion for plants was, for many of the people I was getting to know, more potent than any drug at all.

———

Laroche's ghost-orchid scheme made more sense to me once I understood the nature of international smuggling. CITES has made it illegal to export or sell wild orchids—which obviously includes all native Florida species, including ghost orchids. Most wild species are not being commercially raised. Since CITES, anyone who wanted a wild orchid would have to poach it out of the swamp or buy it from someone who had. Laroche was convinced that there was a big market for Fakahatchee orchids. He told me that he knew lots of people in Australia who were dying for any native American orchids, and that the English were crazy for them, too. To support his theory he sent me a newspaper article about an English nurseryman who was arrested at Heathrow airport with almost nine hundred wild American lady's slipper orchids in his hand luggage. Laroche believed that if he could poach a few plants from the swamp—protected from federal endangered-species law by the Seminoles' immunity—he could clone them using his secret cloning technique and end up with millions of ghost orchids and clamshell orchids and crooked spur orchids that would be legal for him to market anywhere in the world because they would have been produced in a lab and not taken from the wild. Collectors would then have no reason to buy from poachers because they could get a ghost orchid from Laroche, and thus he would scuttle the black-market trade in the species. He seemed so fluent in the laws and prohibitions regarding international plant trade that I had to ask him if he'd ever done any outlaw collecting outside Florida—in other words, if he'd ever smuggled things *in* to Florida rather than smuggling them out. I believe we were driving to the swamp at the time, and he stared at the road for a mile or so before answering. At last he said he had been "involved in some activity in South America," but he refused to say anything more about it. He said that his father didn't know anything about this "activity in South America" and he didn't want him to. He said that someday he might tell me about his activities, but he wouldn't say anything more while his father was still alive.

Since Laroche wouldn't talk to me, I asked other orchid people in Florida if they could introduce me to an international smuggler. All of them suggested I call a man named Lee Moore the Adventurer, an orchid collector and smuggler, a former pre-Columbian-art collector and smuggler, an anarchist, and onetime pot smoker, who was on the brink of leaving south Florida forever and moving to Peru. Someone showed me a photograph of Lee Moore before I met him. The picture had been taken in Iquitos, Peru, and in it he was standing with two Peruvian kids, and the three of them were holding up a staghorn fern that is as big as a Volkswagen Beetle. Lee was twenty-two when the picture was taken, and he looked like a jubilant and beautiful boy, long-stemmed, lean, sandy-haired, tanned. He was from a family of Washington blue bloods. His father, Phillips Moore, had been Truman's assistant secretary of commerce, the director of the Federal Aviation Administration, and at one time a congressman. The Moores moved to Florida when Lee was still a kid. Lee took right to it; while his high school classmates were riding around in their hot rods, he was running around in the Everglades. For spending money, he collected water moccasins to sell to the Miami Serpentarium and rattlesnakes to sell to a venom-extraction company. After high school he got in his car and drove to Central America. A friend of his was already there, setting up a tropical-fish importing business, so Lee began flying back and forth from Central America to Miami with him, and later he went to Peru with another friend, Ronald Wagner, who planned to start a snake-venom business, collecting poison from snakes that could then be processed into snakebite antidote. Lee's own dream was to discover new plants. He used to tell the old south Florida orchid growers like Fred Fuchs and Tom Fennell that he was going to venture into the jungles and find new species. "They would mock my folly," he likes to say. "They would say, 'Oh, here's Lee, the adventurer.' That's how I got my name."

———

I called Lee one humid afternoon when Laroche and his Seminole crew were out collecting waterweeds. Lee sounded careworn on the phone and gave me painstaking directions to his apartment. When he was done he said, "By the way, you better come right away. I'm moving to Peru soon. I hate living here."

At the time of my visit, Lee and his wife, Chady, were living in Miami's Kendall neighborhood, in a small apartment in a shadeless clump of townhouses that had the pebbly walls and hollow doors of places that are built on the fly. The apartment's front yard was a non-yard, just a concrete landing behind an iron gate. The landing was smaller than a picnic table. There was no garden at all, but the day I went to visit there were a dozen potted bromeliad plants near the front door. According to the United States government and CITES, Lee's chief line of work was plant smuggling. When I met him, he was awaiting trial in a case titled *United States of America v. 493 Orchids, more or less (Orchidaceae) from Vivero "Agro-Oriente" Moyobamba, Peru; 680 Orchids, more or less (Orchidaceae) from Vivero "Agro-Oriente" Moyobamba, Peru*, which involved some cattleyas he brought from Peru. The government claimed he had collected them illegally in the wild and purposely mislabeled them as nursery plants. Lee, in turn, was suing the U.S. Department of Agriculture and Miami's Plant Protection and Quarantine Facility for a million dollars. According to his complaint, USDA inspectors had wrongly seized and then neglected another shipment of his Peruvian plants and while the disputed plants were in de-

tention they died. He'd tried to get a law firm to take the case
pro bono but had no luck, so he was going to represent himself.

—

Lee was now close to sixty and his sandy hair had turned silver, but otherwise he still looked like the boy with the
staghorn fern I'd seen in the photograph—long-stemmed,
lean, tanned. The day I came by he was wearing some sort of
loose trousers and the type of light-colored short-sleeved
shirt that Cuban men favor. His wife was at home when I arrived. She was about half Lee's height, dark-haired, action-
packed, and dressed in a hot-pink button-front blouse,
achingly tight white Capri pants, and white high-heeled
pumps. As soon I stepped into the apartment, she positioned
herself in the middle of the living room and started talking a
mile a minute. She had an excess of verbal energy. Even un-
exciting things she was saying sounded very exciting. "Lee,
you should tell her about the art! About our pre-Columbian!"
she declared, pointing at me. "Tell her about all the back and
forth and, oh my God, the situations we were in!"

"I'm telling her now, Mama," Lee said.

"We were very big, very big, very *very* big into art," she said
to me. "We were always smuggling something! Or paying
someone to smuggle for us!"

Lee turned to me and said, "Would you like to sit down?" I
nodded and sat down.

"We were on the Ten Most Wanted list in Mexico!" Chady
said. "We had more adventures, more situations, oh my
God!"

"We were making a fortune with the pre-Columbian art,"
Lee said. "It was just getting harder and harder with plants.
It used to be that you would pick an orchid in the jungle,
pack it, fly it, and have it inspected once you got to Miami.

Then they got in these goddamn yuppie types as administrators, and now they make you wash the plants and fumigate them and have them inspected while you're still in the jungle, and then I had to transport them by truck to Lima, and because it's in a drug area they'd inspect you for drugs, then you'd get inspected again by a botanist, and then you have to get your CITES permit and your phytosanitary certificate. By then about a third of your plants would be dead. These customs guys were always giving me a hard time because my plants are real rough-looking. They're jungle plants. They look wild but they're not. I work with a nursery in Moyobamba that has the plants growing in rough conditions, almost like naturalized conditions. Collecting the pre-Columbian art was so much easier. We started in about 1966 and it just . . . *took off.* We got started and then in a minute we were selling in Europe and Australia to all the top collectors."

Chady stamped one of her high-heeled feet. "We had so many adventures, you wouldn't believe. Lee, you should tell her about being fugitives in Mexico!"

"I *am* telling her, Mama," Lee said.

"Policemen, agents, smuggling, everyone coming after us, it was unbelievable!" Chady said. "You know what? Indiana—what's his name?—Indiana Jones, you know him? Well, Indiana Jones is, is *bullshit!* Butch Cassidy is *bullshit* compared to the adventures we had. Isn't that true, Lee? We had more going on, more situations than Indiana Jones! Oh my God!"

Lee got up and said he was going to find some newspaper clippings about his current legal battles. He said the reason he'd been so determined to sue the government for killing his plants was that one of the *Cattleya mooreana* had formed a seedpod and could have produced millions of seedlings for him. "It took me more than thirty years to find one with a seedpod," he said. "I was the only person in the world with a mature seedpod from the *mooreana*. I would have had fifty thousand plants that would have sold for a hundred or a hundred and fifty dollars a piece. I would be making a fortune now, if it weren't for those goddamn yuppies."

"Well, we *were* making a fortune on the art," Chady said. "Millions! Lee had a Lincoln, no, *two* Lincoln Continental cars! But you know, it was patrimony we were taking. It was illegal to take it out of the country of origin!" Outside the apartment, a truck squealed by and blasted its air horn. A screen door slammed, making a shimmery clatter. A bored-sounding dog barked once and then quit. Inside the Moores' apartment it felt flat and plain and hemmed in. "We were outlaws!" Chady said, tapping her foot. "Oh my God, you wouldn't *believe*."

In fact, Lee Moore the Adventurer did have adventures and he did discover new plants. He found the last species of *Cattleya* to be discovered—a fantastic chartreuse orchid with red splashes and wavy edges that he named *Cattleya mooreana*. He discovered *Catasetum moorei* and *Encyclia lemorea*, two orchid species that are now used regularly in commercial hybridizing. He found an almost black bromeliad, *Aechmea chantinii*, and a striking crimson one he named *Neoregelia moorei* and one shaped like a firecracker explosion that he named *Guzmania bismarkii*. While on a collecting trip in Peru with a Baptist minister from Japan, he rediscovered a species of giant-sized staghorn fern, *Platycerium andinum*, that hadn't been seen in a hundred years. In 1962 he was the Bromeliad Society's Man of the Year. In 1965 he discovered a tall, branching bromeliad with powder-pink and light blue flowers. He named it *Tillandsia wagneriana* in memory of his friend Ronald Wagner, the snake-venom entrepreneur, who died in a plane crash on one of their collecting trips in Colombia. According to Lee, the doomed plane had had only one empty seat, so he and Ronald had flipped a coin for it and Ronald won. All that survived the trip was Lee's dog, Buck, and a metal box containing Lee's customer list. The accident inspired Lee to start a newsletter. He called it *Lee Moore's Armchair Adventurer,* and it included chronicles of his collecting trips, his life in the jungle, and photographs of unusual plants, indigenous jungle people, spiders, tapirs, and Amazon scenes. The first issue contained a photograph of his then wife, Helen, wearing a luncheon dress and playing with a parrot, and a photo of Lee's baby daughter stroking her pet capybara, the largest species of rodent in the world. He devoted the entire first issue of the newsletter to the story of the plane crash that killed Ronald Wagner. Sometimes in the newsletter he included travel suggestions. In his second issue he explained how blowguns work and that the only antidote to their deadly poison was a sugar solution: "So if you are ever hit by a poison dart . . . remember, drink sugar water . . . *if you have time." Lee Moore's Armchair Adventurer* had a limited life span. By the third issue Lee wrote that he was suspending publication because "I find I am so far behind in my work due to disasters." One of those disasters happened to be another plane crash in Peru in which seven friends of his died. Once again he had intended to be on the flight, and this time he missed it because he got delayed en route. Because his name was on the airplane's manifest he was listed as one of the casualties. His friends and family were surprised when he showed up alive. He devoted his final issue to telling the story of the crash. In the editor's note he wrote:

This is a gruesome tale of bitter truth in which the price that is paid during the quest of bringing these exotic plants to you

plant adventurers comes high, horrible, and beyond your fur-
thest imagination. All of the facts cannot be revealed at this
time because the things I know are too dangerous to publish
at this time.

Have you ever seen broken, torn, headless bodies splat-
tered over the ground while buzzards finish what is left of the
people you once knew? Seven of them, just like myself, in
quest of something . . . I am almost ready to get off now, but
before I do, I want you to know why so Lee Moore will not
have reason to be called a quitter.

My business is for sale. Are you interested?

On his plant-collecting trips, Lee became acquainted with
pre-Columbian art and pre-Incan artifacts. "In other words,"
he once said to me, "buried treasure." At the time, there was
no prohibition on dealing in historical artifacts and no duty
on imported antiquities. Lee thought artifact collecting
would complement his plant collecting. His first project was
the removal of a priceless frescoed wall from an ancient
Mayan temple. The dig took three months. During the dig,
Lee and his wife at the time, a Peruvian woman named Za-
dith who was seven months pregnant, camped at the site and
lived on a diet of barbecued doves. The excavation of the
temple was financed by a crooked Armenian businessman
with drug and prostitution affiliations and a Hungarian art
dealer, who arranged to have part of the wall shipped to his
New York gallery and the rest to the Metropolitan Museum
of Art in New York. The wall was in fact stolen property. One
evening a Mexican government official at a reception at the
Met found out that one of his nation's precious artifacts was
in the museum's basement; he demanded its immediate return. The Hungarian art dealer had no choice but to pack up
the wall and ship it back to Mexico City, where it is prominently displayed in the Museum of Anthropology. Lee was

never paid for the wall job, but he wrote it off as a good learning experience. Now that he knew something about the art-
smuggling business he and his new wife, Chady, planned to
loot another Mayan site filled with frescoes, but they called
it off when Lee discovered that federal agents planned to follow him there and arrest him. After that, Lee and Chady decided to focus their smuggling on things that could fit in a
suitcase—Mayan vases, ancient Peruvian artifacts, golden
death masks, antique silver. During this period Lee flew back
and forth from South America to Miami hundreds of times.
Art smuggling was going so well that he got out of the plant
business altogether. He quickly became one of the top five
pre-Columbian dealers in the world. He had his own plane,
two Lincoln Continentals, a fancy house, and a million dollars in the bank.

Now, though, Lee was back in the plant business. He had
returned to it after a downturn in his art smuggling, brought
about by disputes with U.S. customs, most of which customs
won. He had lost a fortune on a large collection of ancient
Peruvian silver because customs confiscated it and forced
him to make a charitable donation of it to a museum in Peru.
He lost even more money on a shipment of pre-Columbian
art that he was planning to sell in Australia, which customs
agents seized after identifying it as stolen property. One of
his biggest investments, a two-thousand-year-old hammered-
gold pre-Incan burial mask, was seized and sent back to
Peru. He became convinced that customs officials had it in
for him. After the Australian fiasco he had to sell his plane,
sell the Lincoln Continentals, move out of the fancy house,
declare bankruptcy. He fished around for work. He was willing to do anything. After Hurricane Andrew he even worked
as a day laborer at local nurseries that were rebuilding their
greenhouses. He gradually became a sort of plant broker,
buying interesting plants from Miami nurseries and then

trucking them upstate and selling them to small nurseries along the way—he would just stop in a town like Jacksonville, find a phone booth at a gas station, stand in the hot sun flipping through the Yellow Pages, and then call the local nurseries to see if they wanted any plants. It was dreary and difficult business and he made hardly any money. But it had also gotten him back into plants, which he had always loved.

—

Lee was leaving early the next morning on one of his plant-peddling trips, so he had to go pick up plants that afternoon and said I could come along. As we were getting into his truck I asked him if he happened to know John Laroche. They seemed as if they were cut from the same flammable cloth, but I suspected they had never met, only because I believe the universe would have exploded if they had ever been in a room together. Lee squinted and rubbed his chin. "Don't think I know the fellow," he said. "I've heard about the case, though. I don't quite understand his passion for the ghost orchid. They're cute, they're cute, all right, but I just don't think they're that special." He started the truck and it creaked out of its parking spot. "I do know pretty much everyone else in the orchid world," he said. "Martin Motes? I gave him his first nursery job. He was my watering boy. And Fred Fuchs, Bob's father, he financed my first orchid-collecting trip, the one where I drove my VW down the Panamanian Highway. And old man Fennell bought the plants I collected for Orchid Jungle." He wiped his forehead. "Those were all the real icons of the orchid world, people like Fred Fuchs. I can't believe I'm now in the category of those icons."

In the stuffy truck we drove down miles of suburban roads with gravel shoulders and no sidewalks, lined with cigar-box bungalows and chain-link fences. We stopped first at a place called Bullis Bromeliads. Lee parked and went to find the manager. "I had four Blue Moons and eight Purple Rains picked out," Lee said. The manager led us through the green-house to the spot where Lee had put his plants a few days earlier. He counted them and then clucked his tongue and said, "You know, it looks like someone made off with one of my 'Blue Moons.' " On to the next nursery. "Harvey, I want a case of Charms," Lee said to this nursery's manager. "Big, big, *big* plants. And not too many orchids today because I put them in the truck and they start blasting in the heat and then no one wants them and I got to eat them." On to DeLeon's Bromeliads. "State-of-the-art place," Lee said to me on our way in. He pointed across the lot. "Look at this new shade-house going up. Whew." In the office he read a list to the manager. "Let's see, some variegated spineless pineapple *Ramosa.* Oh, and I'm getting twenty-one *Fascini,* thirty-six Eileens, and twelve pineapples." These were different species of bromeliads—spiky, spidery ones, and ones with wide, stiff, mottled green leaves, and little ones with a ruff of leaves with serrated edges. "I'm always looking for something new," Lee said to me. "That's been my goal all along. New things, really special things. If you find a prizewinner, it'll be worth as much as five thousand dollars to you. Per plant, I mean. Some of the plants I discovered—they're producing them by the *billions* now, in tissue culture. How much did I make off of it?" He shook his head. "I made a couple of bucks. I should have made millions." He said that most of the time when he found new species he didn't have the money or fa-cilities to clone them and cash in, so he would sell a hundred or so, and then some major commercial grower would clone the plant and turn it into a supermarket plant, a cheapie, a Kmart product. On one hand he sounded exasperated by his near misses with big money, but on the other hand he sounded scornful of an accomplishment as tame as selling your ten-millionth Kmart bromeliad. It seemed like the story of his life, all the near misses with disaster and wealth and wrecked planes and wild animals. I suspect he would have been very happy to have held on to some of the money, but only if he had come by it adventurously, either by almost dying or almost being thrown in jail or almost losing it the moment it was in his reach. I really wondered what kind of life Lee was so afraid he would be stuck with if he hadn't left home and driven off to South America as soon as he possibly could. My guess is that it wouldn't have been a bad life, just a life that would have been tiresome and dry for a romantic like Lee Moore. Probably, it would have been the kind of life in which he would never have needed to pour tropical fish into a hydraulic pump to help his plane land in Colombia, and would never have had to live in a snake-infested hut with nothing but his dog's cage for furniture, and would never have had to elude federal agents searching for him in Peru, and would never have gotten to see living things no one else had ever seen and then get to introduce them to the world and, like Adam, name the living things himself. More and more, I felt that I was meeting people like Lee who didn't at all seem part of this modern world and this moment in time—the world of petty aggravations and obligations and boundaries, a time of bored cynicism—because how they lived and what they lived for was so optimistic. They sincerely loved something, trusted in the perfectibility of some living thing, lived for a myth about themselves and the idea of adventure, were convinced that certain things were really worth dying for, believed that they could make their lives into whatever they dreamed.

Lee loaded the rest of his plants into the truck and said he wasn't going to stop at any more nurseries. He said he had to get to bed early because his plant-peddling trips start before dawn so the plants don't get hot and start wilting. He doesn't take that many plants with him, so the truck isn't too crowded; if he runs out along the way he calls Chady and has her ship him more so he can continue driving north and selling. To me, roaming around the Amazon is unimaginable, but driving to a strange place and calling people you don't know sounds imaginable and scary. I asked Lee if he thought of himself as brave. He twiddled his fingers. "Oh, I'm not brave. I'm just sure of myself. I just remember when I was a kid, I once was going on a canoeing trip in the Everglades and some of my friends decided not to go because it was going to be too much discomfort and hardship. But they did come to watch the rest of us head off on the trip, and I remember looking up as we pushed off and seeing the forlorn faces of the people left behind looking on. That's what started my life of adventure. I knew I never wanted to be the one left on the shore."

In the final issue of *Lee Moore's Armchair Adventurer*, published in the spring of 1966, he had written:

Many people write letters of envy saying they wish they could be in my place traveling and exploring and that the life I am living is the type of life they have always wanted but could not have because of one thing or another. The types of problems that I have been relating to you do not have to accompany this business or even a normal life for that matter. You have been listening to the problems of an abnormal life about which nothing can be done no matter what business may be involved. A normal person would not have these difficulties. Apparently, adventure was destined to follow me in whatever I do. It is not the business; it is me. Adventure and excitement will follow me the rest of my life. Since a little boy I have escaped violent death nine times. It is in my blood to explore it all.

Osceola's Head

A few weeks later, on one of those thick Florida days when the sun looks as smooth and silver as a nickel and the sky is white, Circuit Judge Brenda Wilson announced that she had reached a decision in the ghost orchid case. Earlier in the month, Laroche and the three Seminole men—Russell Bowers, Dennis Osceola, and Vinson Osceola—had entered pleas of no contest to charges of illegally removing plants from state property. Judge Wilson declared that she would withhold adjudication on the Seminoles and would fine them only one hundred dollars each, but that she found Laroche guilty as charged, would fine him five times as much as she had fined the Seminoles, and had decided to extend his exile from the Fakahatchee for six more months. The next day an article in *The Miami Herald* said:

> NAPLES — A case that could have determined whether Indians can treat plants in Florida public lands as their own came to a

murky conclusion in a Collier County courtroom Monday.

Circuit Judge Brenda Wilson fined three Seminole Indians and a Miami orchid grower for trying to take rare orchids and bromeliads from the Fakahatchee Strand State Preserve in December.

But attorneys for the Indians said tribal members should still feel free to take any endangered plant they please from state parks or preserves because a state statute says they can. "This really doesn't make any sense," said Wesley Johnson, attorney for the Seminole tribe members. "The reason we made the pleas was only for convenience. They're not guilty of anything."

Orchid lovers and managers at state parks and preserves were watching the case closely because they worried a precedent could be set if the Indians and Laroche were allowed to take the plants. Laroche said he was working for the tribe because he knows about orchids and other plants. "I went along to make sure it was being done properly," he said of last year's plant harvesting trip.

Buster Baxley, director of planning and development for the tribe, said based on the exemption in the statute he thought the tribe could take the plants. "But just like any other treaty you guys sign," Baxley said, referring to government treaties with Indian tribes, "it isn't worth the paper it's written on."

The day after the judge's announcement I met with the state's attorney, Randy Merrill, who had prosecuted the case. Merrill had been a police officer before he became a lawyer and was planning to run for state office sometime after he finished the orchid case. When the men were first indicted,

Merrill told me he was determined to convict all of them. He was especially eager to get Laroche, because he found Laroche so maddening. The case itself was maddening. It stretched over a messy patch of laws—two of which may contradict each other. One of the laws is a criminal statute. In Florida it is illegal for anyone to collect endangered wild plants, and there are criminal penalties attached. The only exception is for people the statute refers to as "Florida Indians," who are exempt from this law out of respect for their traditional hunting and fishing practices. This means that under Florida criminal law Seminoles cannot be prosecuted for collecting endangered orchids. On the other hand, all state-owned parks and preserves and other lands, including the Fakahatchee, are governed by a rule that forbids the removal of any and all animals and plants, endangered or not. That means that on a state preserve like the Fakahatchee, anyone who collects anything—an ordinary blade of grass, a worm, a ghost orchid—can be arrested and prosecuted. Considering the contradiction between the criminal statute and the state-park rule, can the Seminoles collect ghost orchids out of the Fakahatchee or not? Does the "Florida Indian" exemption from the endangered species law extend to state lands or does the park rule supersede the Seminoles' exemption?

This ambiguity was exactly what Laroche had been looking for in the law library. He recognized that the criminal endangered-species statute and the park rule were inconsistent, and he bet that if he and the crew were caught, a judge would uphold a criminal statute over an administrative park rule—in other words, that a judge would rule that the Seminoles' exemption from the criminal statute does extend to state park land even though nothing in the statute specifically says that it does, so that collecting ghost orchids in the Fakahatchee was within their rights. He was also betting that most judges in Florida would not want to make a ruling that abrogated Seminole rights and certainly would have created controversy.

Merrill decided that the best way to beat Laroche's plan was to avoid it. First, he dropped the charges against the Seminoles for taking the endangered orchids so that the question of Indian exemption from the law would never arise. But the men had been caught not just with endangered orchids and bromeliads but also with the tree branches the plants had been growing on—Laroche had insisted on taking the plants by leaving them attached to the branches rather than merely prying them off because they would be more likely to survive. The endangered-plant statute does not apply to ordinary trees, so the "Florida Indian" exemption from endangered-plant laws does not apply to ordinary trees, either. Ordinary trees are covered by the park rule that makes it illegal for anyone to take anything out of places like the Fakahatchee State Preserve. If the Seminoles had only taken endangered plants, the judge would have had to decide how to interpret the conflict between the endangered-species laws and the park rules. Taking tree limbs out of a park is a simple legal matter—no one at all, no exceptions, is allowed to take living things out of a state park. Merrill realized he would beat Laroche by pursuing the part of the case that would be indisputable—he would leave reconciling the criminal statute with the state rule to some other judge in some other case. The Seminoles would have to concede that they are not exempt in any way from park rules regarding live oak and pond apple trees and ordinary Florida weeds. They had no choice but to plead no contest to taking trees out of a state park, and they finally did.

Laroche's own personal situation was more convoluted than the Seminoles'. Since he was an employee of the tribe, he thought he would be covered by any exemptions the law made for the Seminoles. Just in case the exemption concept didn't work, he had deliberately avoided touching any plants on the day of the poaching: the Seminoles did the actual collecting—wading close to the trees, cutting the limbs, bagging them, dragging them out—not just because Laroche was lazy, but because he wanted to be able to maintain that he was a hands-off consultant and not a perpetrator, just in case they got caught. Judge Wilson was underwhelmed by both of Laroche's arguments. In her opinion, he was an employee of the tribe but not a member and didn't qualify for any special consideration given to the Seminoles. Furthermore, she felt he was guilty of everything—he was guilty of taking the tree limbs and the orchids and the bromeliads, he was guilty of advising the three other men to do the same, and he was morally guilty of having concocted the whole scheme.

—

"Florida Indians" are the descendants of the Yuchi, Creek, and Cherokee Indians who lived in Georgia and Alabama until the eighteenth century, when white settlers forced them off their fertile land. Once the Indians relocated to Florida they began calling themselves Seminole or Miccosukee, which means "wild wanderers" or "outlanders" or "runaways." After the United States took possession of Florida from Spain in 1821, white settlers made their way south to Florida and soon coveted that Indian land, too, and the federal government responded by spending more than $40 million in three Seminole "subjugation and removal efforts." The last of the three Seminole Wars, the Billy Bowlegs War, ended in 1848; by then the U.S. Army had "subjugated and removed" more than 90 percent of the Seminoles to Oklahoma. The remaining 10 percent—about three hundred members—fled to the Everglades and the Big Cypress

Swamp and set up chikee-hut camps on the edge of the wetlands. The government persisted in the removal efforts, at
one point offering Chief Billy Bowlegs $215,000 to lead the
remaining tribe members to Oklahoma. He refused. He was
later persuaded to come to Washington for negotiations.
Along with another Seminole chief and a team of government "removal specialists," Chief Billy Bowlegs traveled to
the capital on horseback. The group stopped along the way in
Tampa, Palatka, Orange City, and in Savannah, Georgia. At
hotels Chief Billy registered as "Mr. William B. Legs." The
summit was unsuccessful in persuading the Seminoles to
leave, as was a law passed in 1853 that made it illegal for
them to live in Florida, as were further incursions by government soldiers. In 1858 Secretary of War Jefferson Davis admitted that the Seminoles had "baffled the energetic efforts
of our army to effect their subjugation and removal." Because they never surrendered, the Florida Seminoles came to
refer to themselves as the Unconquered. To this day their descendants have never signed a peace treaty with the United
States.

One of the leaders of the Unconquered was a young
fighter named Osceola, the son of a white British trader and
a woman who was part Creek Indian, part black, and part
Scottish. Osceola was born in northern Alabama. In 1818 he
and his mother were captured by Andrew Jackson's soldiers.
When they were released they moved to Silver Springs,
Florida, where they lived with his mother's Creek relatives.
Osceola's given name was Billy Powell. "Osceola" probably
derives from his Creek ceremonial title, "asi yahola," which
means Black Drink Crier. Black drink was a strong, bitter
purgative brewed from holly leaves. A "yahola," a sort of altar
boy, would pass out the black drink at religious ceremonies
and sing. Osceola was tall and slender and nice-looking, and

had a taste for fine jewelry, red leggings, and feathered tur-bans. He had no hereditary claim to leadership and therefore was not technically a chief, but he won supreme respect from the tribe because of his passion for the tribe, his skill at the popular Indian game of stickball, and his personal confi-dence. As a young man, Osceola quickly built a distinguished reputation as an Indian warrior. Nonetheless, he also had many white associates and admirers. He was close friends with a white lieutenant stationed at Fort King in Florida whom he had met during the Second Seminole War, and was very friendly with Frederick Weedon, the white physician who attended him after he was captured and put in a military prison. Osceola also had many supporters among white abo-litionists who believed the Seminole Wars were unjust and were being waged only to benefit plantation owners and to punish the Indians for giving sanctuary to escaped slaves. Coincidentally, the Seminoles owned a large number of slaves themselves, although the relationship between the Seminole master and black slave was unusual—slaves com-mingled and intermarried with tribe members, and both groups lived equally humbly. One of Osceola's wives was a descendant of a fugitive slave who was later recaptured, rousing Osceola's commitment to his war against the white man. Nonetheless, when the Civil War broke out, the tribe entered into a treaty with the Confederacy, probably because they were living in the South, but at least partly because, like the Confederate states, they permitted slavery.

Osceola was esteemed by his tribe for being a clever at-tacker and a ruthless avenger, and yet he was also admired by both Indians and whites for his fairness and gentlemanly conduct and his disdain for petty terrorism. It is said he never stole a single possession from a white settler or sol-dier—not even a horse, which was a customary war trophy.

He loathed disloyalty and corruption and lack of principle in anyone, white or Indian. The act of which Osceola was proudest and for which he was most famous was his assassination of Charley Emanthla, the Seminole chief who had caved in to the government and agreed to move the tribe to Oklahoma. Emanthla had accepted bribes in exchange for his cooperation. After Osceola killed Emanthla, he took the bribe money out of Emanthla's purse and scattered it over his dead body.

In 1837 Osceola and another Seminole leader, Coa Hadjo, agreed to attend peace talks at Fort Peyton, Florida, with General Thomas Jesup. Osceola may have decided to negotiate because he was hoping to buy time for the tribe or perhaps because he felt he could not endure another year of fighting. He and Coa Hadjo traveled to Fort Peyton with a delegation of seventy-one warriors, six women, and four black Seminole tribe members. Osceola had made the arrangements in good faith, but Jesup had not: he had secretly ordered Joseph Hernandez, the Florida delegate to Congress and a general in the Florida militia, to seize the Seminoles when they arrived. As soon as Osceola's delegation reached the fort, they were all hit on the head, bound, and imprisoned. Osceola was put on board the SS *Poinsett,* a steamer, and arrived at the military prison at Fort Moultrie, South Carolina, on New Year's Day. He was removed from Florida because Jesup feared his influence on other Seminoles, even from behind bars. Osceola was a strong figure. Even as a prisoner he was charismatic, and he quickly became a celebrity at the fort. He was permitted to walk freely around the grounds and was always well dressed, especially when the many artists who admired him came to paint his portrait. Two of his wives lived with him in prison. He often visited with Dr. Weedon, chief physician at the fort. According to historical reports, Osceola and the other Seminole warriors were sometimes even allowed to travel outside Fort Moultrie; once they were escorted to Charleston to see a play called either *Halfmoon* or *Honeymoon*. Osceola was only in his early thirties at the time of his arrest, but he was already worn-out and sickly, suffering from a number of grave diseases, including malaria. He developed quinsy, a kind of abscessed tonsillitis, in 1838 and asked for a medicine man to treat him rather than Dr. Weedon. When his illness was at its peak Osceola roused himself from his sickbed and dressed himself in his favorite outfit of large silver earrings, a feathered turban, red war paint, ostrich plumes, silver spurs, a decorated powder horn, a fancy bullet pouch, a striped blanket, and a whalebone cane. As soon as he finished dressing he died. Dr. Weedon prepared Osceola's body for burial in the ordinary fashion, but then when no one was looking he cut off Osceola's head. For the funeral, Weedon put the head back into the casket with the body, concealing the severance with a colorful scarf. The body and detached head were buried at the fort in South Carolina, in spite of Osceola's wish to be buried in Florida.

After the funeral, Weedon sneaked back to the burial site and reopened the casket, removed the head, and smuggled it out of the fort. There exists no authoritative explanation for why he took Osceola's head, but it is true that one of Weedon's great-granddaughters wrote in a memoir that the doctor was "an unusual man." He embalmed the head using his own homemade embalming formula, and for a while displayed it in the window of the drugstore he owned in St. Augustine, Florida. Weedon kept the head at home for a number of years, and would hang it over his young sons' beds as punishment whenever they misbehaved. Eventually Weedon gave the head to one of his sons-in-law, Daniel Whitehurst, who also was a doctor. Whitehurst had studied with a Dr. Valentine Mott, who was then the country's preeminent surgeon and pathologist. Mott was accustomed to dealing with renowned figures; he once examined Edgar Allan Poe for brain lesions. Mott owned a large medical library and an anatomical-specimen museum in New York City that was the largest of its kind in the country and was said to be "particularly rich in tumors, aneurisms, and diseased bones, joints, arteries, and bladders," most of which were products of the doctor's own surgeries; he is said to have amputated more than one thousand body parts in the course of his career. Whitehurst wrote to Mott in 1843 and sent him Osceola's head for inclusion in the museum's "cabinet of heads." The 1858 illustrated catalog of the museum noted that Specimen No. 1132 was "Head of Osceola, the great Seminole chief (*undoubted*). Presented by Dr. Whitehurst, of St. Augustine." (The word "undoubted" referred to the three authentications of the head that Weedon had solicited from army officers who had known Osceola and who were willing to attest that the head was indeed Osceola's.) Mott apparently worried that the specimen was too valuable to keep in the cabinet of heads and, as he wrote to Whitehurst, "the temptation will be so strong for someone to take it" that he promised to keep it in his study at home instead. It is unclear whether he did indeed keep the head at home or whether he kept it in the museum. The museum was located in the University Medical College on Fourteenth Street. It burned down in 1866 and most people believe the head was destroyed in the fire. The rest of Osceola's body remains in its Fort Moultrie grave.

Osceola fought on principle, was captured ignominiously, died prematurely, and left behind an unconquered people. Even though he led the Seminoles only briefly he has never been forgotten. Walt Whitman celebrated him in poetry, the portraits painted of him in prison toured galleries across Europe, his artifacts were preserved in museums around the world. At least twenty towns and counties around the country named themselves Osceola in his honor, and almost half of the Florida Seminoles use Osceola as their last name.

—

Laroche maintained that one of Osceola's many legacies was the right of the Seminoles and their agents—namely, himself—to harvest ghost orchids out of the Fakahatchee Strand. The day after the judge released her ruling he called me to gripe. "I was crucified!" he yelled and then started coughing like a seal. "I told you I would be crucified. Fuckin' crucified. The judge is a moron. She didn't know shit about Indian rights and she doesn't know shit about shit. And if she thinks she can keep me out of the swamp she's insane. And let me tell you something. I swear to you, Buster is going to get himself a bulldozer and go back into the Fakahatchee and tear the whole place apart if he don't calm down." He stopped coughing and started to chuckle. The sound dragged out of his throat slowly as if it were traveling over gravel. Talking to Laroche was always a bountiful aural experience: there was his cigarette hack, and the funny round pronunciation he gave to certain words such as "well," which came out sounding like "wahl," and "Fakahatchee," which came out as "Fok-uh-hawchee," and then there were all his nuanced laughs, such as his "ah-huh-huh-huh," which meant he'd just given a description of himself outsmarting someone, and his "Ha!" which meant something like Wait a minute! and his scratchy chuckle, which he used to highlight something he thought was crazy, which was inevitably something that someone else had done. I thought it was fascinating that a guy who could have easily been considered crazy himself considered so many *other* people crazy. I was coming to realize that Laroche believed all human beings, with the sole exception of one John Laroche, were afflicted with constricted and unsubtle minds—that, for instance, park rangers couldn't think about anything broader than the preservation of the park, and the Seminoles couldn't see beyond their sense of injured pride, and the judge had no grasp of anything outside conventional legal boundaries. Laroche prided himself on possessing flawless logic and reason—the way he saw it, he did poach orchids, which is illegal and unethical, but he would poach only a limited number at a time and he would never strip every one off a single tree and, most important, he would be poaching so that he could help the species in the long run by propagating it in his lab and making the orchids cheap and available. He trusted himself alone to balance out pros and cons, to disregard rules and use real judgment instead. He thought that no one else in the world could see things his way because other people had attitudes that were as narrow as ribbon and they had no common sense at all. For a single-minded lunatic like John Laroche, this seemed like a very bold position to take.

—

I first met Buster Baxley, Laroche's boss at the Seminole nursery, when I'd been at the court hearing in Naples, and I had eaten a steak dinner with him at my hotel the following night. I liked him right away because he seemed smart and funny, but I could never figure out what he made of me. Buster was a husky man with puffy jowls and some freckles and longish hair the color of a basketball. Most of the times I saw him he was dressed in casual cowboy-style clothing, amulets, and mirrored aviator sunglasses. There was an air of deep seriousness about him. He had an unnerving sidelong glance and a skew of his head that felt strongly opinionated. Whenever I'd ask him a question, he would pause a really long time before he answered—during the pause I had no idea whether he was going to mock me or refuse to talk at all or be chatty and cordial and tell me interesting things about his life and the tribe. One time, when he *was* chatty and cordial, he took me to lunch at a restaurant near the reservation called the Black-Eyed Pea. We ordered tacos and iced tea, and while we were eating he told me that he was a member of the Seminole Panther clan and his wife is a member of the Bird clan, and that it had been a controversial match because cross-clan marriages were regarded skeptically; that Seminole clans were matrilineal, so his kids were Birds, not Panthers, but mostly he worried that they wouldn't stay in any clan or in the Indian life at all; that he himself was actually three-quarters white, but he'd grown up on the reservation and felt entirely Indian—maybe even more than people who were all Indian and took it for granted, since they'd never had to choose the way he had to; that he was in charge of the tribe's business, which meant he spent much of his workday dealing with the white world, with white people, feeling like just another south Florida businessman, not a Seminole businessman, but as soon as he was done with work and on his way home he saw himself once again entirely contained within the shell of Indian life.

One of the businesses Buster oversaw was the nursery, so that day at lunch I asked if he'd show me around. He shook his head and said, "Well, I can't right now. I've got those Japanese investors here and I've got to take care of them."

"Is that keeping you busy?"

"Too busy," he said. He picked up the little cardboard tepee listing the desserts of the day and started to read it. He looked up and said, "I told those Japanese to fly from Japan to Orlando so they could have a day at Disney World. Then I picked them up there and drove them to my ranch up in

Brighton, and I fed them just a huge feast of Indian barbecue and swamp cabbage and fry bread and pumpkin bread. They were sort of in shock. They'd never seen so much food in their lives."

A couple of days later he called and said the Japanese were gone, the lemon deal had fallen through, and he had a little time, so he could take me to the nursery. I drove over to meet him at the tribe offices, a group of trailers and small buildings off Stirling Road. Across the street from the offices was a huge construction site where the new permanent tribe headquarters were being built. When I pulled in, there were about half a dozen vehicles in the parking lot, and all except one of them were pickup trucks. The receptionist told Buster I had arrived and then went back to cracking her gum. I thumbed through a couple of rodeo magazines and listened to someone in a nearby office on the telephone saying, "Look, you said you'd be done with it by now and when someone tells me he'll be done with something I assume they mean they'll be *done* with something, do you see what I mean?" After a while Buster came out of his office. He looked a little grouchy and he didn't say much. He led me back to the parking lot and into his pickup truck and turned the ignition, unwrapped a piece of chewing gum, and then roared onto the street. After a series of turns under a highway overpass we drove past a little building with a sign saying IN-DEPENDENT BIBLE BAPTIST CHICKEE CHURCH and past blocks with new sidewalks and small houses that he said belonged to members of the tribe. At a traffic light he took a long look at me and then said, "So what did you think of that judge at that hearing in Naples?"

"I guess she was okay."

"No way was she okay," he said, drumming his fingers on the steering wheel. "By the way, you know, don't you, that the

Seminoles have never signed a peace treaty with the government. We're still at war with the United States." The light changed. We rode along for a moment, and then Buster said, "Look, I know everyone thought John was exploiting those Indian boys so he could do his poaching and set his own nursery up. Well, I was the one who authorized it. I told them to go out and gather what they needed. John brought me the statute he found saying Indians were exempt from laws about plant gathering, and we thought the nursery should have some wild plants for propagation and display. I asked John about it several times because I wanted to be sure about it. I made him wait a month so I could go do the research myself. What we did was within the law. It's our *right*. The state of Florida better not mess around with what's my right." He took a deep breath and said, "Otherwise, if they mess with me, I'll go in there and take every single thing in the Faka-hatchee that's alive."

———

He pulled into a driveway and past a fence that surrounded the nursery. Most of the plants Laroche had ordered hadn't yet arrived, so at the moment the nursery was mostly a couple of acres of gravel and dirt and a few potted things. Near the fence there was a stack of sawhorses and cedar planters and plastic bags of mulch and the skeleton of a shade-house—an upright row of metal hoops that looked like gigantic croquet wickets. There was no shade. The light was so bright that the gravel and dirt glinted. A breeze jiggled the string of plastic flags that Laroche had hung above the gate. At the far end of the lot three men were sorting through a pile of more metal hoops and a stack of nylon shade cloth. After a moment they came over and chatted with Buster. I recognized one of the men from court. His name was Vinson Osceola, and he was one of the three Seminole men who had been arrested along with Laroche. He was a smooth-featured guy with a long black braid and meaty shoulders. That day he was wearing a green T-shirt decorated with dozens of skulls. After Buster introduced us he said hello and then added, "I'm not going to talk to you too much. It's nothing personal. It's the Indian way."

Laroche's office was in a beige trailer set on concrete blocks near the entrance gate. Vinson motioned toward it and said Laroche was inside. On the trailer door was a flyer saying "Maydell's. Best Food on the Res. LUNCH specials Stew Beef or Spam and Tomatoes over Rice $5" and another in Laroche's handwriting that said "Tuesday Jan. 24 GRAND OPENING of the Nursery. All tribe members invited for a free steak cookout." Buster pushed the door open and then we made our way through mounds of papers and boxes and gardening journals to Laroche's office. Laroche was sitting behind a metal desk reading a magician's supplies catalog when we came in. He pushed the catalog aside and held up a postcard. "Hey, look at this postcard I got from my friend Walter. He's in Botswana," he said. "Walter is *crazy* about water lilies. He'll go anywhere the minute he hears about a rare one. Sometimes he collects, mostly he just goes to look at it. I'm happy to report that this is a very cheerful postcard. It says, 'John: Plants are good. See you soon.'" He put down the card. "You know, Walter's pretty crazy."

Buster stood in the doorway of the office and ignored Laroche while he was talking about Walter. That moment I got the feeling that they viewed each other as useful but irritating—a combination of mutual appreciation and mutual disrespect. Buster pointed out the window. "John, how're those boys working out?"

"*Fine,* Buster," Laroche said. He drawled so that it sounded like a longer word—*foi-oi-oin.* "We got orders for thirty-two thousand dollars' worth of weeds and an order for nine thousand saw grass plants. State of Florida. They wanted seventy thousand saw grasses to plant on the median strip of that new highway from Tampa to Naples, but we can only give them nine thousand right now." Laroche put his feet up on the desk and started rocking back and forth in his chair. He has a wispy little mustache that comes and goes, and that day it looked to be gone. He was wearing droopy camouflage pants, a Miami Hurricanes hat, and a Chicago Blackhawks T-shirt with team logo of an Indian chief. He later confessed to me that he has no interest in the Black-hawks at all, but the shirt was only a dollar and he thought it would be fun to wear so he could piss off the Seminoles. "I've got some good stuff on the way," he said. "Pigeon peas, figs, frangipani, governor's plums. I'm going to order some guava. And I got something today called a confetti shrub." He yanked the bill of his cap and said, "You know, Buster, it's hotter than hell out there today."

"It's Florida, man," Buster said. He turned to me. "We're just starting to fill this place up now, but the project has been going on for ages. We were *planning* it for ages. It's been trouble from the beginning, even before these boys got ar-rested. We had to find some land, and then when we found the land we had to get the easements from the power com-pany, and then we had to interview a bunch of people to find someone who could get it going. And then we had to come up with a name for it, for the nursery. John got it into his head that he just couldn't have some regular nursery name. He started pestering me for the Seminole word for everything— every minute it's 'Buster, what's Seminole for *this*? Buster, what's Seminole for *that*?' He wanted the Seminole word for garden and nursery and greenhouse. Some of those words just don't *exist* in the Seminole language. I wanted him to just set the place up and then get out there and start hunting for those orchids. I knew he was itching to get into that swamp, too, but he still kept after me for those Seminole words. Finally I really got fed up and told him, 'Oh, Jesus Christ, John, just *name* the damn thing.' "

—

Of course, not everyone in the world liked Laroche. After I went back to New York that summer and wrote a story for *The New Yorker* about the case, I got a letter from a serious gardener who thought that I had been duped by Laroche. This gardener argued that Laroche was feckless and sinister. "To be gently unspecific, [Laroche] belongs to a milieu whose members turn to horticulture partly as therapy, partly as a convenient refuge from the burdens of responsibility," the gardener wrote. "They are not committed to any rules whatsoever except their own impulses which are uncontrollable. They are not true professionals. . . . They go into the business in a disorderly sort of way and, in general, become notorious rather than 'famous.' They lead no regular mode of life, changing interests and occupations at regular intervals. Where their own interests are concerned no principle plays any role. Only impulse has rights. They survive miraculously and, though always poor, always find money." Some of the Seminoles began to question their feelings about Laroche, too. Around the reservation people were starting to call him Crazy White Man or Troublemaker much more often than they called him John, and they complained that he'd gotten the Seminoles into legal trouble for no particularly good reason. Some tribe members even began to question the fundamental point of Laroche's plans for the nursery, for the two and a half acres of penis-shaped peppers and Moroccan carrot trees and a laboratory bursting with ghost orchid clones. Laroche is good at filtering out dissonance. He ignored them. He proceeded with his nursery plans. He finished building the fourteen thousand square feet of greenhouses and the miles of benches for the bedding plants. He ordered more pink string beans from Argentina, more African palms, more juniper bushes that grow in spirals. He hosted a steak cookout for the nursery's grand opening. He told Buster that while the ghost orchid project was temporarily on hold he had plenty of other things in mind for the nursery. "Time to kick into other plant areas," he had told Buster. "Time to get into plant multiplication of another vein. Buy little ones, turn them into big ones, sell them at a profit. Turn them over, do it again. Simple plant multiplication for the masses."

Summer passed. Fall came, the plants multiplied, but the complaints among tribe members about Seminole Gardens multiplied, too. Around the same time, Laroche started to quarrel with his crew—he accused some of them of smoking marijuana on the job—and he complained about it to Buster and to Buster's brother Carl, who was on the executive board of the tribe. Buster responded by suggesting that Laroche take a long and pleasant vacation anywhere in the world just as long as it was many miles away from the Seminole reservation. Laroche suspected that the tribe had decided that Crazy White Man was no longer welcome on the reservation, but he wasn't sure why. "Goddamn politics, probably," he said at the time. "Christ, I can't even believe I'm dealing with this. Like I could give a damn. If they fire me, I'll sue. I already did some legal research about this when I was researching the endangered-species laws. They can't fire me, and I ain't going to quit. There's nothing they can do."

He took the vacation anyway. On the day he came back, there was a severance check waiting for him in the nursery office and someone else sitting at his desk. Then and there, he decided he would leave the reservation forever. It would be another one of his unconditional combustive endings, just like the end to his turtle phase and his Ice Age fossil phase—it would be the absolute end to his Indian phase. He packed up his papers and catalogs and carried them out to his van. Above him the plastic flags strung across the nursery entrance popped and snapped in the wind. The sun was low, backlighting the plants in the shadehouse, throwing monster-sized shadows on the white shadehouse wall, shadows of gigantic Argentinean peppers, gigantic spinach bushes, gigantic pigeon peas, gigantic cracker roses. The saggy office trailer, the cat's cradle of Florida Power & Light transmission lines above him, the dusty gravel below, the hazy hot light, the lab where the millions of ghost orchids were going to be grown—Laroche just walked away from it, got into his van, skidded over the bumpy driveway and out onto the bleached white street and left it all behind. He declared that in his life he would never step on Indian land again and therefore he would never see his nursery again, the place where he had hoped to create millions of rare flowers and make millions of dollars and permanently change the world. I could have never done it, could never have given up so fast on something to which I'd been so devoted, but Laroche shrugged it off. "Like I could give a damn," he said.

—

After Laroche left, the nursery was abandoned under the hot press of the Florida sky while the tribe debated how to proceed. During the deliberations, more than half of the plants died. Even the cactus—Laroche had stocked up with four thousand cactus—burned up. Finally, Buster agreed to hire another nursery manager, a young muscular guy from Jacksonville named Rick Warren who had been installing sprinkler systems and working in a nursery on the side. Warren was not very much like Laroche. He was not a Crazy White

Man—he was a soft-spoken and courteous white man, and his plans for Seminole Gardens were as earthbound as Laroche's had been balmy. "You can't be a nursery that just does exotics," he told the Seminoles. "You need some solid products like Christmas trees and potted palms." He lobbied to convert Laroche's original nursery on Sixty-fifth Avenue to wholesale plants only and to move the retail portion to a new spot on State Road 441, the heavily traveled state road that runs along the eastern boundary of the reservation. Warren pointed out that at the State Road 441 location he would have rust-free city water for the plants, rather than the hard well water at the old nursery, and he would be in a prime commercial area near a tribal smoke shop, a store selling bird and monkey cages, and the Seminole Casino, rather than the desolate corner Laroche had been in. The lot on Route 441 had in fact once been the site of a produce house. "I saw it sitting there, empty," Rick told me. "I thought it would be neat."

I couldn't imagine the Seminole nursery without Laroche, and Laroche couldn't imagine the Seminole nursery without Laroche, and Laroche also couldn't believe I was actually planning to go to the Laroche-less nursery sometime so that I could meet Rick Warren and see the place. "A *sprinkler* guy, for Chrissake," Laroche hissed. "What a visionary." One afternoon when I was driving through Hollywood on my way to an orchid show I decided to stop by. A shiny white office trailer sat near the entrance to the new nursery, and behind the trailer were single-file rows of plants in plastic tubs. Three men were roaming among the tubs, watering and grooming the plants. All three of them were wearing turquoise T-shirts printed with the slogan SEMINOLE GARDENS PLANT NURSERY SPECIALIZING IN LANDSCAPE DESIGN. GO NATIVE! and wet bandannas on their heads. After a few minutes,

Rick Warren came out and showed me around. He was dressed in one of the turquoise T-shirts and a pair of grass-stained gardening pants. He led me down the center row of the nursery. "It's really different here now than when you first saw the nursery," he said. "We're doing really solid projects now. The tribe is our number one customer. At Christmas, the tribe buys every member a Christmas tree, so I decided our first project should be Christmas trees. I mean, the way I see it, the tribe's going to buy trees anyway, so they might as well buy them from their own nursery." He paused in front of a humped, knotted knee-high tree in a small black pot. "Bonsai," he said, twiddling one of the tree's little branches. "It's been my hobby since I was a little lad. I did my first bonsai when I was sixteen. This one here's a hydroponic saw palmetto that I've got growing in sphagnum moss. I've done over two hundred bonsai. I got all the guys on the crew their own bonsai, and I'm teaching them how to prune them out and dwarf them. It's a great hobby and it can be a nice little sideline business." He fished a pebble out of the bonsai pot and tossed it on the ground and then tucked the moss around the base of the bonsai. "See, the nursery's just a totally different place now than it was when Laroche was here. We're just more practical than it was before. The tribe wants to make money, so I'm doing sensible planning. I'm stocking salt-tolerant plants and drought-tolerant plants like ponytail palms and dwarf *Ixora* and variegated *Loriope*. We need tough things like fan palms and majesty palms that can survive here. My goal is I want to be able to take a decent seventy-cent plant and grow it for two weeks and sell it for five dollars. I even got my crew started cutting grass, and it's been going so great that now the tribe wants me to start a lawn-maintenance division." One of the men watering the ponytail palms came over to talk to Rick and then introduced himself to me. His name was Herbert Jim, and he had long black hair and a sorrowful face. He told me he had grown up in a chikee in the Big Cypress and that if he could get a break from work he'd take me out there to meet his grandmother and see wild animals. He and Rick talked about the lawn-cutting schedule over the next few days, and then Herbert Jim nodded good-bye and went back to watering the palms. The fronds were sequined with water drops and the mist from the hose looked like a bunch of silvery scribbles in the air. It was a different place now, even though Laroche had been gone only a month or so. None of the men who had been in the Fakahatchee with him were working at the nursery anymore, and one of them had even left the reservation altogether. None of the plants at the nursery now had the mangy, fantastic look that Laroche's plants and vegetables all had— Rick's plants were clean-cut and regular and looked like plants that a normal person would be able to grow. I actually could even identify a few of them. "What Laroche was doing with the nursery, well, to be honest, I didn't find it too realistic," Rick said. "I don't know the man, but it's obvious that he had a lot of pretty impractical plans. He filled the nursery with weird things that were never going to sell. For one thing, he had all those orchids. And he had plants from places like Africa and India, and a whole lot of strange things that grow a million miles long and eighty million feet tall."

—

In 1957 a group of Florida Seminoles, including Bill Osceola, Betty Mae Jumper, Laura Mae Osceola, Jimmy Osceola, John Henry Gopher, Miles Osceola, and Charlotte Osceola, drafted a constitution and charter that was then approved by the Department of the Interior and accepted by a majority of the tribe members. The charter gave federal recognition to the Seminole tribe of Florida and established the Seminole

Tribe of Florida, Incorporated, to oversee tribal businesses and economic development. In 1971 the Seminoles decided to hold an official annual tribal fair and rodeo at the reservation in Hollywood. The first fair offered roping competitions, log-peeling contests, alligator wrestling, a powwow, and craft exhibitions. Over time, the fair grew into a four-day event and included golf and bowling and basketball tournaments; a Miss Seminole, Junior Miss Seminole, and Little Mr. and Little Miss Seminole pageants; a talent show, musical performances, and a snake display. The year Laroche had come and gone from the tribe happened to be the twenty-fifth anniversary of the fair, and people around the reservation told me it was going to be spectacular. I wanted desperately to go, and I especially wanted to go with Laroche, but he was resolute about never returning to the reservation. He was so committed to avoiding all contact with the tribe that he had even started buying his cigarettes at regular retail outlets rather than the tax-free tribal smoke shops, a considerable sacrifice given his smoking habit. "I ain't gonna go back," he said to me the day before the fair opened. "I'm completely over everything with the Indians. Christ, now I can't believe I even put up with the bullshit there for a minute." I asked what he was doing. "Screwing around," he said. I said I meant professionally. He said, "I'm looking for something that doesn't involve Indians. And I'm pretty fed up with plants. I'm going to do something that doesn't involve things that die, that's for sure. I can't stand working with things that die on you all the time."

I could tell I wasn't going to talk him into joining me at the fair, so I drove to the reservation the next morning alone. I was getting accustomed to this drive by now, coming down the highway from West Palm Beach, then driving down Stirling Road past the bus benches advertising the Seminole

Trading Post and Smoke Shop and the Polish American Club
Polka and Food Festival, past all the white-metal gates to all
the condominium developments and past the casino dealer's
school, past the panel truck that was usually parked at the
corner of Stirling Road and Route 441 selling fresh shrimp
for three dollars a pound. The fairgrounds were west of the
shrimp truck and east of the tribal headquarters. It was a
large spread with a rodeo arena, several acres for booths, a
deepwater alligator pit, and a new stadium that was named in
honor of Laura Mae Osceola, who had helped draft the
tribe's constitution in 1957. That morning there were a score
of pickups and horse trailers parked in the lot and people un-
packing merchandise at the food and crafts booths. I spotted
Buster, so I went over to say hello. He was standing near a
rental truck absorbed in conversation with a short man with
thick arms and thick legs and a chest like a file cabinet. The
back of the rental truck was open and appeared mostly
empty, except for a twelve-foot-long alligator that was napping on the tailgate.

"Hey," Buster said to me.

"Hey," the short man said. "Nice to meet you."

"He's the alligator wrestler," Buster explained, jerking his
head toward the man.

"Name's Thomas Storm," the man said to me. "Storm, as
in 'bad weather.' "

"I see," I said.

Storm turned back to Buster. "Can you believe it, I swear
to God," he said, shrugging. "I've been trying to get Lloyd's of
London to insure me and I'll be damned but they won't do
it."

"Long as you don't sue me," Buster said. "That creature
looks pretty nasty." He looked over at the sleeping alligator,
who suddenly shifted on the tailgate and snapped open one of

his eyes. The eye was moss-green and had a pupil shaped like the side of a dime. He also had a big nose and a terrible underbite and claws that looked like surgical tools. "I'm not interested in wrestling gators but I don't mind eating them too much," Buster said. "They taste like fishy chicken. Not so great, really, but anyway, it's a change of pace."

The fair was getting under way; first there was the grand opening processional of dignitaries and former Miss Seminoles, and then the booths opened, selling cowboy accessories like lariats and toy handcuffs and whips and spurs and Indian accessories like silver belt buckles and embroidered dirndl skirts, and other booths selling odds and ends like alligator feet, plastic slingshots, rubber tomahawks, silver-and-turquoise brooches, incense, and small buffaloes carved out of pine. The food you could buy was fry bread and barbecued beef and Eskimo Pies and an alligator-meat basket (seven dollars) and a frog-legs basket (seven dollars) and a frog-and-gator combo basket (ten dollars) and hot dogs and fries (two dollars, with a student discount). The biggest of the alligator-food booths was called Gator Hut, and hanging over it was a sign that said CARNE DE COCODRILOS. When I walked past, a fat man with a beard was studying the sign and then said to the salesgirl, "I'll have a small gator and a large Coke, please." At a small picnic table in the shade, four wrinkly old ladies wearing woolen mufflers and Seminole skirts and knee socks were sitting wordlessly and eating pumpkin bread. A young man sitting with them had on a Cleveland Indians baseball cap with its goofy Chief Wahoo insignia, and a woman standing behind the young man was wearing an Indians cap, too, as well as a Bob Marley T-shirt, a beautiful embroidered traditional Seminole skirt, and a wristwatch with a neon face. No one spoke to me and I didn't speak to anyone; I just spent the next few hours walking through the drizzle of conversations—"I'm real busy these days. We got a Spanish ministry now." "I heard a fella shot himself in the face!" "I'm sewing this deerskin. You got a problem with a man doing woman's work?" "Hi, Molly, where've ya been? France? Or outer space?" "I'll meet you in a minute, I'm still dressing up my tomahawk here." Over the public-address system a solemn masculine voice boomed: "Walking Buffalo to the security booth, please." "Red River and Otter Trail, report to the front gate immediately." "Buddy Big Mountain to the stadium now, please." While I was lingering at a booth selling bundles of sagebrush and lavender a girl passed by walking an iguana on a leash, and a troop of Hollywood, Florida, Girl Scouts in full uniform marched by, single file. As the morning went on, some other white people trickled in, dressed in buckskin and jeans, or Mississippi State University shirts and shorts, or pastel leisure clothes and plastic visors, and they made their way over to the rodeo arena or browsed shyly at the booths.

In the stadium, the Little Mr. and Miss Seminole Pageant started. The Little Misses were waiting in the stands and the Little Mr. contestants were lined up onstage, a few dressed in dazzling Seminole costumes and the others in miniature business suits. In the yellow sun the little boys glowed like lightbulbs. Silver-tinsel flags rustled over the stage and somewhere out of sight a bass drum was thudding. Onstage, the master of ceremonies began: "Okay, ladies and gentlemen, this is Contestant Number Six, Randy Osceola, who is five years of age and comes to us from the Hollywood reservation. . . . Next is Justin Troy Osceola, three years of age. Justin is a member of the Panther clan and comes to us from the Hollywood reservation. . . . Keith Kelly Jumper is of the Big Town clan and comes to us from the Big Cypress reservation. . . ." The three judges were sitting on folding chairs in the middle of the stadium, chewing on pencils and whispering to one another. "Okay, let's applaud these little boys," the master of ceremonies went on. "They don't know what's going on, but they're doing a great job anyway. It's a big job for a little kid, even though they don't know what's going on. Some Little Miss and Mr. Seminoles travel to powwows out of state, and some don't. It depends on moneywise. But they represent their tribe and we're proud of them all." Just then a couple of Little Mr. Seminoles broke rank and started chasing each other around the stage with sticks. "While the judges are tallying their scores I want to introduce Ginger Tiger, the 1980 past princess," the master of ceremonies called out. A woman stood up in her seat and gave a wide sweeping wave of her hand. The crowd applauded. Someone behind me said, "Hey, who's that baby who won? It's bald-headed."

"Are there any more Miss Seminoles out there hiding from me?" the master of ceremonies asked. "Rita Gopher? Are you out there? Stand up and raise your hand! Stand up and give that princess wave!"

I was sitting up in the bleachers next to one of the pow-wow dancers. She was a tall, lean girl, maybe sixteen or so, with wide-set eyes and long, tight braids. She said she wasn't a Seminole—she was an Ojibwa Indian and lived in Manitoba, Canada, but she had come to Florida with a group of Ojibwas to dance at the powwow. She said she attended some powwow somewhere almost every weekend; powwows were her passion. She was wearing an amazing dress of stiff deep-purple satin that had a high neck and long sleeves and a wide, long skirt. The entire surface of the skirt was covered with the thin silver-colored lids from Copenhagen and McPherson snuff tins. Each tin lid had one hole punched in it near the edge and was stitched onto the skirt through this hole so that the rest of the lid could hang loose and jingle. The girl said that powwow skirts are supposed to have exactly 365 jingles on them, one for each calendar day, but her skirt needed an extra 150 to cover it completely because of her exceptional height. The skirt draped as heavily as chain mail. She said it weighed more than ten pounds but that the weight didn't bother her at all. After a few minutes she stood up to give me a better look at her costume. The purple satin gleamed, and as she twirled, her thin braids whipped around and the five hundred tin snuff lids clinked against one another, making a light, flat, icy sound that cascaded from her skirt to the ground.

—

Thomas Storm had unloaded the alligator beside the deepwater pit and was getting ready for his first show of the day. A half-dozen people were hanging around, watching him get ready and testing their cameras. The deepwater pit was surrounded by sand. Storm was barefoot. The alligator was trussed up and looked as if he was still napping. "Hey!" Storm suddenly hollered. "There are all sorts of ants in this sand. Anybody got any bug spray? Anybody?" No one near the pit moved. Storm's wife, a slight woman with curly blond hair, was standing nearby holding a little girl. "Thomas," she said, "I am going over to get something to eat and I am leaving Chelsea here. I do not want her in the water, you hear me?" Storm was kicking around in the sand looking for ants. "Thomas!" his wife said sharply. "You heard me! You know my temper! I do *not* want Chelsea in the water!" The alligator stretched one of its leathery legs. Most everyone jumped. Thomas rolled his eyes at his wife and said he had heard her. She placed the baby on the sand and walked away slowly, watching over her shoulder the entire time. From the other direction a television crew appeared, and Buster was with them, talking to the guy in a charcoal suit who looked as if he was in charge. "We need some kind of action for the background," the guy said to Buster. "What can you give me?"

"I can put together something for you, for sure," Buster answered. "I've got all sorts of powwow dancers and my gator wrestler's right here."

Storm raised his hand in salute. His daughter was dangling her feet in the alligator pit. "Okay, for the weather segment, we'll go with the gators," the television guy said. "We're going to need to get the timing down. I'd like to have him get the alligator in a good clinch right when we zoom in. I'd also really like to see some of those dancers. I think that'd be nice action."

"I can get you some dancers, but it's going to take a little more time," Buster said. He pulled a cellular phone out of his pocket and dialed a number. "Yeah, it's me," he said into the phone. "I need some dancers for Channel Ten . . . well, call Charlotte Gopher, then! Have her get them together!" He snapped the phone shut. "Done," he said to the television guy. "I've also got an Indian ventriloquist, if you're interested."

"That's okay," the guy said. "With the wrestler and the dancers, I think I've got all I need."

—

The next morning I went back to the fair to see tribe chairman Chief James Billie perform with his country-rock band. It was the first time I'd seen Chief Billie in the flesh, although I had seen the Chief Billie portrait that covers one entire wall in the Seminole casino and his Chief Billie Swamp Safari signs on the road to the Fakahatchee and his Swamp Safari continuous-loop promotional video playing at one of the booths at the fair. He never seemed to be around, but you couldn't talk to a member of the tribe without hear-

The Orchid Thief 🙷 233

ing Chief Billie's name; he was omnipresent, fabled, but always just out of sight, sort of the human equivalent of the omnipresent, fabled, and always just-out-of-sight ghost orchid. James E. Billie was born in Hollywood in 1943 and was adopted at birth by Max Osceola, a cattle rancher and prominent member of the Seminole Bird Clan. Billie grew up in a traditional manner on the reservation but always refers to himself as a bowlegged half-breed because he is bowlegged and his biological father was Irish. After high school Billie served as a paratrooper in Vietnam. When he returned to Florida he became a hairdresser and a hunting guide. By his own description, he was a young fuzzy-headed Vietnam-veteran alligator-wrestling hippie-looking guy wearing bell-bottoms. In his spare time he tried to cook up ways for the tribe to earn money. At that point, the Florida Seminoles were poor and unemployed and received only about a hundred dollars a quarter in dividends from federal land-claim settlements and tribe businesses. One of Billie's first notions was to set up a coin-diving tourist concession in the Everglades. In 1976 he took note of a Supreme Court ruling that confirmed the status of Indian reservations as sovereign nations. Along with a Miami lawyer, Billie researched whether sovereignty would extend to such issues as low-stakes bingo and poker. In 1979 the tribe opened a bingo hall in Hollywood and won a court decision against the state of Florida, making it legal for the tribe to set its own casino hours and jackpots, something that had never been done before on an American Indian reservation. The next year, Billie ran for the office of tribal chairman, campaigning by flying from reservation to reservation in his own four-seat Cessna. He spent election night hunting alligators with his dog, Bingo. The election was his by a landslide. During Billie's next ten years as chairman, the tribe increased its cattle holdings, started its citrus business, established its shrimp and turtle farms, hired John Laroche to set up a tribal nursery. The Seminole casinos were built in Tampa, Hollywood, and Immokalee, and the actor Burt Reynolds, who is half Cherokee and whose first television job was playing a half-breed on *Gunsmoke,* agreed to be the casinos' celebrity spokesman. The Seminole Tribe of Florida, Inc., had become a $35-million-a-year business. The average Seminole's quarterly dividends rose from $100 to $600, and the tribe's income from its businesses rose from $500,000 annually to more than $10 million. Chief Billie and the tribe began to be approached regularly by businesses looking for joint-venture opportunities. Donald Trump approached them in 1996 with his eye on the tribe's casinos; Chief Billie said he would talk with Trump only if the meeting was held in the Big Cypress Swamp and if Trump agreed to spend the night watching alligator wrestling and eating Seminole fry bread and frog legs. The meeting took place on Chief Billie's terms. No deals were made, but the next year Trump invited Chief Billie to be a judge in the Miss Universe pageant, which he owns.

———

Once Billie became the chairman of the Seminole Tribe of Florida, he often toured the reservations in his gold Corvette. He also recorded several albums of his particular musical hybrid of rock, bluegrass, country, and salsa. They were released on a small independent label called Seminole Records. *Big Alligator* and *Old Ways* received especially good reviews. He toured with his band the Shack Daddies, playing at clubs and at country- and folk-music festivals. Otherwise his lifestyle remained rustic. Hunting and guiding in the swamp were his principal enterprises. On the evening of December 1, 1983, Billie and a friend of his named Miguel Contu met for hamburgers at Ruby's, a snack bar on the reservation. Because they were bored after their hamburgers they decided to go spotlight some deer. They drove Billie's pickup into the Cowbone section of the Big Cypress Reservation. Billy got his guns ready while Contu sat in the back of the truck shining a light into the woods. On a gravel road in the thick brush, Contu spotted a pair of eyes that were the green-gold color of lightning bugs. Billie, using a pistol, shot the animal and wounded it in the shoulder.

In the light the animal appeared to be not a deer at all but some sort of panther, probably the subspecies *Felis concolor coryi*, the Florida panther, which is the state's official animal. At the time there were only twenty-six known to exist. Florida panthers once ranged throughout the Southeast, as far north as Tennessee, but around the turn of the century farmers and developers began a program of extermination—of subjugation and removal—that was so successful that by 1960 wildlife biologists believed the subspecies to be extinct. Apparently a small number managed to hide successfully in the Florida swamps, and in 1973 about thirty survivors were discovered. Their territory had shrunk from one third of the entire United States of America to just five thousand square miles of Everglades, Big Cypress Swamp, and Fakahatchee Strand, and they were so inbred that they had developed several distinct, abnormal traits: a kink at the end of the tail, a cowlick swirl of hair on the back of the neck, a compromised immune system, and in males an extremely low sperm count and a testicular defect known as cryptorchidism.

Just two years before Chief Billie shot the panther, the state of Florida had begun to try to save the species. Panthers were captured and fitted with radio collars and treated by mobile veterinary units carrying antibiotics, vitamins, bottled oxygen, endotracheal tubes, and balloon splints. Their movements were tracked by radio telemetry and published over the Internet on the Florida panther website, http://supernet.net/chrisd/gene15/html. For a while the state planned to catch all the remaining wild Florida panthers and then move them to zoos, where scientists could oversee and assist their breeding and eventually reintroduce them to the wild. That plan was rejected when animal rights activists complained that it was too much of a gamble, and that if the species was going to die out, it should be allowed to die out with dignity in the swamp. The state then adopted a crossbreeding program. Texas cougars, close genetic relatives of the Florida panther, were released into the panthers' habitat and encouraged to mingle. The cougar-panther offspring should have the benefit of possessing new genetic material, rather than the recycled and abnormal genes of the panthers alone; the diversity ought to strengthen the animals and eventually revive the population. Some people object to the crossbreeding program because it means the Florida panther might survive but it will no longer be genetically pure. As it happens, the Florida panther isn't pure anyway. Scientists have studied the mitochondrial DNA of seven of the Fakahatchee panthers and traced some of their genes to Chilean and Brazilian cougars, which were imported to Florida for local menageries and then released into the wild in the 1950s and 1960s.

———

After Chief Billie wounded the animal, he fired his pistol again, missing. Then he took out a high-powered rifle and killed the animal with a shot to the head. Back at his lodge in the Big Cypress he posed with his dog, Bingo, and the panther, which he held up by its ears.

On December 7 Florida Game and Fresh Water Fish Commission officers acting on a tip went to Billie's lodge and spotted the panther hide and skull hanging out to dry. On

December 13, a Hendry County judge signed an arrest warrant for Chief James E. Billie, charging him with killing a Florida panther, a third-degree felony punishable by five years in jail or a five-thousand-dollar fine or both. Billie announced that he would plead innocent to the charges on the grounds that Seminoles had the right to kill endangered species on reservation land and that panther hunting was part of tribal spiritual and healing ceremonies and therefore was protected as a religious freedom. During oral arguments in May, Chief Billie told the judge he had been studying to be a medicine man for two years, and that killing a panther was required to attain such a rank. One of the tribe's medicine men, Sonny Billie, told a reporter: "There is very powerful medicine in the panther. I will say that I am very proud of James Billie."

The legal story of Chief Billie and the panther spread and tangled as time went on. Soon after he was charged, Billie filed a federal lawsuit challenging the Florida laws protecting the panther because they impose on Seminole religious freedom. Then Hendry County Circuit Judge Hugh Hayes wrote a twenty-three-page order dismissing the charges against Billie, but the Florida Court of Appeals reversed Judge Hayes's decision and reinstated the charges. Billie was then arraigned on federal misdemeanor violations of the Endangered Species Act in addition to having to face trial on the reinstated Florida charges. Federal prosecutors had been awaiting the outcome of a Supreme Court review of a South Dakota case involving a Yankton Sioux who had killed a bald eagle. Once the Supreme Court held that the Bald Eagle Protection Act overruled Indian treaty rights, they charged Billie, and the federal trial began before the state trial, in August of 1987. All this time, no one had bothered to preserve the remains of the panther. When the animal was introduced into evidence it smelled so awful that it made some people in the courtroom faint. Billie sat through the proceedings with a black kerchief over his mouth and nose because of the odor and complained to a newspaper reporter, "They ruined it! They didn't salt it!" In fact, one of the game officers had boiled the skull and another had kept the panther's hide in his home freezer for a year and a half. The rest of the carcass was missing because Billie had eaten it. Even though during the trial he maintained that he'd never seen a panther before the night he shot one and that he had believed he was shooting a deer, he told the *St. Petersburg Times* that he knew he had been aiming at a panther, and that he wanted to shoot it so he could have a sacred hide to show his children and that he thought the criminal charges and the government's attitude were stupid. He also said that panther meat tasted fine with Progresso sauce and a little seasoning.

The arguments in Billie's defense were diverse. His lawyer contended that the Endangered Species Act did not apply to noncommercial hunting on the reservation, and that the charges violated Billie's freedom of religion because panther claws were used by medicine men and panther hides and skulls were used as Seminole power tokens, and that the panther hide had been seized unlawfully because the game officers had no warrant when they first came to his lodge in Big Cypress, and that, finally, Billie didn't know he was shooting a panther—he thought he was shooting a deer, and even if he had known it was a panther he had no way of knowing it was one of the endangered Florida subspecies rather than merely an ordinary panther. Moreover, Chief Billie's attorney argued, the government couldn't definitively prove that the animal really was a protected Florida panther, since the protected subspecies *Felis concolor coryi* is almost impossible to distinguish from other subspecies. This was not a novel legal tactic in Florida. For years, accused hog thieves had defended themselves in court by claiming that they thought the domesticated hog they'd stolen was actually a wild razorback and therefore ownerless and therefore they hadn't stolen it from anybody, and if they had, they certainly hadn't *meant* to—it was just an honest case of zoological misidentification. Eventually, the Florida legislature in 1937 did away with the I-didn't-know-it-was-a-farm-hog-I-thought-it-was-wild defense by decreeing that as a matter of law, particularly laws applying to pig theft, there *were* no wild razorback hogs in the state. The federal jury in the Billie case deliberated for two days and then informed the judge that they were hopelessly divided over the question of whether the prosecution had absolutely proved that the animal was a Florida panther. Consequently the federal district judge declared a mistrial. The state prosecution—*State of Florida v. James E. Billie*—went to trial the following month. After less than two hours of deliberation the state jury acquitted him, and jurors later said that they were not convinced that the animal had been positively identified as a *Felis concolor coryi.* The day after the state acquitted him, the federal charges against Billie were dropped, probably because federal prosecutors took the state acquittal as a bad omen. At that point, Chief Billie demanded that the U.S. Fish and Wildlife Service return the panther hide to him, but his demand was refused because according to the Fish and Wildlife agents the hide was contraband. The flurry of prosecution was finally over at the end of October. In May, Chief Billie was reelected to a new four-year term as chairman of the Seminole Tribe. Shortly after, the federal government announced that it would be applying the Endangered Species Act's Similarity of Appearance provision to any big cats in Florida; that is, anything in the state that could possibly be mistaken for an endangered *Felis concolor coryi* was now also protected under federal law.

—

While his band was warming up, Chief Billie told jokes to the crowd. He was speaking either Hitchiti or Muskogee—I don't know which because I don't speak either one. It was a brilliant morning and the grandstand seats were as warm as griddles. After the jokes Billie said in English, "Now, you Indians better be careful about buying bear claws here at the fair! I hear a game warden's looking to give you a hard time!" He let his guitar dangle against his hip and winked to the crowd. His hair was longish and choppy and he had high cheekbones and black eyebrows and a foxy, sharp-chinned face that looked good onstage. That morning he was dressed in a fancy cowboy shirt, black jeans, and a string tie. He winked again. "Boy, I'd sure love to have some sardines and crackers right now," he said in an intimate tone. "Funny with us Seminoles, isn't it? Now we got a casino and we got big dividends but instead of having a *new* lifestyle, we've just elevated our *old* lifestyle. We grew up on sardines and crackers. Now we have all our newfound wealth and what do we do with it? Well, we just buy *lots* of sardines and crackers, right?" He laughed. "As long as I can remember, I was always out in the swamp with my grandparents. What we killed that day we ate that night. It's kind of hard to get that out of your system. It's just the way I am. It's the way we are." The band started playing "Down in the Boondocks." The crowd clapped along through the entire song. Toward the end of the final verse, a little boy—Chief Billie's youngest son—ran out into the middle of the arena followed by a small, fat alligator whose jaws were held shut with duct tape. The boy was slight, bare-chested, and barefoot. In a moment he cornered the alligator and then straddled it. The crowd cheered and

Chief Billie smiled, brushing his lips against the microphone. The boy arched his back. The alligator arched his back. With one hand the boy grabbed the alligator's snout and raised it in the air. With his other hand he reached up and flashed a victory sign.

———

In the middle of the afternoon I ran into Vinson Osceola near the front gate. Vinson was the only one of the defendants in the orchid case besides Laroche I'd gotten to know a little bit and I liked him a lot, even though he was quiet and sardonic and had never been particularly friendly. I happened to have met his girlfriend, Sandy, at the Little Mr. and Miss Seminole talent contest the first day of the fair, and between the Little Mr. Seminole who performed "Jailhouse Rock" and the Little Mr. who sang a squeaky, rueful version of "It's My Desire to Live for Jesus," she told me what it had been like to grow up on the Big Cypress Reservation in a shack with her grandparents and uncles, what it had been like hearing the Florida rain strike the tin roof like buckshot and staying up all night, all of them, making up stories about what the rain was trying to say. Now she lived in Hollywood, which she said was nice but too fast—too much of an urban place, too many cars and drugs and bars and street corners that made it too hard to have kids grow up in the Indian way.

When I ran into Vinson he was waiting for Sandy so they could go together to the community dinner. She was helping set up the dinner and he had agreed to oversee the grilling of two thousand steaks. As usual, Vinson was wearing mirror sunglasses, so I couldn't tell whether he was looking at me or through me or around me, although he seemed to at least be listening to me. I asked him whether he had been back to the Fakahatchee since the judge's decision, and he said, "Nah, nah, not since then." I wondered if he'd seen or talked to

Laroche since Laroche had left the reservation. "Nope, haven't seen or talked to the dude," he said, running his finger back and forth under his chin. "He's what got us in trouble." Had he collected any orchids since Laroche left? "Nah, none, no way," he said. "Before we got in trouble with Crazy White Man, the orchids are what got us into trouble in the first place." I wanted to go to the community dinner, but it was Indians-only, and no one I appealed to for permission would budge. Vinson explained that it would bother the older people to have a white person at the dinner—that no matter how many years they'd been mixing in the non-Indian world, they still felt separate and suspicious. "White people, it's your job to make money," he said to me. "Indians, we have our own job. Our job is to take care of the earth. We are different from you and we always will be."

Instead I went to watch the end of the rodeo. The first night's rodeo had been restricted to Indians, but Saturday night was open to any kind of cowboy or cowgirl, and a lot of the roping teams were made up of one Seminole and one non-Seminole. I watched the team of Wildcat Jumper and Sean John storm around after a thick-necked bull named Jimmy Lee while the sun fell behind the palm trees. I had a long drive ahead of me and it was late, so I watched one more team try to rope a bull named Risky Business and then I walked back to my car. I passed the Seminole Casino on the way, the acres of parking lots with guard towers raised like hackles here and there, the plain gray facade of the casino building. There was not one empty parking spot in the place. It was nearly midnight, but people were still streaming in—couples in dinner clothes, a broad-backed older woman with an aluminum walker, a pair of white-blond big-breasted girls in cowboy shirts and boots, a man with thick plastic glasses and the heedful face of a night watchman. The casino wasn't much to look at inside, except for the painting of Chief Billie on the wall with the Seminole greeting "Sho-naa-bish" in giant script beside him. Otherwise it was a big, quiet cavern with tables and tables of men playing Texas Hold-Em and 7-Card Stud beside a sign that said POKER IS FUN AND RELAX-ING. The only sound was the clicking of poker chips. It was a room filled with a million precise, intense, noiseless move-ments, like an operating theater during brain surgery. In an-other room, hundreds of people seated at long tables were playing bingo. Many of them had collections of lucky totems next to their bingo cards—rabbits' feet, plastic elephants, statuettes of the Virgin Mary, snapshots, small plush toys, rosaries—and they were silent, too, until the man at the head of the room called out "B-twenty-three" or "O-seven," and then there would be a murmur and a shifting, like the sound of water running out of a tub, and when someone yelled out "Bingo!" there was the sound of hands slapping down on cardboard game cards as the exasperated losers swept their chips away so they could start again. The waiters and the waitresses and the poker dealers and the bingo callers and the valet parkers and the casino cashiers were all white peo-ple, all with fluorescent-tinted skin and stiff hairdos, and all the customers were white and some had tourist tans and bloodshot eyes, and even though the twenty-fifth anniversary of the Seminole tribe's annual powwow was being celebrated only a few yards away and the chief of the Seminole tribe was peering down on every single table of Texas Hold-Em and 7-Card Stud, you felt nothing of that world at all in here— you felt only the fever and focus of the games and the hard heat of people wanting to win.

Fortunes

As much as I marveled at Laroche's devotion to the things he was devoted to, I marveled even more at his capacity for detachment. For instance, my account of the tribal fair and the new nursery barely registered with him since he had now completely renounced the Seminoles. For two years he had been absorbed by them. He had sunk himself deep. I could understand that he was angry with the tribe for firing him and stung by realizing he was never part of it and never would be, but it was something more than that—for him, it was as if the tribe had disappeared from the face of the earth.

He had also completely renounced the kingdom of plants. He hinted that he was fed up with the orchid world when I had first talked to him about the pow-wow, but I hadn't believed him. But that is just what he had done. He was no longer devoted to the ghost orchids he'd poached from the Fakahatchee or the hoyas he'd tried to wheedle out of his friend at the nursery or the *Cattleya* mutants he had created in the microwave or the collection of exceptional bromeliads and orchids that he'd been assembling since his first collection was wrecked in Hurricane Andrew or the plants he'd saved from being bulldozed at construction sites or the rare ones he'd traded for or had nearly gone broke to get his hands on. He had forsaken them all. When we first met, he had told me that this kind of finish was his style, but I had never pictured that his transit from one passion to another would be so complete. "Done," he said to me the day after the powwow, after I'd been going on for a while about Chief Billie's band and the fried alligator. "I told you, when I'm done, I'm done." From the first time I'd heard of Laroche, I had been fascinated by how he managed to find the fullness and satisfaction of life in narrow desires—the Ice Age fossils, the turtles, the old mirrors, the orchids. I suppose that is exactly what I was doing in Florida, figuring out how people found order and contentment and a sense of purpose in the universe by fixing their sights on one single thing or one belief or one desire. Now I was also trying to understand how someone could end such intense desire without leaving a trace. If you had really loved something, wouldn't a little bit of it always linger? A couple of houseplants? A dinky Home Depot *Phalaenopsis* in a coffee can? I personally have always found giving up on something a thousand times harder than getting it started, but evidently Laroche's finishes were downright and absolute, and what's more, he also shut off any chance of amends. He had the same emotional pitch as the kind of guy who would permanently misplace his ex-wife's phone number, which as a matter of fact Laroche had done: he had no idea of where his ex-wife was living and no clue of her phone number and he claimed he didn't care. He really seemed to mean it, although he made a habit of insulting her favorite flowers whenever we saw them at orchid shows.

How this came up was that the South Florida Orchid Society Show was scheduled shortly after the Seminole tribal fair, and I assumed that Laroche and I were going to go together until he informed me that these days he couldn't care less about orchids and orchid shows and therefore wasn't planning to go. He had a new preoccupation. In the time between his dismissal by the Seminoles and the powwow, he had taught himself everything there was to know about computers and was now making money by building websites for businesses and, as a private sideline, posting pornography on the Internet. He was in love with computers. He even loved the pornography part of his computer work. This was not because he loved pornography; it was because being an Internet pornography publisher was, in his mind, another opportunity to profit from human weakness, something he especially liked to do. He said that he couldn't believe people were paying him to post pictures of naked fat people on the Internet, just the way he couldn't believe people had paid to buy the worthless guide to growing marijuana he was selling when we first met. "People spend a fortune on this junk, and I just keep charging them more and more," he explained to me one morning on the phone. "Maybe at some point it will dawn on these shitheads that they're wasting their money posting these lousy pictures and they'll cut it out. I'm doing them a favor by helping them realize how ridiculous it is. That's why the more I charge, the more helpful I'm being. Anyway, in the meantime, I'm making a *shitload* of money." He happened to sound awful that day, as if he were dying, but he assured me that it was just kidney trouble from his pesticide poisoning and that he'd been sick for about four months but was probably getting better. Anyway, he said, he was in a great frame of mind. "Look, the main thing is, the Internet is cool," he said. "It's not going to *die* on me, like some plant, and it's not going to fuck me over like the Seminoles." He worked building legitimate businesses' websites for a company called NetRunner. His Internet alias was Sabercat. I found his website one day, which said: "Some of you may know me as Sabercat: Lord and Master of the now dead SaberSpace. . . . If you've called the NetRunner office and spoken to a somewhat arrogant and 'different' individual, that would be me. Unlike most of the 'strange' characters you may run across on the Internet, I am not strange *because* of the anonomity of the Internet, I'm just bizarre, period."

We talked for another few minutes, and once again I raised the idea of our going together to the orchid show. He wouldn't change his mind, but he finally agreed that I could keep him posted about my plans and that he might meet me for a few minutes if I was really desperate for his company. That's the way it was with Laroche. Everything with him was extremes. The regular world was too modulated for him. It wasn't enough for me to merely want him to go, the way an ordinary person might want another ordinary person to do something. On the other hand, if I was really *desperate*, then perhaps he would keep it in mind.

———

Except for Laroche, nearly everyone I'd met in Florida was going to the show, including Martin Motes, Tom Fennell, Bob Fuchs, Frank Smith, and all the American Orchid Society people I'd been introduced to at the gala. The South Florida Orchid Society show is the biggest show in Florida, and except for the orchid show in Santa Barbara, California, it is the most important one in the country. I didn't have much hope that it would finally afford me a chance to see a ghost orchid in bloom, but I still wouldn't have missed it for the world. A few days after my conversation with Laroche I called my vanda-breeder friend Martin Motes and told him how Laroche was bucking my invitation, and Martin said I should forget about Laroche and come hang out at the show with him instead. I knew it would be fun to go with Martin in spite of my recent unhappy experience with his dog, because he had always shown me interesting things. Besides, he swore that lately the dog had been in a better mood.

I went over to his house the next day. "Bless my heart, I have a million things to do," Martin said in greeting. He and his wife, Mary, had been English professors before devoting themselves to orchids; in fact, Martin returned from a senior Fulbright lectureship in Yugoslavia in 1976 to set up Motes Orchids. Even in the greenhouse, dressed in his worn-out khakis, up to his knuckles in moss and vermiculite, he looked like a man who would be at ease in front of a chalkboard spinning theories about Yeats. His house, his yard, his wardrobe all were academically shabby. His one nonprofessorial accessory was a BMW sedan. It was a Benlate BMW. Martin, like many other Florida orchid growers, lost a lot of plants after using the Du Pont fungicide Benlate, and even though Du Pont still insists that Benlate was not responsible, it settled with hundreds of growers for millions of dollars; the company's payments were almost $400 million in Florida alone. Martin had a droll attitude toward catastrophe. When he bought the BMW with his settlement money, he put a bumper sticker on it that said BETTER LIVING THROUGH CHEMISTRY. Du Pont is still settling Benlate claims. Orchids are risky business. In some cases, Benlate settlements have been far more remunerative. Some growers took their Du Pont money and retired on it, and it was rumored that people were selling half-used bags of the fungicide to growers who might or might not have actually used it but wanted credible-looking evidence to present to Du Pont.

Since my last visit to Martin's dozens more of his orchids had bloomed. Blue and lavender buoys bobbed in the dark green sea of leaves and stems. Beside them, a row of creamy pink ones, like a set of Wedgwood teacups. "I have an errand to do this morning, pronto," Martin added. "We will be visiting a prince of the tropical fruit industry, should you care to come along." I did, so we climbed into a van with his VANDAI license plates and headed down his driveway onto the road. "I'm going to visit a gentleman by the name of Gary Zill," he explained. "I'm doing this because I believe a man should really find a way to have avocados seven months a year, preferably from his own tree." Gary Zill owned many avocado trees. Martin said he was going to trade budwood from one of his plum trees for one of Gary's avocados. The pieces of budwood were in soggy Baggies on the front seat of the van. There were many times in Florida when I felt I was in another world, and this was one of those times: I was in another world in which fruits and vegetables and budwood are legal tender—a plum bud is the market equivalent of an avocado tree and bananas are down sharply against the orange. Martin pulled up past a sign that said ZILL HIGH PERFORMANCE PLANTS and parked. As soon as he stepped out he got excited and said there was a tree on his side of the van that he wanted me to see. "It's a Cuban fruit, a *Mamey colorado*," he said, pulling a leathery, roundish fruit off a branch. "They retail for about twelve dollars apiece. They're so valuable that no one grows them anymore because they always get stolen." He bit into the fruit. The flesh was the color of brick. "My dear neighbor has twenty acres with these growing and he's selling off all of them," Martin said after he swallowed. "Even with full-time security he couldn't keep them."

Gary Zill had come up behind the van while Martin was eating the mamey and had opened the back doors and seen the hundred or so orchids Martin had in the van. "Ohhhhhh, what a gorgeous cross!" Gary yelled. "Martin, what the hell are these?" In a moment, he materialized beside us. He was as blond as a surfer and was holding a clipboard in one hand and another fruit I'd never seen before in the other. This one was bulging and olive-drab and about the size of a baseball. When he bit into it, he tore away a piece that was as red as a wound. He saw me staring. "Bullock's heart," he said, gesturing with it. "It came from the Yucatan. I ate one down there about fifteen years ago and saved the seeds. I didn't really know what to expect when I planted them here."

"We saw them down there once, too," Martin said. "*Huge* fruits. Size of a young child's head."

Gary squinted up at the sky for a moment and then said, "Martin, we should try propagating these. I brought a species back from Guatemala last week and it was bright orange inside, and it was just *beautiful*. We'll even name it for you. We'll call it the *motes reticulata*. We'll make a fortune." Martin tilted his head like a sparrow. "Ah-ha," he said. "Bless its bright orange heart." Just then, one of Gary's nurserymen came up to talk to Gary. He was a slight, shy man with a Hebrew name who said he had been born in Michigan and grew up in Brazil. It was not a very ordinary personal history, but nothing here seemed ordinary. The fruits were alien. Everyone and everything had an exotic pedigree. Sometimes in Florida you feel that you are on the edge of the world, and that the rest of the world sloshes in as regularly as the tide and produces strange and peerless things—for instance, a Hebrew Brazilian Michigander raising salmon-colored Guatemalan fruit. I talked for a while with the nurseryman, and Gary and Martin began discussing their avocado-for-plum trade and headed down the path from the tropical-fruit nursery to Gary's house. He said he had about twenty thousand plants at home, mostly orchids, and he wanted Martin to take a quick look at them before we left. "They're a mess," he warned us. "The computer that controls the watering system got hit by lightning the night I left for Costa Rica to collect mango seeds."

"I can imagine," I said.

"Martin, listen, if you're interested in any pollen, help yourself. There's plenty. Just help yourself."

Martin smiled. "Yes, well, life is short and art is long. Perhaps we can cook up something artful." We stepped into Gary's shadehouse, walking under a canopy of orchids growing in latticework boxes, some drooping over like seasick sailors, some upright as soldiers and wearing hot pink or hot yellow or cool purple blooms. "Ain't it a caution," Martin said, glancing from plant to plant. He stopped in front of a cobalt-blue *Vanda* and gave it a long look. Gary watched him. "I do believe," Martin said. "Oh yes, I do believe that I made this plant twenty-five years ago. How does it come to be in your home, Senor Zill?"

"I got it from my aunt," Gary said. "And I think my aunt got it from Mona Church."

"Ah-*ha*," Martin said. "And *I* myself gave it to Mona." He rubbed a leaf between his fingers. "And it will live long after you, Mr. Zill. The marvelous plant world. We are but visitors in it."

———

That evening, Martin drove up to the Convention Center to start building his display for the show. Miami was celebrating its centennial that year, and that was the orchid show's theme, which meant that the displays were supposed to illustrate something about Florida history. Martin said he was going to build a swamp scene with lots of vandas and a child-sized wooden dugout canoe. "It doesn't have much connection to reality," he said. "But then again, what does?" Martin's display area was a smallish square in a back row near Tom Fennell, Jr.'s, and around the corner from Bob

Fuchs's. Martin's assistant, Viv, had covered the floor of the display with two inches of beach sand before we arrived. "Very attractive," Martin said to her. "But, Viv, we do need a little negative space here." He started raking some sand out of the way. He had trucked in nearly three hundred vandas and cattleyas to use in the scene and had a few special hybrids that he particularly wanted to show off. He and Viv began placing the plants and then patting sand around to cover the base of the pots.

They muttered to each other as they worked: "I think I'm going to use this little bamboo fence, even though it's a new concept for us."

"Oh, Martin, this *Oncidium* is beautiful, but it's too red."

"It *is* too red. Use this white one. It'll blend if you play it against the canoe."

The vast, hollow Miami Convention Center was now full of other growers building their displays, hollering instructions to their helpers; it brimmed with the clang of hammers against metal frames and the groan of boxes being dragged across the floor and the faint brassy smell of dirt and the fresh sugary aroma of flowers and the squawk of truck tires in the loading dock. Martin mentioned that his display contained about forty thousand dollars' worth of flowers. There were about sixty displays being put up that night, some with twice as many plants as Martin's, which meant that the total value of the displays in the Convention Center might have been as much as $4 million, and I thought to myself: *I am standing amid millions of dollars' worth of flowers.* I breathed in deep and held my breath while I swung my head so that the $4 million of flower colors smeared like lipstick. It was in the nature of Florida, this kind of abundance, the overrichness of living things—so many of everything that all of it blurs together and you have to decide whether to be part of the blur or to be a distinct and separate being.

Martin and Viv worked for about an hour, and all around were other orchid people and their assistants working for hours. When they had positioned the last plant, Martin stepped back and surveyed the display, his index finger resting on his nose. His face settled into broody deliberation. "Viv," he said, finally, pointing at an especially big and bright orange *Cattleya,* "we should take that big honker out of there. I do fear that it's a little like nuclear overkill."

All around the Convention Center, people dropped by to see how other people's displays were doing. They borrowed sphagnum moss and bamboo fencing and loaned out four-inch ferns and filler plants. A nurseryman from Hawaii who was building a huge display stopped by to say hello to Martin. "I'm not doing the New York show this year," he said. "I got all showed out. When you have a minute, come see this new electronic mist generator I've got." Martin took a break and wandered a few displays down to the South Florida Fern Society. The man working on it was named Jack. In the center of the display was a six-foot-long alligator. "That's a good alligator, isn't it, Martin?" Jack asked. "He's concrete. I'm calling the display 'Dangerous Attraction.' That's a good name, isn't it?"

The next display, from a nursery called Grow-Mor, had been made to look like a Victorian sitting room. It included a gilded fireplace, two armchairs, an antique mantel, a French side table, and two good-quality oil paintings. "The furniture's all from our home," Mr. Grow-Mor told Martin. "We tore the mantel out of our dining room because we thought it would look great here. Damn it, Martin, can you believe my best Toledo Blue isn't blooming? It's about two weeks off. Oh, by the way, Martin, do you have any extra moss?"

"We have three boxes of Spanish moss, help yourself," Martin answered. "It's from a very good commercial-moss business in Kentucky. I'd like to think that somewhere they're raping the mossy banks of pristine forest streams for this stuff." We walked by the bottom half of a mannequin dressed in period Florida pioneer clothes, and then a two-hundred-pound stuffed crocodile sitting on a ten-foot-high Styrofoam replica of a famous place called Portrait Rock. "I roughed it out with a chain saw," the man at the display said. "It's amazing what you can do with Styrofoam and acetone." We passed displays named ORCHIDS OVER MIAMI and RAINBOW OF LIVING DIAMONDS and THE MAGICAL ORCHID CITY and GATOR TRAIL and PARADISE LOST. Martin said he thought quite a few orchid people were really crazy. Right after that he introduced me to an orchid grower with wild hair and wild eyes named Waymon Bussey, who had just flown in from Mexico.

"What am I doing these days, Martin?" Waymon hollered when he saw us. "I'm doing *great*. Life is great. I'm growing mini-cymbidiums at an altitude of six thousand feet in Mexico." Martin raised his eyebrows. "Plus I just recovered from a killer-bee attack," Waymon went on. "They got me when I was out rescuing plants. I was rescuing orchids. Wild orchids. They were screaming out to me, I swear, Martin. The bees were swarming all around them. I *had* to help those orchids. I wasn't poaching! I was on a rescue mission!"

Martin twirled his beard. After a moment Waymon said, "Martin, I want you to know I've given up nicotine, alcohol, and fornication. The only addiction I have left is orchids."

"It was said of Dante that he always had time for lechery," Martin said, nodding solemnly. "Don't disappoint me, Waymon."

Waymon turned to me and winked. He had a fevery, cock-eyed grin on his face. "Hey, do you want to know something?" he asked me. "Do you know that I'm only forty-one years old and I've already seen *two* flying saucers?"

Around another corner we came upon Bob Fuchs. Bob was famous for doing grand R. F. Orchids displays. This time he had erected a nearly full-size Florida cabin circa 1886. The cabin was trim and had a small porch and a little peaked roof, and orchids hung from the railings and covered the little front lawn and lined the cabin's winding stone path and wrapped around the cabin's foundation. There were flowers of practically every single natural color. The cabin itself was authentic-looking 1886 brown. Bob greeted us, and Martin said he would leave me with Bob. "I need to go back to the Motes territory and add mulch," he said. " 'The time has come, the walrus said, to speak of many things/Of shoes and ships and sealing wax' *and* mulch. My accountant said he would come assist me in the process." Martin and Bob always looked for excuses to stay away from each other. Martin nodded at Bob and turned on his heel.

A lot of orchid growers don't like each other, just the way a lot of people don't like each other, or more precisely, the way a lot of family members don't get along. They like different orchids or they have different philosophies about breeding; for instance, Bob wanted to breed bigger and more gorgeous vandas, whereas Martin wanted to breed vandas that looked more as they had when Carl Roebelin first discovered them in the Philippines. Or one grower thinks his or her plants are better than anyone else's and are not sufficiently appreciated, or better than anyone else's and therefore the object of bitter envy, or some growers just rub one another the wrong way. This year, no one at the show hired bodyguards, as they did the year of Bob Fuchs's indictment, but you could still feel the kind of prickly tightness between certain people, as if they were about to make each other break out in a rash. If I had ever doubted whether the orchid world was really as much a world, a culture, a *family* as I imagined it was, this antagonism was perfect proof. The orchid world had the intimacy of a family and the fights of a family. Like a family, it provided a way to fit into the world, to place yourself inside a small and sometimes crowded and sometimes bickering circle, and that circle would be surrounded by a bigger circle, and then an even bigger circle, and then finally by the whole wide world; it was some kind of way to scratch out a balance between being an individual and being a part of something bigger than yourself, even though each side of the equation put the other in jeopardy. This has always been a puzzlement to me, how to have a community but remain individual—how you could manage to be separate but joined, and somehow, amazingly, not lose sight of either your separateness or your togetherness. The two conditions go up and down like a teeter-totter, first one and then the other tipping the balance back. If you set out alone and sovereign, unconnected to a family, a religion, a nationality, a tradition, a class, then pretty soon you are *too* lonely, too self-invented and unique, and too much aware that there is no one else like you in the world. If you submerge yourself completely in something—your town or your profession or your hobby—then pretty soon you have to struggle up to the surface because you need to be sure that even though you are a part of something big, some community, you still exist as a single unit with a single mind. It is the fundamental contradictoriness of the United States of America—the illogical but optimistic notion that you can create a union of individuals in which every man is king. I envied the orchid people all around me in the Convention Center, and all the orchid people who were going to swarm in here tomorrow, and I envied the Seminole tribe members for the same reason, for having found and fitted themselves into a small and crowded circle, and if any of them had moments when they had to step outside it and vouch for their independence from it, they seemed to be able to do it and then step happily back in. I even envied people like Laroche and Lee Moore who belonged to the cult of not belonging, which is its own small and crowded circle that gave them a shape for their lives, even if it was in bas-relief.

———

People often show up early at orchid shows; serious orchid people, people who want to scoot in and find the best plants before anyone else. They line up early, armed with shopping bags and wire baskets, locked on their targets.

"I want a white *Phalaenopsis* with a one hundred percent red lip. I already have one, but it has a little white mottling on the exterior of the lip *which I do not want*."

"I want a *Paphiopedilum concolor*, it's a specific one, it's a 'Walter' crossed with a 'Krull's Fat Boy' and it's the color of butter with maroon speckles."

"I have to wear handcuffs to these shows because I want everything."

"If I haven't been to a show for a few months I just *have* to go."

"I hear that cymbidiums are falling out of favor."

"I would spend ten thousand dollars on a single plant if I liked it well enough. If you see something you like and you can't get it, you get crazy."

"I love these! I want these! I brought a whole bunch of these back from Jamaica in my bra, but most of them died."

"I want a really good-sized *magnificum*. This one's pretty good-sized, but I am not leaving here until I get one that's *really* good-sized."

———

I wanted a Fakahatchee ghost orchid, in full bloom, maybe attached to a gnarled piece of custard apple tree, and I wanted its roots to spread as broad as my hand and each root to be only as wide as a toothpick. I wanted the bloom to be snow-white, white as sugar, white as lather, white as teeth. I knew its shape by heart, the peaked face with the droopy mustache of petals, the albino toad with its springy legs. It would not be the biggest or the showiest or the rarest or the finest flower here, except to me, because I wanted it. In the universe there are only a few absolutes of value; something is valuable because it can be eaten for nourishment or used as a weapon or made into clothes or it is valuable if you want it and you believe it will make you happy. Then it is worth anything as well as nothing, worth as much as you will give to have something you think you want. It saved me all sorts of trouble knowing I wouldn't find a ghost orchid here, since then I didn't even need to look. It was a relief to have no hope because then I had no fear; looking for something you want is a comfort in the clutter of the universe, but knowing you don't have to look means you can't be disappointed. It just so happened that a few days earlier, I met a man who said he'd been to a street fair in Lake Worth and that one of the vendors was selling macramé baskets, and inside the baskets were jumbles of roots growing on chunks of wild wood. He was sure that the roots were ghost orchid roots, but at the time none of them were blooming and the vendor claimed he had no idea of what the plants were, he'd just gotten them from some guy who had gotten them from some other guy. I didn't expect to see any macramé baskets of anything at the show. I saw books like *Bishop's Interim List of Orchid Hybrids Registered during 1991–1994,* and *Descriptive Terminology for the Orchid Judge,* and *You Can Grow Cattleya Orchids,* and *You Can Grow Phalaenopsis Orchids,* and orchid sweaters and T-shirts and earrings and ties. There were orchids for sale, for one and two and three and five hundred dollars, a madhouse of orchids in every color, in every shape, with wide leaves and skinny leaves and no leaves at all, with fat jutting lips and lips cupped like thimbles, and with blackish-red hoods and freckles, with ruffles, with pleats, with corkscrew curls, big as fists, small as fingernails, smelling of honey, grass, citrus, cinnamon, or of nothing, not a smell at all but just the heavy warm quality that air has after it has been sitting inside a flower.

At Martin's booth a man was squawking. "Hey, I got a bad plant from you last year!" he said. "It was a mutation. It's in the car. I'll go get it."

"I believe you," Martin said. "I don't need to see it. Why don't you choose another beauty for yourself?"

"Hey!" another man at the booth said. He held up one of the lavender vandas. "How much salt will this take? I mean, how much salt can it handle? And is it called Mood Indigo or Indigo Mood? And should I water the hell out of it?" Martin conferred with him while wrapping the plant that the man with the mutant had chosen. Another man, tall and bemused, wandered by. "Beautiful," he said to Martin. "Absolutely beautiful. By the way, Martin, you need your teeth cleaned."

"Lord," Martin sighed, "you can never hide from your dental hygienist."

Martin's canoe scene hadn't won anything in the display competition. In fact, the show committee clerk confided to me that the judges hadn't liked it at all. "In fact," she whispered, "they *hated* it." She told me that the judges thought Martin's plant labels were homely and that overall the display was too cluttered, and that when it came down to giving awards they hadn't even given Motes Orchids a second thought. I asked her about the other displays. The Hawaiians they liked, she said, but they didn't like the moss on top of the orchids, and one display called YESTERDAY they loved because "they loved the fake water." The Victorian sitting room failed because Mr. Grow-Mor had used an ugly white backdrop and the colors of his plants didn't flow. It was a long, critical list. On the other hand, the judges did like Bob Fuchs. All the major awards went to the R. F. Orchids Florida cabin—the artistic trophy, the five-hundred-square-foot-display trophy, and the ultimate award, the show trophy. It was a matter of pride, of professional respect, of personal satisfaction, to win at a show, and it was a matter of money, because plants with show ribbons command higher prices, and also it was a matter of something unimaginably profound—it was a matter of shaping evolution, because plants that win in shows become popular, and other breeders will use them as parents for new hybrids and as a model for the kind of plants they will try to produce on their own. Winner take all, including the future. All day, the first day of the show, every time I turned around I saw Bob's orangey hair and luminous pale face and the cool bright composure on it of someone who knew he'd won.

For a while I walked around with a man who was looking for a white *Phalaenopsis* with a gold and red lip and no mottling, who said he used to be an avid bridge player but finally quit because he thought bridge people were too weird, had too many emotional problems, and that he was much happier in the orchid world, and he had three different alarm systems in his greenhouse in case anything went wrong with the temperature or the light or the humidity, so he was usually very relaxed. By this time it was late and it was dark outside. I remembered that Laroche had said I could try to call him if I felt desperate. I didn't really feel desperate but I really wanted to see him here in the world that he had planned to conquer, even though in his mind he was already a million miles away from it. He was home when I called and said he'd see about coming by to meet me after he took his girlfriend and her son to a soccer game or a birthday party or something—I couldn't quite hear. He said I should just stick around in the Convention Center and he'd find me, which I knew would be impossible because it was as big as a planet and you could be lost in it for hours. I didn't for a minute expect Laroche to come and I didn't wait to see. I just flitted from one orchid to another, from one orchid display to another, from one orchid person to another, until I was as dizzy as a bee.

A Kind of Direction

A ranger at the Fakahatchee once told me a story about a woman from Georgia who had called one morning and asked if there were any ghost orchids in bloom in the swamp. The ranger told her he had just spotted a few flowering near Deep Lake. This woman was madly in love with ghost orchids and said she would go anywhere to see them, so as soon as the ranger told her this, she got into her car, drove to Atlanta, caught a flight the next morning to Miami, rented a car at the airport, drove to the Fakahatchee, got directions from the ranger, and spent the next several hours hiking toward Deep Lake, toward the ghost orchids. Less than a day had passed since the woman had first called, but orchids are changeful things, and by the time she reached the plants their flowers had shriveled up and were finished for the year. She took a long look at the green coil of roots that remained. Then she turned around and hiked out of the swamp and returned to Georgia that afternoon. I assumed the woman had been disappointed to have traveled all that way for nothing. The ranger said no, she hadn't seemed disappointed at all, and in fact she had told him she was glad she had come, and she made him promise to call her anytime he saw a ghost orchid flowering; she would happily come back again.

Laroche promised that he would go with me to the Faka-hatchee before I left Florida, and he promised that when he went with me to the Fakahatchee we would see ghost orchids. I took this under advisement. I had begun to doubt that I would ever see a ghost orchid flower. For that matter, I had begun to suspect that Laroche and I might never even hike the Fakahatchee together. It just seemed as if every attempt I made had been thwarted. When I first asked Laroche to go with me he couldn't because he was prohibited by court order from entering the area, and then he couldn't because he got too busy with the Seminole nursery, and then he couldn't because he refused to enter the swamp as a protest against the Seminoles and against the orchid world and against the world itself, and then he got busy with his new computer business and couldn't take the time. In the meantime, winter was passing and a sharp new spring heat was rushing in—the sun was higher and more ferocious every day, and I knew that if we didn't go soon the weather would become unbearable and we would have to wait until next season.

A few days after the South Florida Orchid Society show, I called Laroche and told him all about the experience, and about Bob Fuchs's win and Martin Motes's disappointment, and then I raised the question of our trip to the Faka-hatchee. He announced that he was now ready to go, and that he wanted to plan the trip for the upcoming Saturday. I was astonished. I packed up my belongings in West Palm

Beach and checked into a hotel in Miami Beach so I'd be a little closer to Laroche. On Friday night I could hardly sleep. I didn't want to think about the hike but I couldn't help myself; I kept dreaming of my initial trip to the Faka-hatchee, the time I went with Tony the ranger and saw for the first time the lavish dome of bromeliads and the trees swathed in orchid roots, but in the dream I was alone, and when I had walked deep into the swamp I stepped into one of the black sinkholes and in an instant something ropey wrapped around my legs like a lasso and I toppled over, arms flapping against the luminous enamel surface of the lake. I snapped awake, eyes wide open, blankets braided around my legs. I don't remember how I spent the next several hours, but at last it was morning. Laroche and I were planning to leave for the swamp in the early afternoon. While I was get-ting dressed I turned on the radio and heard a news bulletin reporting that Valujet Flight 592 en route from Miami to At-lanta had crashed into the Everglades and vanished beneath eighteen inches of marl and sand and mud. The crash site was only twelve miles from the city of Miami, only twelve miles from valet parking at a shopping mall, close enough to ride a bicycle from the Biltmore Hotel, but it was really a world away, wild and severe and almost inaccessible. The plane crashed on the edge of the Miccosukee Reservation, between Everglades Canal L-67A and L-67C, in an area of the swamp that local people called the Pocket. All the nearby roads, including the roads to the Fakahatchee, were closed. I stopped dressing when I heard the bulletin and im-mediately called Laroche, who had obviously still been sleeping, even though according to the schedule he had de-creed I was already running late. We agreed that we couldn't possibly get to the swamp now and that we'd try Sunday in-stead. I told Laroche that we absolutely had to make it that day, because I had booked myself on a Monday flight to go home.

———

I spent Saturday watching news of the plane crash and an interview on CNN with a Miccosukee named Buffalo Tiger, who said that the crash was caused by the spirits of nature who are angry over the damage that man has done to the Everglades. He said that the Everglades had often swallowed people for spite—that sometimes even tribe members who'd headed out into the swamp were never seen again. Laroche called me during the Buffalo Tiger interview and suggested that I meet him for a few hours at an orchid show at Fairchild Garden in Miami. He hadn't been to a show since the Seminoles had fired him and I wasn't sure why he wanted to go to one now, but I was glad of it. I drove to the garden and waited for him in the Fairchild parking lot. He showed up only a little late in a bright, bouncy mood, and insisted we first stop in the gift shop, and then, once we were in the shop, he insisted on buying me a red rubber fish I admired. Then we ambled around. The Fairchild show was in a busy room full of displays and the cool vegetal smell that rises off plants and the hollow *pop!* of shopping bags being snapped open and loaded with hundred-dollar seedlings. We surveyed row after row of orchids, stopping to admire a table of peach-colored polka-dotted dendrobiums and then to examine a *Laeliocattleya* that from a distance looked remarkably like a buck-toothed blond kid I'd known in grammar school. At one point Laroche dragged me over to see some clamshell orchids that are native to Florida. "We'll see a million of these tomorrow," he said, twiddling the plant's roots. "The Faka-hatchee is just *lousy* with these fuckers."

The proprietor of the clamshell booth had her back to us, and just as he said that she spun around and gave Laroche a look. Then she gave him a second look and lit up. "John Laroche!" she said. "John, how the heck have you been? What are you up to these days, John?"

"Barbara!" he said. He turned to me. "This is the woman I told you about, remember? The one who I took to the Faka-hatchee and then had to hack up a couple of snakes that got between her and a ghost orchid."

Barbara grinned. "John, how have you been?"

"Great," Laroche said to her. "You know, I'm an Internet publisher now. I don't have a single orchid anymore. I don't even have a single *plant*." He sounded proud.

"I'm glad for you, John," she said, in a tender voice. "I was worried about you. It was beginning to wear and tear on you. Like a bad marriage."

Laroche nodded. "Well, I love computers now." He stroked one of her orchids and added, "It's really such a relief not having to rely on living things anymore." He became preoc-cupied with a bromeliad at the next table. Barbara watched him for a moment and then whispered to me, "He seems so much better now. For some people, it's just too intense, this whole orchid thing. It infects their whole being. John was just being eaten up by it."

A few minutes later when we were at the other end of the room, another dealer recognized him. "I'm an Internet pub-lisher now!" Laroche declared. "I don't have even a single or-chid anymore!" It was almost a boast. "I kicked the habit!" he said to another acquaintance. "I gave it up!" After an hour or so we left the show and went walking around the grounds. Hurricane Andrew had ripped up acres of the Fairchild prop-erty, and even though there had been some replanting, it still had the shocked look of a newly shaved head. The busted garden seemed to make Laroche morose. "You should have seen this before the hurricane," he said, looking around.

"Christ, it looks like hell now." He patted the trunk of a bottle palm. "I love these," he said. "I always loved plants that were silvery and different. I used to have this silvery-gray hibiscus, it was just a crummy little runt I found at a nursery, and I brought it home and doctored it up and fuck if it didn't turn out to be one of my favorite plants! It was the coolest color." He leaned against another tree. "Name this tree," he said. "Forget it. You'll never know it. It's a zombie palm. Now why do you think a plant would look like this? That's how I'd always get caught up in this stuff. Botany by imagination. I'd put myself in the plant's point of view and try to figure them out. I'm a plant. Why do I want rough bark instead of smooth bark? Why do I want narrow leaves instead of wide leaves? I was always really good at feeling things out that way."

"Do you miss it?" I asked.

Laroche snorted and lit a cigarette. "Of course I miss it," he muttered. "I mean, *Jesus Christ*. You just have to find something else to fill up your life."

On the way home Laroche wanted me to come with him and visit a friend of his named Dewey Fisk. He thought I would find Dewey illuminating. "Dewey's place is right near here," he said. "You should meet him. Really. He's got tons of shit, really cool shit, and he's just plant crazy. You'll see what I mean when I tell you that there is a whole universe of people who just live for their plants."

I said I'd slept badly the last few nights and thought I should go back to my hotel and rest up for our hike.

"Look, I think this will be really good for you," Laroche continued. "And anyway, it'll only take a minute. *Less* than a minute. Dewey's place is right around the corner. I know exactly where it is." An hour later, after driving up and down many of the obscure and unmarked streets in Dade County, we finally pulled into Dewey's driveway. His house was on a moth-eaten back road, one of those old Florida roads with rain ruts and grassy edges, and rows of one-floor bungalows with screened porches and dead cars and dead bicycles and dead appliances lying out in the open to molder, the way the Seminoles lay out their dead. This was one of those parts of Florida that have nothing to do with the other Florida, the brassy, booming Florida of superstores and tall hotels. This was the low, simmering part of the state, as quiet as a shrine except for crickets keeping time and the creak of trees bending and the crackly slam of a screen door and the clatter of a car now and then. Dewey was in his shadehouse when we arrived. He strolled out when he heard the car. He was dressed in a pair of saggy khaki pants and a chewed-up plaid shirt and was brandishing a pair of rose shears. In appearance he reminded me of Laroche—an older, grizzled Laroche with more meat on his bones, but the same rough-knuckled look and the same strange air of benign derangement.

He and Laroche hadn't seen each other in months. "Hey, Dewey," Laroche said in greeting. "You quit smoking?"

Dewey glowered at him and said, "Hell, *no.*" He searched his pockets until he found a dented pack of cigarettes. Laroche introduced us and said I was interested in plants. Dewey gave off not one glint of interest. After a moment he cocked his head toward me and said, "See that yellow dog there?" He motioned with his chin toward a rangy dog with strawberry-blond hair. "That dog will bite." He paused. "I'm not saying '*can* bite.' I'm saying '*will* bite.'"

"Thanks," I said. I thought maybe I should wait in the car.

"Oh, for Chrissakes, come *on*," Dewey said, walking toward the shadehouse. He stopped after a second and handed me a business card that said

THE PHILODENDRON PHREAQUE
Rare and Unusual Plants
DEWEY FISK, PLANT NUT

He spun around and continued toward the shadehouse and Laroche and I followed, stepping around heaps of green plastic pots and piles of plant cuttings and then ducking under hanging baskets of curly ferns and then finally squeezing past a rotting old garden bench on which there were dozens of plants, including miniature trees with bronze bark and blush-pink flowers.

"See this?" Dewey said, pointing at a shoot in a gallon pot. "This was collected in Vietnam by a friend of mine. *Amorphaphallus henrii*. And that? Over there? Julius collected that in Trinidad. Remember Julius, John? And there, that tree has the flower that is used in that perfume, Chanel No. Five." He riffled through the stuff on the bench and then picked something up. "Holy Christ! I don't know if this is a bloom or *what*. What do you make of this, John?"

Laroche was examining another plant and barely looked over. "Well, damn it to hell, Dewey," he said, shaking his head at the plant he was examining. "This was always my favorite little aeroid."

"A guy sent it to me," Dewey said. "He said it was slightly nonaggressive." He was still holding the plant he'd picked up off the bench and suddenly remembered it. "*Laroche!*" he growled, holding it high. "Name this."

Laroche studied the plant for an instant and then said something Latin.

Dewey smirked. "Small form or large form?"

"Let's see," Laroche said, squinting. "Jesus, Dewey, I'm an Internet publisher now! I'm not as fast as I used to be. I'd say that's the large form."

"Bullshit," Dewey said, triumphantly. "You're losing it, buddy. You're through."

It was a dazed, shambling kind of afternoon, a day seen through a scrim, the time gliding by. It had to have something to do with the plants. When I first met a lot of orchid people, they all said that time spent in a greenhouse had a rare, shapeless quality—a day could go by and they wouldn't even notice it had passed if they had spent it among their orchids. That afternoon at Dewey's the light shifted and dropped, and then dusk drifted in, and the time passed, and still we roved around the shadehouse picking up plants, smelling things, rubbing fingers on slick leaves, poking thumbs into dirt, and every couple of minutes Dewey and Laroche would pause and both would light cigarettes and stand in front of some delicate green sprig of something, smoking hard and wordlessly admiring it. I wasn't in any hurry to leave, even though I should have been. Being in the shadehouse was restful in a way that being around people can never be, and it was vivid the way being around lifeless objects can never be, and in the veil of evening air it was as fantastic as a dream.

———

Before we each went home, Laroche and I made our plans for the next day. It was about a two-and-a-half-hour drive from the Miami area to the Fakahatchee, and Laroche wanted to start before dawn. "Otherwise we'll get there late in the day and the bugs will be miserable and you'll just get burned," he said. "Believe me, I'm warning you. I think you should pick me up around four-thirty tomorrow morning. Or five, at the latest. I'll be up and waiting for you at four-thirty. And what about food? I'll get all our supplies. What kind of stuff do you like?"

I said I liked pretzels, and he said, "Well, that's not enough. How about pretzels and those crackers with peanut butter and maybe some kind of cheese. Maybe some candy, too. And *lots* of water. And we should have some sunscreen and dry clothes. Look, I'll get everything. I'll get the supplies for both of us." He ticked off on his fingers: "Pretzels, peanut butter crackers, Hershey bars, cheese."

"How about a compass?" I said. The rangers carried compasses. "Or a map?"

Laroche glared at me. "We don't need a map. I've got everything under control. I know the Fakahatchee like the back of my hand. I mean, you *have* to know it to go in there. It's dangerous. All those pits of mud and those big sheets of water. You can disappear and die in the swamp."

I slept through my 3:00 A.M. alarm and then jerked awake at 4:30, imagining Laroche standing in his driveway, chewing on a cigarette and fuming. It took me only a minute to get ready. The night before, I had laid out my swamp clothes—leggings, cheap tennis shoes, long-sleeved white shirt—and a set of clean clothes to put on when we emerged and a little camera to photograph the flowering ghost orchids I was quite sure that I wasn't going to see. I threw on my swamp outfit and raced down through the hotel lobby, deserted and dim at that hour except for the glow of a pink neon wall clock. The street was deserted and dim, too, and all the hotels along it were still, and the surf was low and miles out, barely licking at the hard brown edge of sand. The beach itself was vacant except for a cluster of furled beach umbrellas and a bony-looking beach chair missing a seat. There is nothing more melancholy than empty festive places, and I was glad when I got to my car and started down the highway to pick up Laroche.

He was not standing in his driveway when I arrived. I guess he had been in the front hall, and when he heard my car pull in he cracked open the door and signaled me to be quiet and then stepped out. Every time I saw Laroche I was freshly amazed. His tallness, thinness, and paleness seemed always to be growing taller, thinner, and paler. He had the bulk and shape of a coat hanger. Even though he had spent a lot of time in his life walking around the woods he was wispy and unmuscled. The aura of peacefulness and repose was not anywhere around him. Instead he had the composure of a jackrabbit.

He didn't look dressed for the woods. He was wearing a Miami Hurricanes hat, a pair of thin corduroy pants, a flimsy short-sleeved shirt, and aerobics shoes. He wasn't carrying anything—no pretzels, crackers, water, Hershey bars, cheese, maps, compasses, emergency flares. I asked him where our stuff was, all the stuff we'd need in the Faka-hatchee. He tapped his shirt pocket and then pulled out a pack of Marlboros. "Brand-new pack. I just bought it last night," he said. "I've got everything I need."

I turned off the ignition and sat staring at the steering wheel. Laroche looked at me and shrugged. "Look, don't worry about it," he said. "We'll stop and get stuff at the Indian trading post on Alligator Alley. Hey, do you want me to drive?"

—

It was not even 7:00 A.M. when we started out, but it was already warm outside. The road gleamed in the bright light and melting tar around potholes made a bubbly sound under the tires. Laroche was steering with one half of one finger on the wheel. He was able to do this because Alligator Alley is so straight, rolling over the land like a hall runner, but more because he didn't seem to care if we veered onto the shoulder now and then. I knew him to be one of those people who are really sour in the morning, but that day he was very talkative. He described his new computer work to me and some new software he was writing that he was convinced would make him rich. As he was talking he saw a car coming in the other direction that reminded him of his mother's car, so he began reminiscing about slogging around the swamp with her and recalled the time they walked through a charred prairie in the Fakahatchee and came upon a single snowy *Polyrrhiza lindenii* in bloom. The way he recited this made it sound like a fairy tale or Bible story—the bleak journey with the radiant finale, the hopeful journey through darkness into light. A more conventional, more comfortable story wouldn't have this rhythm of struggle and victory, and instead it would have had the unswinging tempo of usualness and habit, a kind of deadly incessancy. I never thought very many people in the world were very much like John Laroche, but I realized more and more that he was only an extreme, not an aberration— that most people in some way or another do strive for something exceptional, something to pursue, even at their peril, rather than abide an ordinary life.

Just then we crested a little rise in the road. On our right was the Indian trading post. Laroche swerved onto the exit ramp and into the parking lot.

"Go ahead and get whatever you want," he said. "I'll meet you inside." He peered out the windshield. "This will be interesting. They hate me here."

In the store I picked up some crackers and bottled water, and soon Laroche came in and bought cigarettes and some Doritos, and then we stood in the sweltering parking lot for a few minutes before we got back in the car and onto the road. "Nobody in there gave me any shit," he said. "I'm surprised. All the Indians recognize me and they all hate me now because of the orchid case. We used to stop here all the time on our way to the swamp." He shaded his eyes and looked out over the highway. "You know, I had really big plans for the Seminoles. What I really wanted was to get the orchid lab going. The nursery was fine, but the real money was going to be in the lab. We could have been cloning orchids day and night, really made it into a huge operation. Eventually I wanted to chuck the nursery completely and just have a huge lab the size of the Seminole bingo hall. That was the master plan. Then we wouldn't really need the nursery. We'd just be cloning native Florida orchids and wholesaling them around the world, and then we'd expand and not just clone orchids but clone everything. And in the meantime I'd be training my guys in some basic botany. They would have really gotten something out of it. We would do some mutation, some bizarre hybridizing. We were going to weird people out. It would have really been cool. Cool as hell."

He sped down Alligator Alley and then onto State Road 29, the road that leads under three elevated panther crossings and past Copeland Road Prison to the entrance of the Faka-hatchee Strand State Preserve. At Laroche's chosen speed the trees looked like green streamers. When he slowed down to eighty or so, a dirty orange blur in the sky resolved into a column of slow-moving smoke, maybe from a torched sugar-cane field or maybe from the plane crash. We whipped past abandoned bungalows melting into woodpiles, and past NO TRESPASSING signs that were all shot up like Swiss cheese, and past a rusty boat run aground on someone's driveway, and past fences leaning like old ladies, and then almost past a hand-lettered sign that interested Laroche, so he smashed the brakes and craned his neck to read it. "Look at this!" he exclaimed. The sign read FOR SALE: BABY GOATS, GUAVA JAM, CACTUS. "That's pretty fucking weird, don't you think?" he asked. "Now, how would you end up with those three things for sale? Is it random or do you wake up one day and say, Hey, honey, let's have a baby goat and guava jam business. Why not something else? How about lambs, ferns, and raspberries? Or, Christ, I don't know—cows and tulips and orange juice?" He sighed. "What the hell," he muttered after a moment. "People are so strange."

At last we were at the Fakahatchee entrance. The car bounced onto the hard road and past the houses and trailers you go by before you cross the boundary of the preserve. The road bent around a creek and then cut diagonally through the swamp, through brush and weeds and trees that were woven together like wool. Every few yards there was a clearing on the side of the road that led to a flat-topped levee— the old tramways built by the Lee Tidewater Cypress Company when they came here in 1947 for the Fakahatchee's cypress trees. Each levee looked exactly like the next levee, and each stretch of swamp looked exactly like the next. I glanced over at Laroche. His face was puckered with concentration. He caught me looking at him and broke into a smile. He had mentioned a few weeks earlier that he was thinking about buying teeth to replace all of the ones he had knocked out in the car crash that had killed his mother, but he hadn't gotten around to it yet, so his smile was still holey, a fence missing pickets. "Don't worry. I know exactly where we are," he said. "I know this place like the back of my hand." We drove a few miles more. The road was empty in every direction. At last he steered into one of the clearings and gunned the engine before turning it off. He pointed ahead into the green thicket and said this was the trail we wanted and that we'd better get moving before the day got too hot.

———

The levee was high and dry and we walked for a mile or two before we stepped off. The water we stepped into was as black as coffee. It was hard to tell how far down we would go, and when our feet touched the bottom it yielded like pudding. Duckweed floating on the water's surface wound

around our calves. There is a deep stillness in the Fakahatchee, but there is not a moment of physical peace. Something is always brushing against you or lapping at you or
snagging you or tangling in your legs, and the sun is always
pummeling your skin, and the wetness in the air makes your
hair coil like a phone cord. You never smell plain *air* in a
swamp—you smell the tang of mud and the sourness of rotting leaves and the cool musk of new leaves and the per-
fumes of a million different flowers floating by, each distinct
but transparent, like soap bubbles. The biggest number in
the universe would not be big enough to count the things
your eyes see. Every inch of land holds up a thatch of tall
grass or a bush or a tree, and every bush or tree is girdled
with another plant's roots, and every root is topped with a
flower or a fern or a swollen bulb, and every one of those
flowers and ferns is the pivot around which a world of bees
and gnats and spiders and dragonflies revolve. The sounds
you hear are twigs cracking underfoot and branches
whistling past you and leaves murmuring and water slopping
over the trunks of old dead trees and every imaginable and
unimaginable insect noise and every kind of bird peep and
screech and tootle, and then all those unclaimed sounds of
something moving in a hurry, something low to the ground
and heavy, maybe the size of a horse in the shape of a lizard,
or maybe the size, shape, and essential character of a snake.
In the swamp you feel as if someone had plugged all of your
senses into a light socket. A swamp is logy and slow-moving
but at the same time highly overstimulating. Even in the dim,
sultry places deep within it, it is easy to stay awake.

—

The first orchid we saw was a butterfly orchid, *Encyclia tam-
pensis,* that was growing in a crotch of a pop ash tree. It was
a little plant with lustrous green pseudobulbs. The flower

was yellow with a lip that was white with purplish veins. After Laroche pointed it out to me, he lit a cigarette and clenched it between his teeth. "Nice little sucker, isn't it?" he asked, examining the flower. "Cute." I appreciated it from a distance because I could feel the land sloping downward as I moved toward the tree and I had decided I'd be happier if the swamp water never went above my waist. We turned north and slogged on. It was slow going. The water was heavy and the mucky bottom held tight, and each step was really three steps—a test step to feel for alligators and a second test to feel for cypress knees, those shin-cracking knuckles of wood that cypress trees send out from their roots to help them breathe. Then finally you commit the real step. After an hour of inching through the water we moved onto slightly higher ground, where we followed a path of palm fronds and fallen limbs so swollen with swamp water that they crumbled under our feet. Laroche stopped under a laurel oak that was draped with vines. "Toward the end of my plant career, flowering vines were my new love," he said. "It was, sad to say, unrequited." He frowned for an instant and then noticed a tiny clamshell orchid on a nearby tree he wanted me to see. "I found you two already," he said excitedly. "I'm going to show you one of every orchid you want today. I'll show you a fucking ghost orchid if it kills me." A few minutes later he stopped and pointed triumphantly at a pond apple tree with ghost orchid roots around a low branch. I loved the look of the roots, the glossy greenness of them and their squashed tubular shape and the way they wrapped around the branch like a bandage. "Already flowered," Laroche said. "Well, there'll be more to see. We're definitely going to see one in bloom." We circled around a sinkhole, then through a tunnel of cabbage palms, then into a stand of willows. We stopped by one shrubby tree. "Here's an ugly-ass orchid," Laroche said, reaching up. "Rigid *Epidendrum*. Ugly-ass. But I'm not a snob. I was always interested in all orchids, not just pretty ones. When we poached we took pretty ones and drab ones, not just the showy ones. They're all cool, if you ask me."

By this time a few hours had gone by since we had started walking and the sun had slid above the trees. It was getting hotter and hotter, and a haze of mosquitoes had settled around me. Even my fingers were sweating. Ahead and behind and on either side of me was a snarl of brush and palm fronds and sedge, and above were the moptops of bromeliads and the gray trunks of trees. The land was as level as a pool table. I had no bearings. I wondered if we were getting close to the ghost orchids. "They're right nearby," Laroche said. "Just follow me."

He set out in one direction and then paused and changed course and then paused and changed again. This depressed me. "Laroche," I said, "can I ask you a personal question?"

He turned and scowled. "We're not lost, if that's what you plan to ask," he said. "It's *this* way. We passed on the right of this tree before, didn't we?" The tree he was referring to had a thick, bumpy trunk and green leaves—the same thick, bumpy trunk and green leaves of at least ten thousand other trees in the Fakahatchee. He started toward the left of this particular tree. I followed. I was getting tired and clumsy. We started moving faster and recklessly, making a racket as we pushed through the underbrush and splashed through the sinkholes. I had the powerful feeling we were walking in a spiral. The Fakahatchee consists of eighty thousand acres, and I was sure you could walk a lot of spirals in eighty thousand acres without crossing the boundary.

We came to a small clearing where the ground was mostly dry, so we stopped to eat something and consider our whereabouts. The fact is we were lost. Laroche knew it and I knew it. "We're not lost," Laroche said. He fumbled around for a cigarette. "I'm just turned around a little. Anyway, here's what we'll do." He sifted through stuff on the ground until he found a short straight twig. "I'll make a sundial," he explained. "We'll just set this up and wait a few minutes and we'll be able to tell which way the sun is moving. We want to be heading southeast." He glanced at me. "This is no big deal."

He stuck the twig in the dirt and sat on his heels. "You know, I was thinking that it would be really cool to have a little amusement park for orchids," he said. "No snakes, no critters, nothing but orchids, sort of like an orchid safari." He laughed. "My feeling is that anything is interesting, especially if there's even a slight chance to make money at it." He stretched out his leg and accidentally knocked over our sundial. Without looking up he found another section of twig and poked it into the ground.

"Do you collect anything?" he asked.

"Not really," I said.

"It's not really about collecting the thing itself," Laroche went on. "It's about getting immersed in something, and learning about it, and having it become part of your life. It's a kind of direction." He stopped on the word "direction" and chortled. "If anybody had a plant I didn't have, I made sure to get it. It was like a heroin addiction. If I ever had money I would spend it on plants. When my wife and I had our nursery, we had forty thousand just totally unimaginable plants."

"Your favorite?"

He scuffed his heel in the dirt. "I think it would have to be this little *Boesenbergia ornata*, this gorgeous little ginger plant a friend got me in New Zealand. It had first been collected a hundred years ago, and I think I had the only one in cultivation. It had these tiny round leaves, sort of brownish,

with silver chevron markings. I swear it looked like it was
made out of crystal. And it had an amazing huge orange
flower, too."

I asked if he still had it. "I don't have *any* plants anymore,"
he said, crossly. "I sold that one for nine hundred dollars and
sent a cutting of it to Kew Gardens."

"The sundial isn't working."

He looked at it and squinted up at the sun and then narrowed his eyes at me. "It is so working," he said.

A wave of wind pushed by. It felt like the exhaust from a
pizza shop, oily and thick and hot. My cheeks were pulsing. I
felt extremely uncomposed, like many other Fakahatchee
wanderers: *The place looked wild and lonely. About three
o'clock it seemed to get on Henry's nerves and we saw him crying, he could not tell us why, he was just plain scared.* I did
want desperately to see a ghost orchid in bloom, to complete
the cycle, to make sense of everything I'd been doing in
Florida, but at that moment I wanted even more not to spend
the night in the swamp. I also very much wanted to kill
Laroche, to actually murder him and leave his body here, not
because murder is part of my nature or upbringing and
not because I thought it would help me find the way out of
the swamp but just because I was furious with him and I
was wrought up and had a lot of nervous energy. The sundial
was definitely not working. Something whirred in the underbrush, and a crow dipped down from above and cawed.
A hundred years ago plume hunters would come here
and gather enough feathers to decorate ten thousand fash-
ionable ladies' hats. If a ranger interfered with them, they
would kill him. "The thing about computers," Laroche said,
"the thing that I like is that I'm immersed in it but it's not a
living thing that's going to leave or die or something. I like
having the minimum number of living things to worry about
in my life."

"John, do you actually have any living things that you *do* worry about?" I asked.

"Yeah, well, my girlfriend and my dad," he said. "I have four cats, too—Puffy, Zippy, Bill, and Bob. But that's it for now. I don't know if I could ever stand to have plants again."

I suddenly felt sorry for him, for having had his heart broken again and again, and then I felt sorry for everything, sorry for the people who didn't win anything at the orchid show even though they had groomed and doted on their plants, and sorry for the way the Fakahatchee had been plowed and burned and stripped, and sorry for all the people who'd bought a piece of imagined paradise in the muddy stretch of the Blocks, and for the Seminoles who wished they still lived in chikees in the wetlands, and for all the crumpled-up bingo players at the casino, and for the hundreds and hundreds of Elaine bromeliads that turned out ugly and were dumped, and for Lee Moore, who was just then on his way to Jacksonville with orchids in his van but instead of seeing the drab interstate in front of him was dreaming of his city of gold in Peru, and sorry for anyone who ever cared about something that didn't work out, and I felt sorry for myself for being lost in the Fakahatchee Strand with no idea of what to do. Then like all sorriness it hardened into something less stifling, and I suddenly decided that I would rather walk, no matter which way we went, than to sit here idle and frantic, spinning my mind like a tire in sand. I knew Laroche wanted me to see a ghost orchid as much or maybe even more than I wanted to see it myself, but now I really wanted most of all to go home. At this point I realized it was just as well that I never saw a ghost orchid, so that it could never disappoint me, and so it would remain forever something I wanted to see.

"Okay, fuck the sundial," Laroche said. "We'll just go straight and eventually we'll get there. What I mean is that we'll get *somewhere*. Out of here. I mean, logically, we have to get out as long as we walk straight. I've done this millions of times. Whenever everything's killing me I just say to myself, Screw it, and go straight ahead."

We left the clearing and walked back into the thick brush. It was acre after acre of sameness, of too many living things to notice any single one, and we didn't notice any of them. We just went as straight as we could for as long as we could, dodging the vines, the canopy of branches, the imperturbable ancient trees. It was pure vivid gorgeousness, a bounty, a place so rich no one could help but pass through it and say to himself, I will find something here. After hours or minutes or forever, we splashed through the last black water and onto the dry levee. First we turned to the right but saw only more cypress and palm and saw grass, so we turned to the left, and there, far down the diagonal of the levee, we could see the gleam of a car fender, and we followed it like a beacon all the way to the road.

Bibliography

The following books were helpful to me as source material:

Blanchan, Nelte. *Nature's Garden*. Doubleday, Doran & Co., 1926.

Covington, James W. *The Seminoles of Florida*. University Press of Florida, 1993.

Dodrill, David E. *Selling the Dream*. University of Alabama Press, 1993.

Douglas, Marjory Stoneman. *The Everglades: River of Grass*. Mockingbird Books, 1947.

Lamme, Vernon. *Florida Lore not found in the history books!* Star Publishing, 1973.

Luer, Carlyle A. *The Native Orchids of Florida*. New York Botanical Garden, 1972.

Neill, Wilfred. *The Story of Florida's Seminole Indians*. Great Outdoors Publishing Co., 1956.

Reinikka, Merle A. *A History of the Orchid*. Timber Press, 1995.

Silver, Doris. *Papa Fuchs' Family 1881–1981*. Jane Fuchs Wilson, 1982.

Swinson, Arthur. *Frederick Sander: The Orchid King*. Hodder Publishing, 1970.

Tebeau, Charlton W. *Florida's Last Frontier*. University of Miami Press, 1957.

———. *Man in the Everglades*. University of Miami Press, 1968.

Whittle, Michael Tyler. *The Plant Hunters*. Lyons & Burford, 1997.

Wickman, Patricia R. *Osceola's Legacy*. University of Alabama Press, 1991.

Willoughby, Hugh. *Across the Everglades: A Canoe Journey of Exploration,* 1898. Florida Classics Library Edition, 1992.

Wright, J. Leitch, Jr. *Creeks and Seminoles*. University of Nebraska Press, 1986.

THE
ORCHID
THIEF

Susan Orlean

A Reader's Guide

A Conversation with Susan Orlean, Author of *THE ORCHID THIEF*

Q: If there were one question you wished an interviewer would ask, but never has, what would it be?

A: There is no question I wish I had been asked. There is a question I wish I could answer: how does the creative process work? Often people will say, where in the world did you get the idea for that lead? And I wish I could answer it, because it is very intuitive, and I think it would be a comfort to imagine that it wasn't sheer accident, that there was a very specific process by which writing took place, but there isn't.

Q: This book had its gestation as a report in a Florida newspaper article. Then you wrote a piece on the subject for *The New Yorker*. What was it that made you decide that it warranted 282 pages?

A: When I originally went down to write about it for *The New Yorker* I felt like I was peeling an onion. Every aspect of the story seemed richer than I imagined. For instance, at the Fakahatchee Strand where the original poaching took place, I casually asked one of the rangers how long it had been a preserve and what had been there before it was a preserve, and I stumbled on an entire story of Florida land scams that I felt was fascinating. I loved the idea of taking a single event, something very specific and examining it thoroughly and deeply rather than a big, sprawling event. That's a task, to take a very tight focus and make a book out of it.

Q: Your published work is all based on actual happenings; it is reportage. Have you ever considered novelizing your experiences?

A: I never have. People have asked me this, but I think real life is so interesting. I don't think I could have imagined a character as eccentric and fascinating as John Laroche. I also think there is a discipline in taking true stories and making them engaging to a reader. You have to deal with what really exists. That is a greater challenge than thinking, "Gee, it would have worked out better if he had gone to jail for a year; I think I'll just have him go to jail for a year." Instead, this is reality.

There is also a part of me that likes the pedagogical part of writing. I like that challenge of bringing knowledge to readers, material they didn't know they would actually want to know.

Q: One of the themes of the book is: what is the nature of passion, how it is that people can shape their lives around a particular obsession. Are you a passionate collector?

A: No. I am fascinated by it, partly because I never have had that kind of devotion to a single interest. Obviously at the end of the book, I realize I do have a single-minded passion. It is the passion to be a writer and a reporter. But I think the detachment was to my advantage. I don't like writing about things I am too invested in initially. For me, part of the process of writing is the journey to understanding. Orchids were to me a complete cipher—just flowers; how could anybody care about them? The journey was to try and understand how people could come to care about them, and why.

I am not being perfectly honest when I say I am not a collector. I am not an orchid collector. I collect many things, many kind of strange things. I have just never surrendered my sense of myself to say that I am a collector of things. I have a lot of odd collections: for years I collected toothpaste from around the world, American pottery of a certain color, tin globes. I have started lately to collect dice. And yet I would never describe myself as a dice collector or a pottery collector. That's the big difference between me and the orchid people who think of themselves as Orchid-people. It defines their lives

Q: John Laroche may be the title character of the book, but he is only its object; Susan Orlean is its subject. It is about you; it is a form of autobiography. If you were to consciously write an autobiography, which element of your life would you focus on?

A: I can't even imagine.

When people say, "you always put yourself in your stories," well, I am in my stories. It is a matter of acknowledging it. The fact is I do not write news that must be reported. I choose to write about whatever captures my curiosity. Simply choosing what you write about is a subjective choice.

Q: In the context of orchids—interdependence between species, their parasitic or epiphytic relationships—you might consider your focus to be living off the desires, aspirations, happenings of others. That is how you make your living. As a common parasite, really.

A: Thank you. My subject is, in one form or another, 'family' (in a very loose way). We are put on earth, we don't know why and we need to figure out how to make it feel meaningful, how to find some niche that we fit into comfortably. People go to great lengths to do this. They might focus on work or some interest like orchids, or be propelled by a desire to make lots of money or to raise their children in a certain way. And my passion is to examine and interpret that and convey it to other people. And yes, it is very much a matter of connection and disconnection and belonging and not belonging.

Q: **Beneath the overriding theme of the nature of passion, the thought that surfaces with regularity is the nature of the parasite. You describe Florida as "less like a state than a sponge." John Laroche himself lives off other people's weaknesses. What is your ultimate estimation of his parasitic pursuits?**

A: I think his whole episode in pornography was very telling. If people were foolish enough to come to him and offer him lots of money to post naked pictures of themselves on the web, he felt that his mission in life would be to charge them as much as possible. That's parasitic profiteering: making money off of people's fantasies.

Q: **With the title *The Orchid Thief*, you immediately raise the question of John Laroche's morality.**

A: This was the question that dogged me throughout my reporting. There were certainly moments when I thought: this is really just an ordinary greedy guy who is a little bit more clever than the ordinary greedy guy. Yet, there was a certain strange logic in this greediness. He had discovered a law that was so badly written that he could abuse it and take advantage [of it]. I also think it was a way for him to justify his own ends which were fairly simple: he wanted to make a million dollars. But he would not have wanted to do it had there not been an interesting complexity to it. I don't think he is a charlatan. I think he's a person who can't seem to live within the conventional bounds that most of us feel comfortable living within. And it is probably something to do with needing attention. He can't just succeed, he needs to succeed in a complicated, interesting, unusual way.

Q: **John Laroche shares with so many Americans a "lotto" mentality of getting rich quick. But not every get-rich-quick scheme ignites the same degree of passion in him. Although he recognizes its**

potential, he disdains, for example, the white-striped lawn grass that he is offered from South America with "Oh, I'm not into lawn grass." It is like him looking for a Friesian cash cow in a meadow full of Holsteins. Like Don Quixote, he is the ultimate loser. Do you regard Laroche's particular fetish as a noble, quixotic trait?

A: I think noble would dignify it too much. I think he has a grand self-image. It would be enough for an ordinary person to get rich with something unspectacular like lawn grass. But Laroche has a vision of himself as something larger than life. When he steals orchids, it isn't sufficient that he steals orchids, it is also necessary that the Florida State legislature stops dead in its tracks and rewrites the law, recognizing what he has done.

He is a loser if you compare him to normal standards of success. In his own mind he is not a loser because he really is living the life he wants to lead.

Q: You paint Florida as the ultimate America, the land of plenty, and yet one gets the strong sense that you find its profuseness more than just a little vulgar. Did you retain a sense of remaining a distinct and separate being, or were you ever in danger of becoming part of the exotic blur?

A: I will forever be an outsider to Florida. I am not a hot weather person. I think you have to learn to melt into the Florida landscape if you are to learn to become 'Floridian'. On the other hand I think I am a person who is typical of Florida. I came down there to find my own fortune. Like so many people I came to Florida with a scheme in mind: I wanted to write this book about this peculiar event that had taken place. But my connection was impermanent. It surprises me to realize I have written easily over half a dozen pieces down there. Part of that is the fact that interesting, strange things happen in Florida. It is a bubbling-stew of a place. And the kinds of stories that interest me, people starting new lives, creating new communities, happened in Florida.

Q: Let's talk about your relief when you know that you will not be seeing the ghost orchid after all. Fate intervenes. Disappointment is deflected. And you are grateful. Is that how you rule your life?

A: I think about this all the time. I try to figure out if there is destiny and fate or if life is just haphazard. What we search for is a kind of order and logic in what is the chaotic and illogical experience of being alive. I think you grab on to little footholds that make you think that there is logic and that there is some sense of order in your life. It is very funny how much we crave that. I am almost delighted to have a fortune teller say to me, "Nothing is going to happen until January" because I feel relieved of that anticipation. I can't believe there isn't a grand design that is always unfolding in front of us. It is a comfort to think that there is something. Sometimes I wonder how it is that I ended up as a writer. It seems, looking back on it, almost fated. On the other hand I am not sure. Do I believe that? Or, aren't we all inventions of our own choices and decisions?

Q: Do you still have the desire, unrequited as it was at the end of the book, to see a ghost orchid?

A: Now I am a little afraid to see one. I had gone for such a long time thinking I was going to see one, and being thwarted over and over again, that towards the end of my reporting, I began to think it was better that I didn't see one. It could never have matched all of the expectations that I was bringing to it. A ranger from the Fakahatchee called me after the book came out and said, "If you want to see a ghost orchid, I will take you to see one. I'll call you when I know there's one in bloom. You can come down." And I realized I didn't really want to. I like just imagining it, as something irresistible and unattainable. One of these days I suspect I will see one. It would be nice if it were by accident.

Q: Have you seen or talked to John Laroche since the book was published?

A: I haven't seen him. I have talked to him. In fact he called me after the book was first published and he said, "Well, I've read the book."

And I said, "U-huh," and naturally I was a little apprehensive. I wasn't sure what his reaction would be. It wasn't an entirely flattering portrait.

And he said to me in his usual way, "You know, if you write a couple more books, you could turn into a pretty good writer."

Q: There is never anything in the book that unambiguously paints Laroche as an attractive individual, yet he seems to have exerted a

strong almost pseudo-antagonist influence on you amid the sexual imagery that pervades the descriptions and activities of orchids—growing in the crotches of a pop ash tree—Laroche lusting after orchids—the passion for them being the catalyst for divorce and so on. Did you analyze your fascination with Laroche going beyond the objective interest in his passion?

A: There was a lot of sexual imagery in the book. I only realize this now. As a matter of fact, it was a bit of a challenge to find a photograph of an orchid for the cover that wasn't too sexual. Certainly, when I set out to write a book about flowers, I never thought it would be sexy.

But our relationship was strictly reporter and subject. It is certainly true that you develop a kind of intimacy with someone you are writing about. You spend an enormous amount of time with them. You want to hear everything they have to say. It is a kind of idealized relationship. By definition, everything he had to say was interesting to me, because that is what I was there to do: to find out about him. I think you can become very attached, very connected to each other. Going back to the parasitic theme: you are each serving a purpose. He was my subject. His cooperation made it possible for me to write a book. I was his witness to whom he could describe his life's ambitions and get attention for them. I think one of the great questions in non-fiction is: what does that relationship mean? Because the relationship ends when the book ends, is that a betrayal? There was never any flicker of romantic interest on my side, and I suspect on both sides. But you do develop a connection that is unusual. It is hard to imagine any relationship that is similar, except that of a confessor, I suppose.

There was a great piece years ago written by Janet Malcolm, that argued that there is a mutually exploitative relationship between a reporter and a subject. I have to agree with her. That does not mean that it is evil and corrupt. It just means that to not acknowledge that you are each using each other for a reason and that that is the context of the relationship, is just naïve. It is not a natural relationship. It is a very unnatural relationship. You are not having a friendship with John Laroche. You are having a relationship within the context of the reportage. I don't think it means that it is false. It means that you always have to be aware that it is an unnatural circumstance.

A Reader's Guide

Q: **Has a subject ever fallen in love with you?**

A: Yes. And I felt great affection for him, but I understood what was going on. Let me explain transference to you. I knew he was confusing the circumstance with the specific emotion. He was in love with the sense of attention and interest, real attention and curiosity. It is a great feeling to have someone who simply wants to know everything about you but isn't demanding in return. It is like therapy. I was flattered but I also knew it is contextual. You do have a sort of magical power when you write about people. I sometimes forget what it means when you write a story and have it published in *The New Yorker* and 800,000 people read it.

I often write about people who don't get written about. They are not press-savvy, they are not used to this. To them it is usually a once-in-a-lifetime experience. I never go with a set of questions. I will sit and wait and listen and watch. I take notes. The intimacy that I develop with people makes the end of the process sometimes very jarring. I have come to terms with the fact that people feel, if not betrayed, then kind of shocked after spending two or three weeks with me and having a sense of closeness.

I remember the hardest thing for me was when I did a piece about a ten-year-old boy. When I was done with the reporting I was under a lot of deadline pressure, so I told him that I had to go and write the piece.

And he said to me, "Are you going to come over tomorrow?"

And I replied, "Of course I am not going to come over tomorrow. I am on deadline." Then I thought: I have spent two weeks with this kid saying, "Whatever you want to do I want to do; whatever you have to say I am interested in." It is not that it was false, it was just that I had moved on to the next part of the process, writing my story. For him, it was very abrupt and very confusing. For an adult it is easier to understand, but for a kid, attention and friendship equals attention and friendship.

Q: **Have you ever been smitten by a subject?**

A: Yes. He was a show dog. I fell in love with him. But he was a tough interview.

Tim McHenry edited and contributed to the *Bloomsbury* publication *The Lost Voices of World War I*. His travel writing on Madagascar, Borneo and East Timor has appeared in *The Daily Telegraph*, London.

Reading Group Questions
and Topics for Discussion

1. Is there a hero in *The Orchid Thief*? An anti-hero?

2. Is the book subjective? Objective? Or a different genre altogether? Some people describe this as "literary non-fiction." Is that how you would characterize it?

3. Susan Orlean resists the temptation to feel possessed by the orchids but she is willing to undergo great trials in order to satisfy her passion for reporting. Is this passion evident in her writing?

4. The passion for collecting is described in the book as a means of infusing meaning into life, subjecting the vicissitudes to some order, acquiring the ability to mold and change the nature of things, i.e. create life itself. What other means do humans employ to achieve the same ends, and how effective are they?

5. John Laroche would not describe himself as an orchid person. To him the orchid is a temporary albeit very intense passion, a means to an end, not an end in itself. How would you analyze the difference between Laroche's motives in collecting orchids and the regular orchid collectors we visit in the course of the book?

6. Laroche wrestles verbally with the thought that acting within what he considered the bounds of the law for his own immediate gain was ultimately an act of altruism. His rape of the Fakahatchee would force the law to be changed and close the loophole that allowed him to poach rare and wild orchids from an Indian reservation in the first place, thus protecting the species in the wild, and securing it for the marketplace at the same time. Is this the thought process of an amoral character? Or is he just an everyday charlatan? Discuss.

7. Laroche makes a very telling statement: "When I had my own nursery I sometimes felt like all the people swarming around were going to eat me alive. I felt like they were that gigantic parasitic plant and I was the dying host tree." Is Laroche playing the role of the victim, the martyr to a (preferably lost, but grand) cause or is he in control of his life by making a living off other people's weaknesses, whether it be a passion for orchids or pornography? Discuss.

8. Orlean seems fascinated by the story of Darwin and the study of the orchid with the eighteen inch nectary and the moth with the eighteen inch proboscis to feed on it: the idea that two totally different

life forms evolved specifically to serve each other; that neither could have existed without the other. What has the evidence of the orchid's adaptability altered your perception of the theories of evolution?

9. Orlean interrupts her central narrative of John Laroche with stories of the orchid hunters of the past, the contemporary state of Florida and other histories. How does this affect the pace of the work? Is the framework she has devised successful?

10. The Native Americans on the reservation are entitled by one law to remove protected species from their land. Is this law justified?

11. Orlean seems surprised by the abundance of sexual references to orchids in her book. Yet the flower is the prime sexual organ of most plants. Seek out a florist with a good representation of orchids. What alternative descriptions of these exotic flowers can you devise?

12. What is the real core, the central character, of the book: Laroche? Florida? Orchids? Native Americans? Darwin? Orlean?

13. As a reader, what did you expect from a book about orchids? How did your experience of reading *The Orchid Thief* compare to what you expected?

14. The working title of *The Orchid Thief* was "Passion." What does that suggest about the themes in the book?

15. What, besides orchids, could generate a book like this? Are there other subcultures or other objects of desire that might be as provocative?

ABOUT THE AUTHOR

Susan Orlean has been a staff writer for *The New Yorker* since 1992 and has also written for *Outside, Esquire, Rolling Stone,* and *Vogue*. She graduated from the University of Michigan and worked as a reporter in Portland, Oregon, and Boston, Massachusetts. She now lives in New York City.